Managing Content in the Cloud

Tom Jenkins

This book is dedicated to the staff, partners and customers of
Open Text Corporation and its subsidiaries.
This book is possible due to their combined efforts, innovation and collective vision.

We would like to thank the staff, users and partners of
Open Text Corporation for their contributions to this book.

Special thanks go out to writer and editor: Elizabeth Chestney-Hanson; editor Ian Wilson;
and the following contributors:

Chapter	Title	Content Owners
1	The Business Needs	Lubor Ptacek, James Latham
2	ECM 2.0 Technologies	Lubor Ptacek, Richard Anstey
3	Compliance and Information Governance	Jeremy Barnes, Adrian Butcher, Nelson Chen, Stephen Ludlow, Liz Kofsky, Donald Lazar, Chris Mak, Hugh Ritchie
4	Information Discovery	Mei Dent, Charles-Olivier Simard
5	Content Lifecycle Management	Liz Kofsky, Lynn Elwood
6	Email Management	Jeremy Barnes
7	Web Content Management	Jens Rabe
8	Collaboration and E2.0	Vinit Doshi, Conleth O'Connell
9	Social Media	Vinit Doshi, Craig Hepburn
10	Digital Media	Damian Saccocio, Anthony Gallo
11	Business Process Management	Roland Jäger, Nicholas Carter
12	The ECM Ecosystem	Patrick Barnert, Ron Vangell, Ute Schullan
13	Cloud Computing	Martin Sumner-Smith
14	Mobility	Adam Howatson
15	Enterprise Adoption	Martin Sumner-Smith, Suzanne Lawrence
16	ECM and the Future	Ian Wilson

Also: Ginny Bartosek, Alex Benay, Lucia Bonatesta, Travis Cain, Michael Cybala,
Marten Den Haring, Bertrand De Coatpont, Margaret Dobbin, Joe Dwyer, Thorsten Fischer,
Anna Fleet, Rohit Gupta, Tiffany Janes, Toby Jenkins, Agnes Kolkiewicz, Detlev Legler,
Agnes Leung, Stewart Lynch, Alex Martinez, Jennifer McCredie, John Myers, Donna Pearson,
Patrick Pidduck, Jeremy Reed, Craig Reidel, Keith Sauve, Jacqueline Saayman,
Helga Schmid, Michele Stevenson, Sam Trieu, Trevor Unruh, Jason Varmazis,
Dave Wareham, Terry Whyte, Greg Williams, Neil Wilson, Sheila Woo, Dave Wormald
and designers: Alex Mohammed, Sabrina Prudham and Gary Smith.

Specific resources are accredited in the Bibliography.

Jenkins, Tom

Managing Content in the Cloud

First Printing, May 2010

Printed in Canada

ISBN

978-0-9730662-8-9

$29.00 U.S.

Published by

Open Text Corporation

275 Frank Tompa Drive

Waterloo, Ontario, Canada

N2L 0A1

(519) 888-7111

info@opentext.com

www.opentext.com

FOREWORD

On first reading, this book is a comprehensive presentation of the technologies underlying the latest Enterprise Content Management (ECM) 2.0 solutions. It provides a clear description of the developments over the last decade in harnessing the wild proliferation of digital content in a modern corporate environment. From creation at the keyboard to mobile cameras, from email and the early Web through to interactive social media, from word search to retrieval in context and from isolated business process solutions through to enterprise-wide fully integrated collaborative systems, this volume is the guidebook to the technology necessary to the knowledge organization. It may be mistaken for a text for technology enthusiasts. It is that but much more.

For the thoughtful manager in any large organization or bureaucracy, in the private or the public sector, this volume is a manual for transformation. The practical examples given in each chapter demonstrate how these technologies have been used to integrate a dispersed enterprise or to create new responsive relationships in the supply chain and with customers. The chapters on social media suggest the expectations of young digital natives as they emerge from school and university into the workforce and the creative potential their skills offer the organization. Throughout, the challenge to all large organizations is whether to adopt these technologies and realize the benefits of managing as one enterprise, mobilizing all knowledge assets and experience across traditional silos. Silos and hierarchies are traditional ways of defining information and knowledge flows. ECM 2.0 and all it implies, enables, or perhaps even demands a different corporate culture. The latest technological advances in integrating records as a knowledge asset, simplifying e-discovery processes, supporting collaboration to stimulate innovation, encouraging efficiency and agile processes are increasingly reinforced by employee and client expectations.

The technological solutions presented here are transformative. Organizations and managers will require time to adapt and adjust traditional policies, attitudes and approaches to information. Over the past decade, corporations, governments and other major organizations have gradually come to realize that information is a vital asset: one that must be managed throughout its lifecycle and that has the potential to become a strategic knowledge asset. The technology has matured. It is time to implement.

Ian E. Wilson, CM,
Director, Stratford Institute
University of Waterloo

Since the ECM trilogy (*Solutions*, *Technology* and *Methods*) was first written, the Web has evolved from the first generation or Web 1.0 into Web 2.0. This book, *Managing Content in the Cloud*, focuses on the application of Enterprise Content Management (ECM) to Web 2.0 technologies, and eventually to Web 3.0 technologies or the Semantic Web.

As technologies have evolved, so has their delivery. ECM infrastructure and applications are delivered to the workplace as part of the "Enterprise Cloud". Computing services are available in the marketplace as part of the "Internet Cloud". The delivery of computing services can also be a combination of the two forms. The enterprise as the Cloud combines the power and flexibility of infrastructure with the expertise, security and availability required by large organizations with mission-critical computing solutions.

The purpose of this book is to help executives and IT professionals understand how to apply evolving Internet technologies inside their organizations to remain competitive and compliant in a rapidly changing business environment. The book also makes generous use of innovative organizations to illustrate how these technology trends can be used to securely and effectively connect people, processes and information to create new opportunities and competitive advantage in business.

When Web 2.0 technologies are applied to an organization, this is commonly referred to as "Enterprise 2.0" or E2.0. Generally, the use of E2.0 increases levels of productivity which can result in tremendous organizational agility and innovation. Why did YouTube™, Facebook® and Twitter™ become such popular services and become the pillars of Web 2.0? These applications and services became so widely used because they allowed people to find information, collaborate and communicate faster than they could using other services or similar portal sites. The rise of the Internet as a connected network has allowed human beings to connect and generate "virtual" human intelligence on a mass scale. Wikipedia, the product of user generated content, is an excellent example of this.

How do Web 2.0 technologies enable better productivity? To answer this question, consider how online video expedites communication between people when friends are sharing vacation experiences. One individual might choose to blog repeatedly about specific adventures, while the other takes video clips with a mobile phone and uploads them to share experiences with friends, family and colleagues. The old way of sharing information requires a keyboard, an office set up and significant amounts of time and effort; the Web 2.0, is portable and requires considerably less time and effort.

Today's organizations are changing. Traditional management hierarchies have been broken down by the necessity to move further and faster than ever before to stay ahead of the competition. Communities are forming across all levels of the enterprise. Some are traditional, such as the management team that debates corporate policy and determines corporate direction. Others are ad hoc communities that form organically around identified areas of skills and expertise. These are called "Communities of Practice" or CoPs where birds of a feather gather in a social network.

Internet technology has enabled companies to overcome the geographical barriers that prevented collaboration among different office locations. In the Web 2.0 enterprise, individuals can quickly and easily collaborate with peers and work in virtual communities that span the globe. ECM 2.0 manages the content from Web 2.0 technologies. It helps organizations harness talent and nurture knowledge, extending the enterprise to include all stakeholders, from employees to complete marketplaces.

We are witnessing a shift in how people share information on the Internet. As peer-to-peer opinions, recommendations, ratings, commenting and sharing are increasing in importance, Google is being replaced by Facebook for simple fact-finding on the Web. This is because we value people as references over and above machines. No matter how precise search results are, we prefer human intervention. Since the start of modern communications, society has used books, TV, and radio to communicate from one person to many people. Only with letters and the telephone did communications offer one-to-one communications. Now with the Internet, it is possible to have a multitude of "many-to-many" communications.

Driven by this new capacity to communicate, an exponential increase in user generated content has occurred. This complicates the work environment as organizations struggle to balance productivity with risk. Society is demanding higher standards for the accuracy and availability of content. Across many industries, individuals and companies have been penalized for not complying with regulations and mismanaging critical business content.

ECM 2.0 provides the underlying platform to securely manage all structured and unstructured content across the enterprise – from user generated content in Web 2.0 applications to data contained in ERP systems. It describes both a philosophical approach to and the underlying technologies used to help businesses transform their content into competitive advantage.

ECM helps organizations connect departments, applications and repositories to maximize the flow of content across organizations. How? By working on existing infrastructure, being accessible from anywhere in the world, and leveraging peoples' knowledge of common Web technology. ECM significantly increases overall productivity, efficiencies and operational performance. ECM unlocks the true potential of the enterprise by enabling people to transform content into knowledge, creating new possibilities and business opportunities.

This book tells you what you need to know about ECM and how it can help to transform your organization into a more knowledgeable and agile enterprise. It describes the creation of a new approach to data by some of the greatest minds in the world of information technology – a collective vision determined to solve the challenge of managing structured and unstructured information in the midst of emerging Web applications and content types. Each chapter in the book focuses on a technology component of ECM, tracing its origins from early search technologies to the Semantic Web, immersive collaboration and social media. Innovator stories in each chapter illustrate ECM applications in action and paint the picture of an industry in the making. The end of the book explores ECM implementation and what the future of ECM 3.0 holds.

Tom Jenkins

Open Text Corporation

CONTENTS

Part 1: The Business Case

Part 2: ECM Lifecycle Technologies

Part 3: ECM Engagement Technologies

Part 4: ECM Transaction Technologies

Part 5: ECM Solutions and Implementation

INNOVATOR STORIES

Compliance Grid

Company Name	Page Number
M = Methods Book	
S = Solutions Book	
T = Technology	
C = Cloud Book	

Compliance Solutions Map	Education & Government	Health & Pharma	Utilities & Resources	Financial Services	Mfg	Legal & Services
R&D	OSFI C 49	Roche C 17	Southeast Water M 158	NERA T 58	Distell S 6	Ocean Conservancy C 181
Mgmt & Admin	City of Edmonton C 224	GPHIN C 60	CVPS C 39	Deutsche C 194	Sony M 21	Mumbai Airport C 84
Operations	BRZ C 226	Genzyme C 190	Energen C 10	Barclays C 211	Siemens C 255	ECHR C 188
Enterprise - Wide	Junta de Andalucia C 120	NIAID C 43	Halliburton C 99	UBS C 46	Northrop Grumman C 161	STA Travel C 150
Marketplace	Suffolk University C 124	EMP C 239	CPUC C 281	Canopius C 31	Mercedes Benz C 117	RBS 6 Nations C 114

ROI Grid

ROI Solutions Map	Retail & Media	Education & Gov	Health & Pharma	Utilities & Resources	Financial Services	Tech & Telco	AEC	Mfg	Legal & Services
R&D	EA C 169	OSFI C 49	Roche C 17	Southeast Water M 158	NERA T 58	Motorola C 263	Mott MacDonald C 12	Distell S 6	Ocean Conservancy C 181
Mgmt & Admin	Delhaize C 215	City of Edmonton C 224	GPHIN C 60	CVPS C 39	Deutsche C 194	Sony M 21	INVISTA C 206	Sony M 21	Mumbai Airport C 84
Operations	HBO C 177	BRZ C 226	Genzyme C 190	Energen C 10	Barclays C 211	T-Systems C 27	Hatch C 155	Siemens C 255	ECHR C 188
Sales	Time Warner C 6	CDN Heritage C 87	Novartis S 155	Sasol M 98	EIB C 266	Siemens C 255	Deichmann C 104	Fiat S 281	Davis + Henderson C 230
Enterprise - Wide	Cohn & Wolfe C 157	Junta de Andalucia C 120	NIAID C 43	Halliburton C 99	UBS C 46	Motorola C 263	Multiquip C 213	Northrop Grumman C 161	STA Travel C 150
Marketplace	Timberland C 174	Suffolk University C 124	EMP C 239	CPUC C 281	Canopius C 31	Open Text C 283	BEHR C 112	Mercedes Benz C 117	RBS 6 Nations C 114

M = Methods Book
S = Solutions Book
T = Technology
C = Cloud Book

Company Name	Page Number

Figure 1.1: ECM Applications

The business needs for Enterprise Content Management (ECM) 2.0 are outlined in this chapter, along with the benefits of departmental applications across a variety of industries.

Figure 1.1 displays an overview of ECM technologies. This chapter focuses on how ECM helps organizations manage content to improve productivity, reduce risk and lower the total cost of ownership – and how it does so most effectively by delivering a common data model and core applications.

CHAPTER 1

THE BUSINESS NEEDS

Digital media is growing at an amazing rate. Digital cameras were introduced in 1996 and have practically obliterated the market for conventional film. Apple's iPod® and iTunes® music store have changed the way we consume music. Similarly, Amazon's Kindle™ device and the iPad® may transform our access to newspapers, books and magazines. Mobile applications using smartphones such as the BlackBerry® and iPhone® are changing the way we work. Managing digital content has now become a way of life, both for consumers and businesses alike. Those who master it hold a significant competitive advantage.

To demonstrate the volume of digital media on the Internet, let's consider how much content is shared on the Web:

- 4 million+ original songs
- 100,000+ original films
- 40 million+ original books
- 100 billion+ web pages
- 1 million newspapers
- 1.5 billion email users
- 3.5 billion texters

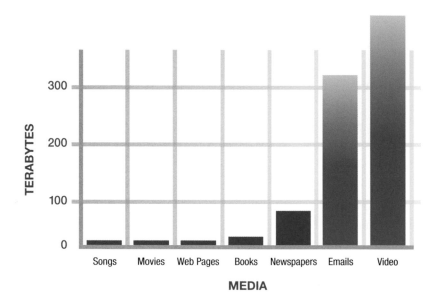

Figure 1.2: The Unchecked Growth of Digital Media is Unsustainable

To put this in perspective, let's examine a traditional medium: the newspaper. Newspapers house the largest repositories for content, requiring 100 terabytes to store information in just one year. Based on this number, the storage of newspaper content over fifty years could total 5 petabytes. When we consider the impact that email and social media could have on storage requirements, it becomes clear that the unchecked growth of digitally stored media is unsustainable. What is key here is that organizations need to do more than store media; they need to manage it as well.

As user generated content proliferates on Web sites like Facebook®, Twitter™ and YouTube®, enterprises are experiencing a similar influx of digital content inside the firewall. This content ranges from large and complex rich media files to granular XML code – and all formats in between, including business documents, vital records, reports, Web content, digital assets (images, audio and video), email, forms, letters, reports and text messages.

All businesses create, distribute, and consume content. As the volume and complexity of this content increases, so does the need to understand, locate, manage and share it. As enterprise content doubles every 9 to 12 months, so does the need to manage it. Organizations require ECM to help control growth while recovering the knowledge that resides in the unstructured content that today makes up more than 80% of enterprise information assets.

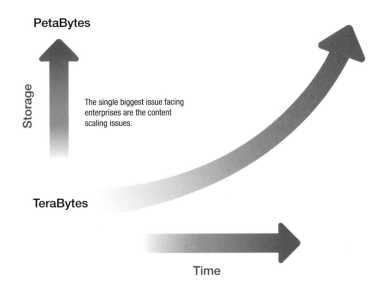

The single biggest issue facing enterprises are the content scaling issues.

Figure 1.3: Digital Content is on A Geometric Progression

Organizations rely on Enterprise Content Management (ECM) to control information overload. From a strategic perspective, ECM brings value to content by encouraging a culture of collaboration, fostering process agility, avoiding duplication and controlling the risk and cost of content.

From a technology perspective, ECM 2.0 describes a collection of inter-related technologies that help organizations create, store, manage, secure, distribute and publish digital content for enterprise use. These technologies address specific content management challenges for organizational departments, providing a valuable service for the business as a whole. ECM technologies are covered in greater detail in Chapter 2.

For ECM systems to be widely adopted, they need to emulate the way people work without disrupting their daily routines. This involves creating a digital place where people can work in much the same way they would work together in departments or at office locations. For ECM to be effective, it needs to be unobtrusive, automatically capturing the content that is produced as a by-product of this work.

The best ECM solutions deliver applications at the departmental level that integrate content management invisibly within the process of collaboration. The transparent combination of content and collaboration benefits organizations tremendously by providing a place where simple ideas take root, are nurtured and finally mature into market-leading innovations. It is a critical point and one that we will explore in detail in this book.

Time Warner
Book Group

With its rich history and vast holdings, Time Warner Book Group looked to media management as a solution to support its publishing, marketing and new media activities. Time Warner Book Group required a solution to enhance its organizational efficiencies by enabling it to find and retrieve assets more quickly and easily, while also simplifying the packaging of promotional materials for distribution to its internal Web sites and external eTailers.

The company's approach was to break its books into their digital components and establish a common meta-data standard to allow asset sharing across the company. Time Warner Book Group was able to bring formally outsourced processes, such as eBook production, in-house. Additionally, the asset management solution enables its sales force to create presentations in the field, tailored to their specific customers.

For Time Warner Book Group, the benefits of establishing such a centralized repository include the elimination of redundancies and islands of information; the ability to repurpose core information; major efficiency gains in the distribution of content and marketing materials to online and brick and mortar trading partners; a vast reduction in hardcopy circulation, photocopying, large email attachments and scanning; and reduced time spent distributing and accessing online assets.

Figure 1.4: Media Management at Time Warner

Interdepartmental Requirements

In every industry there are key steps that need to be taken to create value within an organization. In 1980, Michael Porter published his book *Competitive Advantage*, which used value chain analysis to describe the specific steps businesses could follow to improve business operations and create competitive advantage. Porter's value chain approach is an appropriate way to define the major drivers within an organization.

Value chains differ substantially between industries, but generally describe key steps common to all stakeholders in a given sector, with some organization-specific variations. Within each step, there are typically a number of processes and activities involved to support this step.

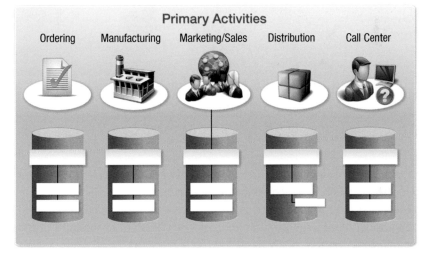

Figure 1.5: Companies Organize to Support their Value Chain

Companies are typically organized in a manner that either explicitly or implicitly supports their value chain. Simply put, if a major value creation step is the manufacturing of a product, a company will have a manufacturing department. Companies are organized by department around specific lines of business – accounting and finance, legal, administration, marketing, sales, information technology, research and development, and so on. Over the years, ECM business solutions have been designed to meet departmental requirements. These solutions are driven by the need to improve efficiency or save money. Examples include: Purchase Order Processing, Invoicing, Project Management, Claims Processing, FDA Compliance, Product Lifecycle Management (PLM), and Sales Readiness.

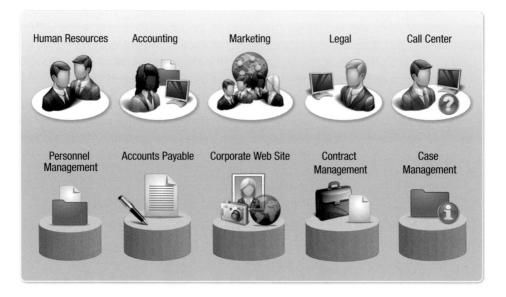

Figure 1.6: ECM Addresses Departmental Solutions

Different types of content created by each department require different content management (CM) functionality. The finance department relies on a transactional content management system to manage the capture and processing of paper invoices; whereas the marketing department uses a media management system to manage branded digital images and corporate videos.

Each of these departmental CM systems works well in isolation. In an enterprise context, however, they create information silos which make it difficult for departments to share information. Each system has its own infrastructure requirements. Often content is duplicated within silos, creating problems of legitimacy and wasted resources. Many processes require access to corporate content and expertise across a number of information silos.

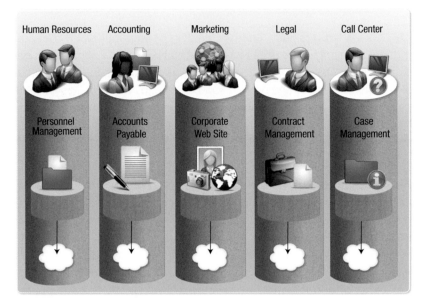

Figure 1.7: Corporate Content Trapped in Application Silos

ECM eliminates these silos by integrating different applications and interfaces to support seamless access to a centralized and secure content repository. No matter how content is created or captured, users can tap into the repository from different applications and different interfaces.

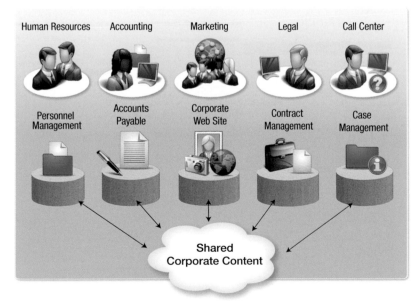

Figure 1.8: Shared Corporate Content

> Energen

Energen is a diversified energy holding company with headquarters in Birmingham, Alabama. One of its two lines of business is the acquisition, development and exploration of domestic, onshore natural gas and oil reserves. The other is natural gas distribution in central and north Alabama through Alabama Gas Corp. In the natural gas business, records have a long life. Government regulations require that service lines, which are typically buried underground, be tracked for the life of the corporation. Other aspects of energy production are also highly regulated, so Energen needed a robust document and records management system.

One criterion for selection was the ability to integrate well with the ERP system used by Energen. Another was the ability to manage very large volumes of data, because Energen wanted to archive all of the emails it sends and receives for the required retention period. "The use of an email archiving system is a component of our overall document management strategy," said General Manager of IT, Lynn Lovelady. "We started our document management program with a single application and continue to expand it to other areas of our company." An archiving system takes out duplicate copies of emails and attachments, reducing the total storage space required.

In the Accounts Payable department, invoices are scanned and meta-data is released to the ERP system. This initiates the Procure-to-Pay process through automated workflows and the documents archived in the ECM system. Use of ECM technology has allowed Energen to consolidate multiple applications so that all the content is stored in the repository, with workflow and authorization handled by the ERP system.

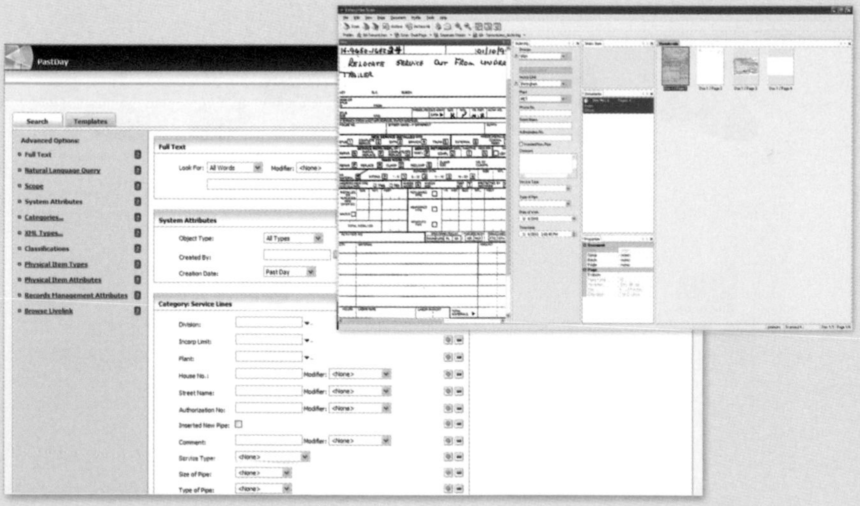

Figure 1.9: ECM Consolidates Multiple Applications at Energen

 www.opentext.com/ecmbook/innovator/energen

The decisive strength of ECM 2.0 is its ability to cross departmental, content and application silos. To illustrate this, let's examine how a sales department interacts with a legal department to process a new customer acquisition. A sales representative uses a CRM system to store information on a prospective customer. Once a contract is signed, the legal department processes the contract in a contract management application. An ECM system connects processes across departments, allowing content to flow from one format (Word) to another (PDF). Although each department might have its own workflow, notifications are used to alert the legal department about the sales contract. The legal department fulfills the next step, transforming content formats to cross departmental silos and repositories.

An enterprise deployment of ECM 2.0 involves more than just a shared repository; effective enterprise adoption of ECM maximizes the flow of information across an organization's value chain. How? By working on existing infrastructure and integrating business processes across silos, being accessible from anywhere in the world, and leveraging peoples' knowledge of common Web technology. Because it is easy to use and improves the way people work together, ECM 2.0 increases overall productivity, employee satisfaction, and the workplace environment. ECM spans departments, applications and repositories to maximize the flow of content across an organization.

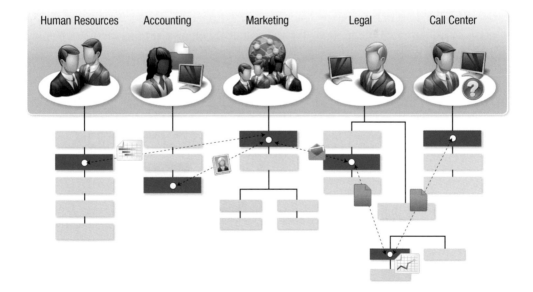

Figure 1.10: ECM Maximizes Content Flow across an Organization's Value Chain

> # Mott MacDonald Group

The Mott MacDonald Group is a management, engineering, and development consultancy serving the public and private sectors worldwide. One of the organization's main currencies is documents – from business case studies to progress reports, from engineering drawings to complex engineering processes. Due to the importance of these documents, coupled with the growth of the company's activities, Mott MacDonald decided it needed an enhanced document management solution to better support its risk management strategy and also improve efficiency in document production.

Document Management with Extended Collaboration has provided Mott MacDonald with a comprehensive information management solution, delivering a consistent approach to the management of documents and information. It has enabled its project teams to share knowledge more efficiently and communicate more effectively.

Integrated with their ERP system, the solution has brought consistency to all of Mott MacDonald's projects and staff no longer needs to learn new methods of working with each project. Mott MacDonald currently has 20 terabytes of information and 14,000 projects stored on the system, which has dramatically increased efficiencies between project teams. Collaboration is now simplified and staff has access to one single, reliable, and verified source that eliminates document duplication. Initially 500 to 600 users had access to the system; following online training and rollout activities, this has been extended to 6,000. In time, this will be further extended to all Mott MacDonald's 14,000 employees.

Figure 1.11: ECM Manages 20 Terabytes and 14,000 Projects

The inter-departmental benefits of deploying an ECM solution include harnessing collective knowledge to break down geographic and organizational boundaries and make a distributed organization more efficient. ECM 2.0 enables teamwork and sparks creativity.

Organizations are changing in fundamental ways. Until now, silos and hierarchies have defined information flow and internal communication. ECM 2.0 provides the rich content and the links which now define the knowledge organization. Communities form across all levels of the hierarchy. Some are traditional, such as the management team that brings the heads of department together once a month to discuss corporate policy and direction. 'Project' communities cross departmental silos on many levels. To illustrate, imagine a project to install a new computer network in your office. IT will be involved with engineering, logistics, administration and finance. In fact, just about every department in the enterprise will be affected in some way and will need to play a role in the project. And even a simple business process, such as raising a purchase order, will touch a virtual community of employees within the business. ECM 2.0 empowers individuals to collaborate with peers and work in virtual communities that span the globe.

ECM Architecture

As demonstrated above, collaborating across departments is essential for many critical business operations and applications. All perspectives are needed, and connecting employees from different backgrounds to address a common problem creates conditions conducive to innovation. In many organizations, achieving this cooperation is the very basis for long term competitive advantage.

The issue of cross-departmental functionality raises two important concerns for ECM architecture:

1. In order for multiple departments to collaborate or work together efficiently, both business and IT staff require infrastructure support.

2. An underlying common data model is required to allow people in different departments to share information contained in separate applications at a cost-effective rate.

While it can be argued that some applications can be delivered within a department, most ECM applications need to be enterprise-wide in nature so that they can be accessed easily across departments.

As organizations move to leverage the same infrastructure for process improvements, finding a solution often results in a long-term, strategic ECM. This involves deploying an integrated series of applications across an entire organization. To make these applications simple to deploy and cost-effective to replicate, a common set of technologies with the same content model is required as an underlying infrastructure.

Figure 1.12: ECM Architecture Simplified

ECM systems that can be easily adapted to meet each department's unique needs, while maintaining a common data model are inherently more flexible and future proof. With this basic architecture, organizations benefit from the common integration layers which enable all elements to communicate and share information, alongside the flexibility of the system which allows it to address specific business requirements. This is demonstrated in the customer example in which Energen standardizes its processes across a common data model with an integrated ECM and ERP system for records management.

Implementing ECM applications on a common data model results in lower total cost of ownership and faster implementation times, leading to greater productivity and higher returns on technology investments.

ECM 2.0 Applications

Departmental applications are models for a phased enterprise rollout of ECM. Once an application has been deployed at the departmental or group level, the IT department involved in implementing the first application can use the lessons learned to solve other content issues in other departments. While the first deployment may take place in the sales department, the next may occur in manufacturing, and so on. Some of the most advanced ECM-enabled organizations in the world today have more than 20 distinct department-level applications supported by a common underlying suite of technologies and a common data model.

Figure 1.13: ECM Applications

Some of the solutions that have been developed for ECM include:

- Accounts Payable
- Case Management
- Collaborative Submissions
- Compliance & Governance
- Conflict Management
- Content Migration
- Contract Management
- Correspondence Tracking
- Data Integration
- eDiscovery
- Email Lifecycle Management
- Engineering Document Management

- Enterprise Portals
- Enterprise Search
- Knowledge Management
- Library & Collection Management
- Management of Change
- Mobility
- Program Management
- Quality Management
- Records Management
- Recruiting Management
- Regulated Documents
- Transactional Content Management

There are hundreds of ECM solutions implemented in organizations in major industries throughout the world. This book profiles many of those ECM success stories.

Industry Requirements

ECM customers are looking for a solution that provides a common technology for many different applications. Departmental applications have evolved to add elements that address specific vertical market needs. An organization's pain points are often specific to a particular industry, so customers prefer a vendor that has expertise in their industry. An ECM solution gains traction in an industry when one organization begins to use a solution and other organizations expect this solution to resolve their issues as well.

Within many industries, managing content is absolutely critical. Pharmaceutical companies are early adopters of ECM because managing documents related to a new drug application is a regulatory requirement for doing business. We have seen how pharmaceutical organizations face stringent compliance standards. The FDA New Drug Application (NDA) requires organizations to provide detailed information about what happens during clinical tests, what the ingredients of a drug are, the results of test studies, how a drug behaves in the body and how a drug is manufactured, processed and packaged. The integrated document and records management, collaboration and workflow functionality of a comprehensive ECM solution enables pharmaceutical organizations to detail the lifecycle of a product from start to finish. Using a comprehensive ECM suite, pharmaceutical employees can seamlessly review new drug markets, deploy personnel and resources, manage drug discovery projects and accelerate time to market.

Productivity Gains

ECM 2.0 is not just about controlling and managing business content and the repositories where it resides. It is about understanding the relationship between people, processes, and content in an organization. It is about documenting how content flows within and across departments, what systems it touches and what processes it affects. In addition, it is about understanding all types of content – from faxes to emails to blogs – and managing their entire lifecycle from creation through disposal. It is about our key competitive asset: knowledge.

ECM addresses the higher-level needs of the knowledge-intensive organization; how to increase overall organizational effectiveness in a volatile business environment. It does so by giving people ready access to the right content, regardless of format or where it is stored – inside the company or outside the firewall. ECM also provides tools that enable collaboration, workflow, and process improvement to help people work more efficiently.

ECM automates manual, content-based processes to increase efficiency and quality. By combining collaboration and social media, ("social collaboration"), ECM 2.0 creates context around content, enabling people to come together to develop ideas that become the foundation for innovation.

Pharmaceutical product development cycles – from conception to marketing – require on average four to ten years longer than in most other industries. Increasing the efficiency at which global development teams cooperate is critical in determining the speed at which new drugs can be readied for the market.

Roche's ECM-based platform for information sharing, entitled ShareWeb, supports the full lifecycle of global team projects. Providing a single point of access to training information, compliance programs and a broad range of documents, ECM helps improve efficiency at each stage of Roche's new product development cycles.

Since the launch of ShareWeb, access to documents is independent of formats, knowledge from previous projects is available and updated at all times, international teams can be assembled faster, and new team members are easily inaugurated. "ShareWeb brings the various countries in the Asia-Pacific region into one community," says Roche's Medical Director, Taiwan.

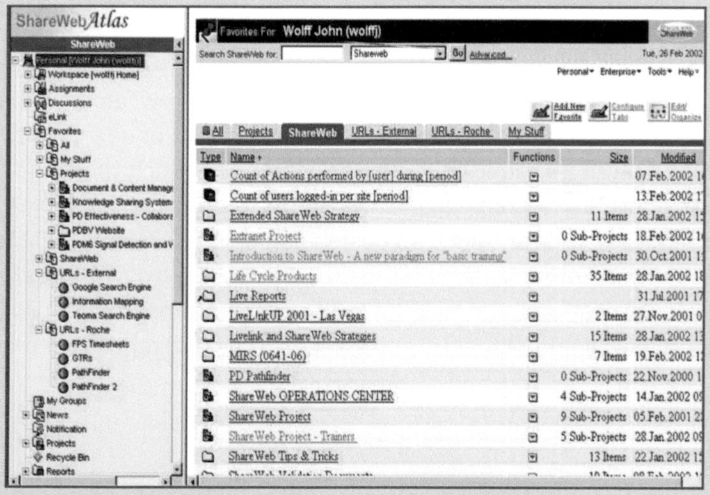

Figure 1.14: Roche's ShareWeb

Figure 1.15: ECM Technologies

As ECM reaches maturity in the market, it has evolved into a blend of proven technologies designed to solve a variety of content and process-centric problems. For global organizations, ECM solutions will simply become part of the cost of doing business.

Within the enterprise, the reliance on content will continue to grow, along with the need to store and manage content effectively. Based on the proliferation of new media, technology and devices, ECM 2.0 will be required to deliver personalized rich media content to any audience using any device – securely and efficiently. As Web 2.0 technologies continue to introduce new methods of delivery, such as hosted content applications (ECM-as-service) and open source software, organizations will need to control the risks and costs associated with content. The enterprise will turn to ECM 2.0 help ensure that content is stored in an optimal, cost-effective way and managed according to legal and regulatory requirements.

While Chapter 1 discussed how ECM applications can be used to address business needs, this chapter will focus on ECM 2.0 technologies. Chapter 2 explores the definition of ECM 2.0 as a combined set of technologies and provides an overview of each technology.

Figure 2.1: ECM Technologies

ECM 2.0 technologies can be grouped into three categories as shown in Figure 2.1:

- Engagement
- Transaction
- Lifecycle

These three categories represent the core groups of technologies required to connect people, processes and content across an organization. We will discuss all of these technologies in much greater detail and provide the terminology used for each of these core ECM components. While the method by which these technologies can be delivered may differ (inside the firewall versus in the "cloud," for example, and across multiple devices and applications), the same core technology components exist.

ECM 2.0 TECHNOLOGIES

As the Internet expands to support increasing amounts of users and content, organizations throughout the world will require Enterprise Content Management technologies to manage digital media. To understand how organizations implement ECM technologies to address their business needs, it is important to examine the impact of the Internet and emerging Web technologies on ECM.

The Emergence of ECM 2.0

Since the mid 1990s, the Internet has overtaken ERP systems to profoundly impact ECM technologies specifically, and society in general, by dramatically changing how people access and share information. The following statistics, based on the number of transactions made and users connected, reflect a remarkable reliance on the Internet for communications and collaboration:

- The Web connects more than 1 billion people

- Web content appears to be doubling month over month

- The rate of connections by people to the Web appear to be doubling in less than one year

The relatively brief history of the modern Internet began decades ago as a much smaller and more restricted network, first among U.S. agencies and then universities. Three eras have been identified to represent the evolution of Internet or Web technologies. As the Internet has progressed from browser-based content access to a platform or system that facilitates dialogue to a highly interactive artificial intelligence system, these three eras have been recognized as Web 1.0, Web 2.0 and Web 3.0 respectively.

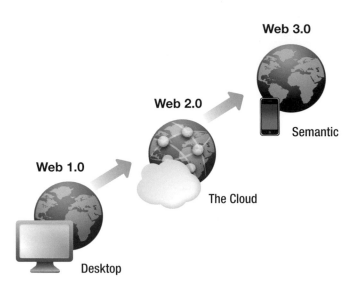

Figure 2.2: Eras of ECM

Each of these three eras of Internet development has affected ECM technologies in different ways. Web 1.0, the earliest version of the Internet, is characterized by Web sites as digitized version of newspapers and corporate brochures. Browser limitations and slow connection speeds (or bandwidth) restricted the types of applications that were possible. In Web 1.0, basic content technologies were created, including search engines, document management and Web content management applications. As the Web grew to support more content, the sophistication of these technologies increased in scale and complexity.

Mainframe and client-server computing systems moved online to connect these content management technologies with enterprise content, making both more accessible than previous LAN (local area network) systems. ECM technologies were then assembled into suites to manage the complete lifecycle of electronic documents, from their creation to archive or eventual deletion. For the first time, these ECM technologies could be accessed using a standard Web browser interface rather than requiring software to be installed on a personal computer. Web 1.0 for ECM provided a Web-based interface for content management technologies and the historical enterprise repository.

> Canada 3.0

Canada 3.0 is organized by the Canadian Digital Media Network (or CDMN) and the University of Waterloo's Stratford Institute. Launched in 2008, the event itself provides a once-a-year opportunity for Canadians in digital media to come together to discuss the key issues and make the plans required to propel Canada to a leadership position in global digital media. The purpose of the CDMN is to link Canada's digital media clusters from coast to coast and create a digital convergence corridor, including a focus on digital media research, commercialization and innovation.

The event is largely focused around building critical connections and networks. The Canada 3.0 Community provides a platform for continuing dialogue, based on a central repository for collecting and sharing the information, discussions, and outcomes of all event-based collaborations. The online community, complete with embedded media, blogs, forums, member profiles, and a Twitter feed on the home page promotes dialogue and maintains momentum around the event all year long – all of which will contribute toward the ultimate development of the CDMN.

The online community is a good example of cross-media integration. The site is driven largely by user generated content and uses social media to integrate online and offline presentations at the event. During its inaugural event, Canada 3.0 gathered feedback and input from attendees in order to accurately determine the goals, mission and objectives of the CDMN. Using social media content, the CDMN was able to generate interest in the show, highlight key events and collect invaluable feedback around key stakeholders, target audience, areas of focus and more.

Figure 2.3: Canada 3.0's Community Facilitates Critical Dialogue and Networking

After a decade, Internet technologies evolved into Web 2.0, which describes the Web as a social platform based on applications that facilitate interactive and instantaneous information sharing and collaboration over the Internet. The Web as a social platform grew to accommodate a growing and diversified community of users, driving the creation of new collaboration technologies including blogs and wikis. As these collaboration tools have risen in popularity, organizations have been forced to consider how people access content outside the firewall. With Web 2.0 technologies, security and privacy have become key issues around content – unlike Web 1.0 technologies – which protected content and applications inside the corporate firewall. At the same time, the enterprise has had to grapple with escalating amounts of email and integrating email management with ECM systems to enable comprehensive content management and ensure compliance.

At present, emerging Web technologies are defining a new era which is sometimes referred to as Web 3.0 or the Semantic Web. This era is characterized by highly intelligent, interconnected and very personal interactions with the multiple device types connected to the Web. Personalization can occur unobtrusively by matching past interactions through many devices. Web applications will be able to build up a digital identity of an individual and target content accordingly. The Web can respond to this real-time "telepresence" as an artificial intelligence (AI) system. Based on new devices and technologies, the Semantic Web is able to interact with users within context to create "meaning" or semantic information that is highly relevant and personalized. The technology developed in this era that will have the greatest effect on ECM is the mobile user interface which will bring greater context to a content transaction through geographical awareness and enable productive use of content anywhere, at any time.

Now that we have described the origins of ECM technologies and the impact of the Internet on these technologies, we can examine the technology components that make up an ECM suite.

Bringing all the Technologies Together

Enterprise Content Management (ECM) is an integrated suite of products comprised of the diverse technologies previously discussed.

The component technologies that underpin ECM are shown in the diagram below.

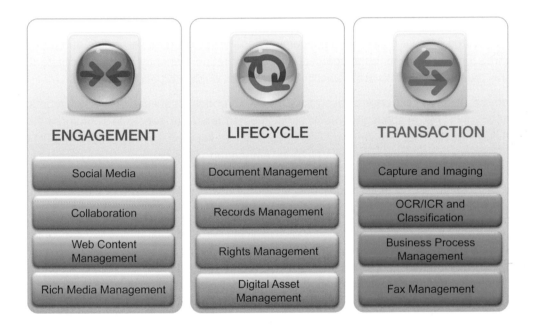

Figure 2.4: ECM Technologies

When combined into a suite, ECM 2.0 technologies help manage and optimize the flow of content throughout the enterprise. Engagement technologies such as social media, collaboration, Web content management and media management drive user engagement; applications that support the full lifecycle of content include document management, records management and archiving, and media management; and finally, processes that are transaction-based and place content in the context of a larger ECM system are enabled by capture and image technologies, fax management and ultimately, business process management.

Making sense of all this technology is a challenge, so let's simplify the picture.

Engagement Technologies

Engagement technologies focus on the productivity of teams and individuals – or people-centric business issues – and require communication and interactions between people. Individual productivity begins with the ability to find the right information at the right time, which is addressed by search, navigation and recommendation technologies. Individuals also need to rely on accessing the most appropriate and up-to-date content assets, which are delivered by core document management capabilities such as versioning and access control. Finally, document management and collaboration technologies also facilitate the active reuse of content to avoid wasting resources on duplicated efforts.

Team productivity can be increased through synchronous (real-time) and asynchronous collaboration that enables geographically distributed teams of people to coordinate their activities. Social media technology takes this ability to the next level by providing a richer collaborative experience with microblogs or embedded video content, and by facilitating joint authoring of content with technologies such as wikis. Individuals can also use social media technologies for expert location – giving organizations new avenues to discover and foster innovation.

Collaboration and social media technologies facilitate communication between team members and groups within an organization. There is also the need, however, to interact with stakeholders outside an organization. This is accomplished with Web content management technologies and multi-channel content delivery. Finally, a variety of rich digital assets can be managed with media management applications.

·· **T** ··Systems·

With branches in more than 20 countries, T-Systems, the busiest customer brand of Deutsche Telekom, is the provider of choice for conducting global business by many major European customers. Around 160,000 companies and public bodies make use of T-Systems' integrated services – everything from managing data centers and global Internet protocol services to developing and administering applications.

T-System's teams needed a platform that would allow them to come together quickly and easily to exchange information and ensure the professional and efficient execution of customer projects. Approximately 40,000 T-Systems employees are now using a company-wide ECM platform for collaboration, document management and knowledge management.

T-Systems is enhancing its collaboration platform with an extranet gateway to facilitate collaboration with customers and partners and a lifecycle management system for project rooms with storage periods of up to 10 years. This second feature will enable T-Systems to meet its compliance obligations in the area of corporate governance, while simultaneously making valuable, but dormant project information searchable at a later date.

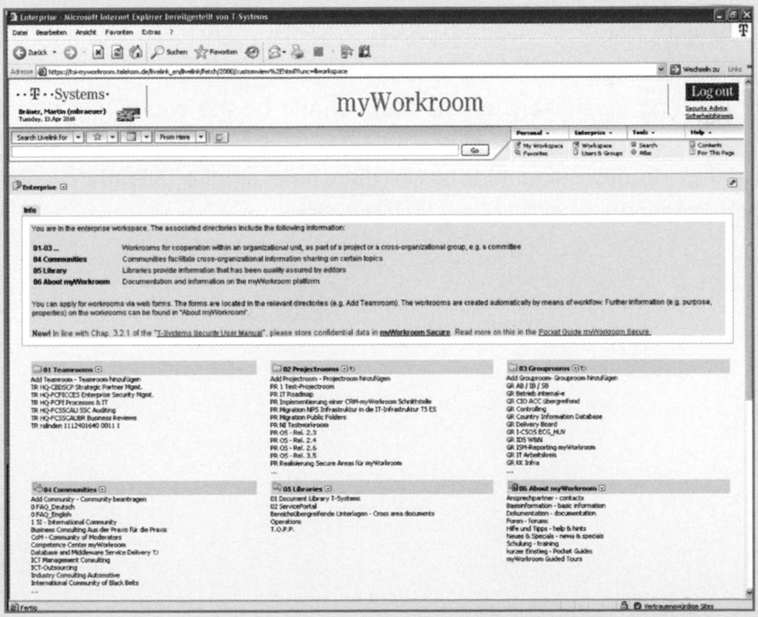

Figure 2.5: T-Systems Company-Wide Collaboration Platform

Lifecycle Technologies

All the information, ideas and data created as a by-product of collaborative work need to be securely captured, managed and made available to others. Lifecycle technologies manage content-centric business issues.

According to research, content volume has been increasing by 67% year over year, and it is now outpacing the storage capacity required to store this content. Enterprise archiving, together with storage management, are technologies that work to resolve this issue. Security and intellectual property protection are also addressed by the security and rights management capabilities of enterprise archives.

Compliance and corporate governance are business drivers behind technologies such as retention and records management, auditing, electronic signatures, and workflow. Compliance typically requires that content is kept for a defined period of time in an irrefutable way, that the organization can trace content back to creation and through modification, that tasks can be explicitly signed off, that certain steps occur in sequence, and of course, that only the appropriate individuals have access to the content they need to do their jobs effectively.

Since the new Federal Rules of Civil Procedures (FRCP) have been adopted in the USA, the litigation landscape has shifted significantly regarding content. In adherence to the FRCP, content can and most likely will be subpoenaed by the courts. Organizations are responsible for producing requested content, along with shouldering the requisite cost and potential for liability. As other countries adopt the same stance, litigation readiness has become a major driver behind eDiscovery technologies.

Buncombe County, a local level of government in North Carolina, needed to enhance information sharing and reduce the amount of paper created and stored. With over 1,900 employees in almost two dozen different areas, Buncombe County needed a way to streamline administrative processes and improve customer service.

In Human Resources, for example, all processes were paper based and each department had their own copies of their employee files; payroll had copies and personnel had the official employee record. There was a tremendous amount of paper that required duplicated file storage and maintenance. By replacing the paper personnel file with an electronic file, the County has created a comprehensive electronic personnel data storehouse that spans the lifecycle of the employee.

Using integrated content and records management systems, Buncombe County shares information between departments, has reduced storage requirements, and has drastically improved efficiencies. There is no more duplication, the amount of work has been greatly reduced, and as a rule, documents do not get lost and departments have the right information. The County is also provided with a complete audit trail of all transactions and personnel who have access to official records.

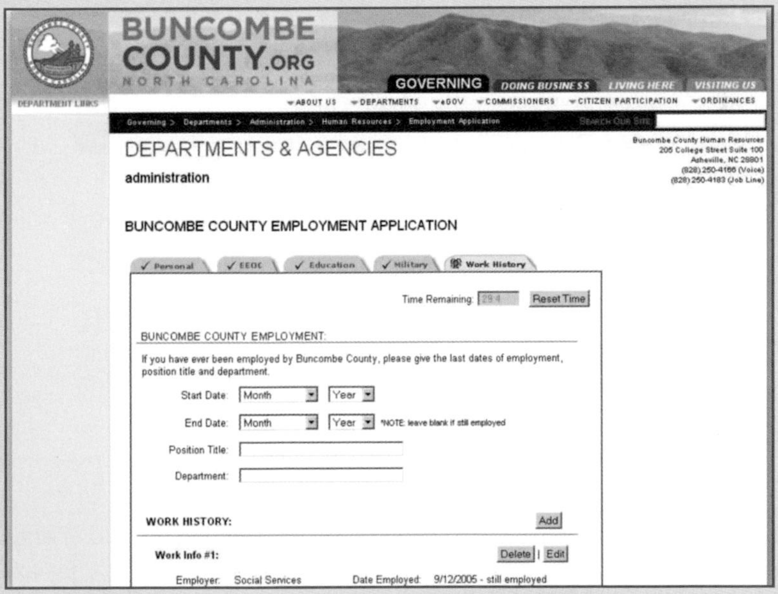

Figure 2.6: Streamlining Administrative Processes at Buncombe County

Transaction Technologies

The third type of business issues are focused around business processes and how they improve efficiencies, shorten cycles, lower costs, reduce resources and increase product or service quality. Business processes are usually initiated by a trigger, which can be a received correspondence, fax, email, online submission, or message from another application. Consequently, technologies such as scanning and imaging, automatic document recognition, optical character recognition and fax management are involved.

Once initiated, business processes are orchestrated by a process engine that also facilitates interactions with other applications. But before processes can be orchestrated, they need to be designed, modeled, and deployed. As a process is completed, a required activity is triggered, which can include passing off information to another application, printing a document stream, sending a message via fax or email, or posting information on a self-service portal. In most cases, all information related to the process – including data and content – is archived and retained for a fixed time period.

User Experience Services

While the above-mentioned foundational technologies form the basis of ECM, user experience also plays an important role in the successful deployment of an ECM solution.

Figure 2.7: User Experience Services

User experience is critical to motivate end users to engage with applications and to stimulate productivity. While the Internet browser is the de facto standard for user experience, many applications require a desktop-based experience, a portal or a mobile device. User interface (UI) development is driven by advances in consumer applications and devices. End users have come to expect richer visualizations with physics engines, 3D modeling of virtual spaces and touch or gesture based interactions.

Canopius is an international insurance and reinsurance group that operates at Lloyd's and through its overseas operations in Bermuda, Singapore, Ireland and Australia. Canopius has selected ECM to improve processes, reduce filing costs and support the implementation of electronic trading.

With technical advances in communications, the London insurance market has introduced an improvement initiative to reduce administrative overheads and improve servicing times. Electronic messages and documents are key elements of this improvement program, and participants in this market are tasked with adopting these new electronic solutions. Canopius was keen to support these improvement initiatives in readiness to trade with business partners on an electronic basis, whilst introducing more immediate efficiencies to its business processes.

Realizing the potential market demand for electronic trading, Canopius identified the need for a solution that would enable the organization to exchange information electronically with brokers and third parties around the world. They had already started work on a series of process models defining improved business functions and required a compatible workflow system to support these processes with minimal IT development effort. Adopting an ECM solution, Canopius relies on integrated business process and content management for long-term benefits such as improved visibility of 'work in progress', reduction in the effort needed for administrative tasks in the underwriting and claims areas, and general process improvements.

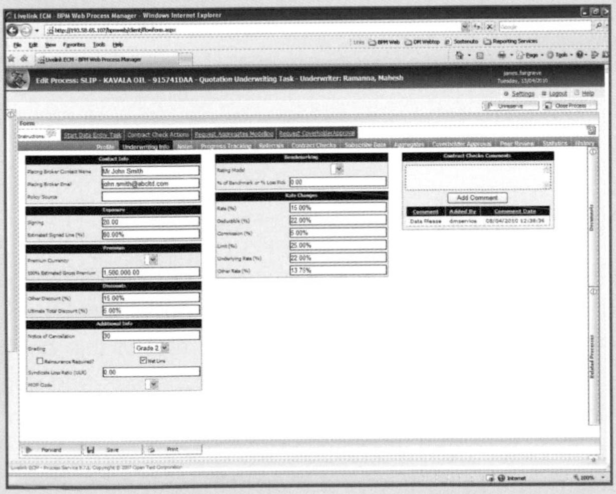

Figure 2.8: Business Process Management at Canopius

An effective ECM solution delivers all of the tools necessary to produce and manage content in any format, by multiple users across unlimited domains. An intuitive UI connects complex functionality to provide an integrated desktop, Web, portal and mobile experience. ECM 2.0 gives end users seamless access to all engagement, transaction and lifecycle based technologies.

Enterprise Library Services

A logical centralized repository is a key requirement for any true, enterprise-scale content management system. Enterprise content is stored, shared and managed inside a shared repository, giving end users access to content, no matter where it resides within the ECM system. Although different applications might require distinct repository abilities for high volume transaction processing, long-term retention, or high performance delivery to Web sites, these repositories must enable common policies and corporate-wide taxonomies. Content is protected in a repository where it is stored in secure, compliant and reusable ways. By ensuring continuity and recovery in the event of disaster, a central repository also protects against accidental loss of critical content.

Figure 2.9: Enterprise Library Services

The ECM Value Proposition

ECM combines the engagement, lifecycle and transaction based technologies to deliver true end-to-end solutions that address three universal requirements: end user empowerment, business agility, and cost and risk reduction. The rest of this book outlines in detail how ECM helps organizations to manage people, processes and content. The value proposition of ECM lies in the effective management of content to mitigate risk and ensure compliance, increase innovation and adoption, streamline efficiencies to fast track critical decision-making and increase agility to create competitive advantage.

Figure 2.10: The Value Proposition of ECM

ECM Solutions Framework

The diagram below shows the technologies that form the framework for a fully integrated ECM suite. The framework provides a layer of repository, process and user experience services which link knowledge workers to an enterprise library of information via multiple user experience services. These user experience services (or interfaces) present customizable views of business content. The enterprise library delivers access to a trusted repository to consistently enforce and manage retention schedules, corporate governance and regulatory compliance policies for all content types in the enterprise.

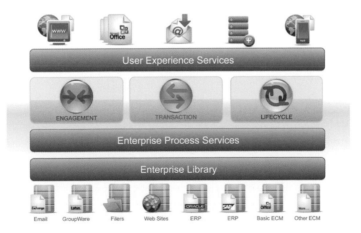

Figure 2.11: ECM Solutions Framework

An ECM framework delivers integrated and secure access to content across the enterprise and supports storing the content on any mix of storage devices from leading vendors. Enterprise process services deliver a common framework for automating the routing of information and documents, entering information via forms and notifying information workers of critical tasks and events via email. An ECM framework facilitates the smooth evolution of existing solutions, speeds development of new solutions and provides agility for the enterprise to be responsive to change.

Now that you are familiar with the fundamental technologies of Enterprise Content Management, we can begin the journey of discovery that led to the creation of a market.

The remaining chapters of the book focus on specific areas of ECM technology. In them, you will learn the history behind each technology and discover how organizations are using ECM 2.0 today as the foundation for innovation, compliance and accelerated growth.

Figure 3.1: Compliance and Information Governance

Compliance and Information Governance is delivered across all of the departments within an ECM driven organization.

This chapter outlines how ECM solutions are helping many of the world's leading companies address compliance and information governance issues. Featured innovator stories demonstrate how businesses across all industries are using ECM solutions to minimize risk, achieve compliance and optimize operations.

CHAPTER 3

COMPLIANCE AND INFORMATION GOVERNANCE

Organizations are under increasing levels of scrutiny. In every industry and in all countries, countless government regulations, industry standards and company procedures exist. How a company manages both its operations and its information has a direct impact on shareholder value. At the risk of losing shareholders, customers and bottom-line profits, organizations must do what they can to manage their intellectual assets and minimize risk.

Poor management and non-compliance can lead to lost business, financial penalties and even criminal charges. In some industries, failing an auditor's inspection can lead to a company being closed down until corrective action is taken. Corporations across the globe are striving to learn from the enormous regulatory failures of companies such as Enron, along with Lehman Brothers, Bear Stearns and AIG in the recent global economic crisis.

Regulations such as the SEC's passage of the mandatory XBRL filing requirements, the Sarbanes-Oxley (SOX) Act, the Data Protection Act and its equivalent European Directive, and amendments made to the Federal Rules of Civil Procedure (FRCP) have driven requirements for organizations to maintain strict control over their data to protect against liability and comply with regulations to ensure business continuity.

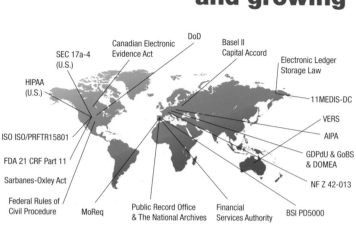

More than 100,000 rules and regulations worldwide...
and growing

Figure 3.2: Global Regulatory Pressures

Organizations are increasingly relying on innovative content management solutions to mitigate risk, make information transparent and collect, refine and distribute best practices. Enterprise content management delivers effective solutions for compliance and information governance, enabling organizations to control information across disparate sources and applications in the enterprise ecosystem.

Compliance Defined

Regardless of industry, regulation, country, or even voluntary regulations like the ISO series, organizations face a number of risks and overlapping requirements that impact almost every aspect of the business. Finding a regulatory best practice "key" that will leverage the balance between efficiency and effectiveness for a company is crucial to enable active compliance across the enterprise.

There are greater benefits associated with compliancy beyond mitigating risks and avoiding penalties. Regulations are based on demands that inherently describe optimal business operations; by practicing "active compliance", organizations are ensuring that their businesses adhere to industry-established best practices and procedures.

> Central Vermont Public Service

Central Vermont Public Service (CVPS) is an independent, investor-owned company that provides energy and energy-related services to 157,000 customers across Vermont. As the largest of the 21 utilities within the state, CVPS has its share of content management opportunities.

"As a high performance company we need to ensure that the right information is in the right place at the right time so we can make the right decision. To do this we have to incorporate compliance mandates, overcome information organization challenges, and constantly improve business processes. Additionally, there are regulations from multiple authorities that mandate how long we need to keep information," says Chuck Piotrowski, Corporate Records Manager for CVPS. "ECM enables us to maintain a good balance between compliance and business need."

Their ECM environment allows them to manage much of their information in one convenient and secure location. They have access to all of their structured and unstructured content, no matter which format it is in – email, spreadsheets, Word documents, PDFs, etc. Using ECM, CVPS is able to meet compliance regulations and manage its operations in a more transparent and efficient manner by ensuring that all content is safe, searchable, and readily accessible – regardless of the application software.

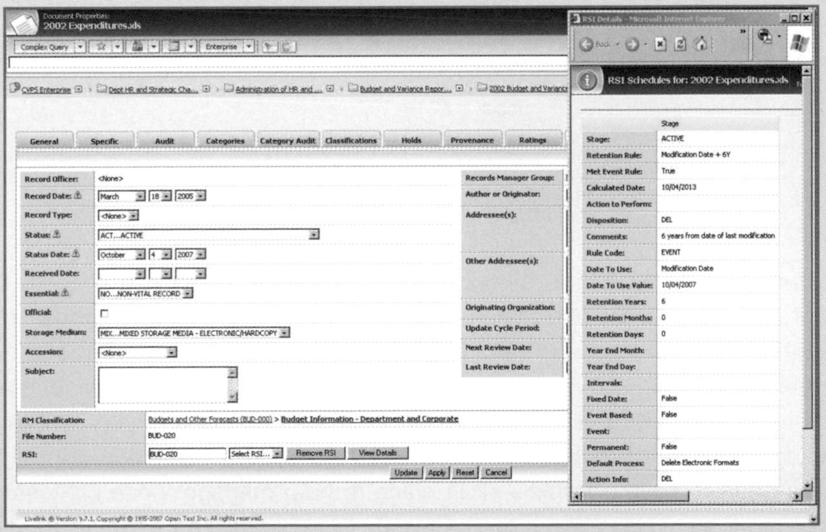

Figure 3.3: Records Management and Archiving Options at CVPS

With active compliance, an organization transforms the burden of compliance into an opportunity to improve the conduct of business. By committing to continuous improvement, visibility, granularity and transparency, an institution assures shareholders that it is focused on their investment and interests. By building a defect-free enterprise… institutions can transform the cost of compliance into an investment. Technologies that automate, standardize, control and optimize business processes provide an opportunity to drive out costs and improve business conduct. [1]

What lies at the heart of compliance is ensuring that people do the "right things" in a particular way or according to a defined level of performance. Accordingly, compliance prevents people from doing the "wrong things" – either deliberately or by accident. But simply complying is not enough; in today's litigious business environment, organizations must also prove their adherence to rules and regulations. Achieving compliance requires the execution of best practices without error and proving this by providing accurate information.

Figure 3.4: A Simplified Compliance Model

ECM platforms play a key role in allowing organizations to comply in a cost-effective and efficient manner. An ECM solution ensures smooth operations, proper delegation of authority and acceptance of risk. ECM can help overcome the inertia of "silos"– organizational, functional, and process silos – and reduce the challenge of tracking, monitoring, reporting and auditing on overlapping and conflicting regulations. It is not enough to implement policies and procedures. To reduce error and control costs, organizations need to have a framework in place to help manage these processes and controls, inform all employees about the necessity of implementing ECM, while meeting reporting and auditing demands.

---

[1] Crump, James. *"Passive vs. active compliance: active compliance mitigates cost, improves business and reduces risk. (Technology Strategies)."* Bank Accounting & Finance. 2007

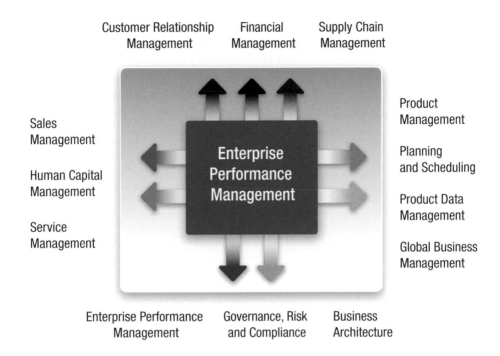

Figure 3.5: ECM Delivers an Integrated Framework for Best Practices

Implementing a Compliance Strategy

As diverse as the various local, national, or global regulations are, they all share common elements:

- Governance structure
- Assured, audited, appropriate delivery of all guidance
- Training records, both as proof of delivered guidance and an inventory of defined skills and competences
- Means to measure ongoing compliance effectiveness and exception handling
- Internal audits and accompanying CAPA (Corrective And Preventive Action) mechanisms
- Records keeping
- Process management tools to improve efficiency and minimize error
- Reporting on compliance processes

ECM as a Platform for Compliance

By bringing together diverse policies, procedures, documents and individuals, it is easy to see how a compliance initiative could be fragmented and hard to manage, monitor and report on. When properly configured, the components of an ECM suite can be implemented to manage all aspects of compliance. ECM delivers a seamless solution which connects procedural guidance with documentation, process execution tools, reporting and audits, integration with ERP systems and the ability to document and prove compliance.

Information Governance Defined

Historically, ECM has provided a proven platform for enabling compliance initiatives across many industries, including financial services, pharmaceutical and life sciences, and energy and utilities. However, such initiatives are often very specific to a given industry, with stringent regulations governing an organization's policies and practices.

In recent years, the need for corporate compliance concerning electronic information has evolved in the wake of numerous legal disputes where content served as the evidentiary centerpiece in highly publicized trials. Approaching information management and retention in terms of ensuring regulatory and corporate compliance has become only a single pillar of the overall information governance needs of organizations. More importantly, to minimize legal costs and risks, companies across all industries are compelled to define and enforce policies and practices governing the creation, retention, preservation, identification, review, and production of all electronically stored information. In today's aggressively litigious environment – intensified by the staggering growth of electronic information – it is critical to have a measured and consistent means of managing corporate data.

Information governance is both an emerging and evolving concept, borne out of the traditional archiving market. Fundamentally, information governance is about bringing consistency and scale to the retention, management, and destruction of electronic information. While the basic premise of archiving electronic information forms the backbone of information governance technology, it is the inclusion of many peripheral concepts – like records management, enterprise search and eDiscovery, and business continuity – that truly defines information governance on a grander scale.

Implementing an Information Governance Strategy

Before considering a technology solution, it is crucial for organizations to articulate a long-term information governance strategy. The strategy must be inclusive of every stakeholder in the organization who is charged with, or impacted by, the efficacy of the program. Typically, this mandates involvement from individuals within the IT department, legal depart-

NIAID is part of the National Institutes of Health (NIH), which is an agency within the U.S. Department of Health and Human Services and the primary federal agency for conducting and supporting biomedical research. NIAID, the second largest NIH Institute with an annual budget of over $4.7B, focuses its research on infectious diseases like HIV/AIDS, flu, tuberculosis, and malaria, as well as tropical diseases and a number of other infectious diseases.

NIAID had been experiencing exponential growth of electronic documents that needed to be shared among thousands of staff and contractors worldwide. The agency had been using a solution to facilitate basic content management and collaboration, but needed to find additional ECM capabilities, including sophisticated workflow and advanced document and records management functions.

To address these requirements, NIAID created a unique, integrated ECM strategy to establish synergy between its existing infrastructure and an ECM suite. This integration enabled NIAID to enhance the Institute's storage, management, and collaboration capabilities. NIAID benefited from important efficiency and accuracy improvements as the Institute can now effectively store and share information among its over 1,600 federal staff and many onsite and offsite contractors and grantees across several divisions and many locations. This approach also ensured the Institute's ability to comply with a complex array of government and industry regulations such as the Federal Drug Administration Act, Freedom of Information Act, and Department of Defense (DoD) records management standards.

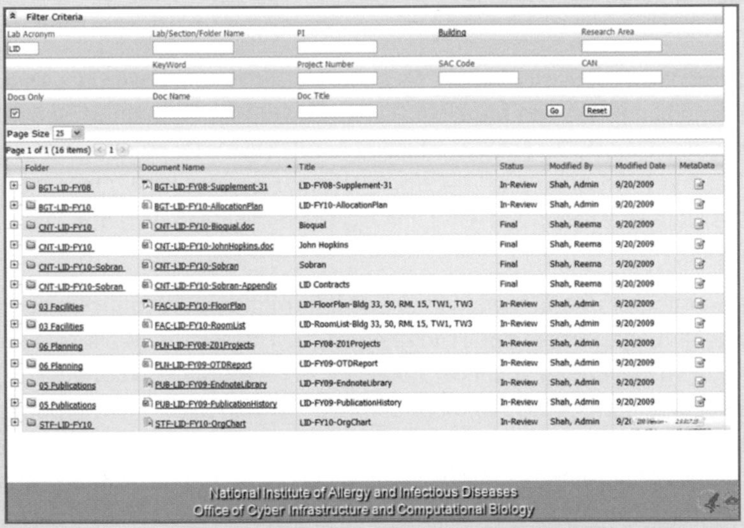

Figure 3.6: NIAID's ECM Dashboard

ment, compliance and records management, as well as business unit. Accordingly, the scope of an information governance initiative is as broad as its purpose is vital.

A steering committee should consider many various aspects of information governance – how the company will endeavor to manage its electronically stored information (along with its paper documents and other physical records). When requirements, goals, and measures of success are understood, technology may be evaluated to meet those needs.

ECM as a Platform for Information Governance

Many technologies are positioned as both dedicated solutions and foundational platforms for compliance and information governance initiatives. Organizations are well-served to consider the long-term goals and interrelation between such activities, rather than investing in point solutions that resolve an immediate need, but ultimately incur costs and challenges in the future. ECM provides a sound platform for implementing an information governance strategy.

Security and Privacy

Security is of paramount concern in any organization given rising incidents of information crime, increases in losses of confidential customer information and intellectual property theft. With the growing capacity of digital storage devices, governments and private corporations around the world have been embarrassed by the theft of computers and hard drives, computers left in buses and the accidental loss of flash drives, containing the personal information of thousands of citizens. Credibility built over decades can be destroyed in a few days.

Many government policy issues today are focused around national security and privacy. In the US, these regulations include the USA PATRIOT Act, the Homeland Security Act and the Health Insurance Portability & Accountability Act (HIPAA). Canada's counterpart is the Personal Information Protection and Electronic Documents Act (PIPEDA). Global equivalents include the Data Protection Act (UK), the EU E-Privacy Directive and Data Protection Directive in Europe.

Security plays an integral role in compliance and information governance, requiring a balance between good management and IT infrastructure. The role ECM plays is critical as an organization's intellectual capital must be protected. For security to be effective, it must address risks, benefits and processes at the enterprise level, to align with corporate strategy, policies and procedures, key stakeholders and required resources. Protecting confidential information is a risk management strategy that should be addressed at the senior management level as an imperative that also helps to effectively optimize business operations.

While governance is the responsibility of senior executives and the board of directors, it should align with an organization's IT governance framework. Senior executives can incorporate security issues and concerns into execution and their daily operations, while the board of directors can make information security and privacy an intrinsic part of the organization's overall governance framework and processes already in place.

To ensure that all relevant elements of security are addressed, various security standards have been developed to provide guidance. Some of the most commonly used standards include Control Objectives for Information and related Technology (COBIT), ISO/IEC 27000 (part of a growing family of ISO/IEC Information Security Management Systems), the PCI DSS: Payment Card Industry Data Security Standard and others such as FIPS Publication 200 and NIST 800-53 in the US. As organizations are increasingly using services that are outsourced to the Cloud (see Chapter 13), strategies around security have expanded to include data loss prevention (DLP) which are systems that identify, monitor, and protect data to minimize both intentional and unintentional data loss.

A formal strategy around security and privacy can be deployed by creating enterprise standards for security policies. As in the cases of compliance and information governance, key resources and stakeholders need to be identified, empowered and supported; policies must be incorporated into relevant processes; education and training should be provided to all employees; technology infrastructure optimized; and the appropriate solutions implemented to support secure and reliable operations.

ECM Technology Components

Technology plays a critical role when integrated into the proper processes and organizational structure. The following ECM technologies are crucial to helping organizations achieve compliance and support information governance:

- Archiving
- Retention Management
- Records Management
- Search
- Business Process Management

Archiving

Archiving is the technology backbone of compliance and information governance. In the past, archiving technologies were deployed to address the storage and IT-related costs concerning electronic information. Historically, archiving enabled electronic documents and data to be offloaded from one system and placed into another. In cases where information was still readily used in day-to-day business, providing continual access to that content through a leading application was preferable.

In response to the new compliance requirements posed by Sections 302 and 906 of the Sarbanes-Oxley Act, UBS, one of the world's leading financial institutions, implemented an internal certification process for financial reports, in which senior executives formally certify their financial figures and processes using a 'sub-confirmation' process.

During the internal certification process, appropriate persons are notified via email when their input is required, and are then granted personalized access to the relevant documents on the UBS intranet. All relevant processes are archived and tracked in a log file. The CEO and Group Controller – generally the CFO – issue a final certification for the Security Exchange Commission only when all internal processes have been completed.

The UBS corporate governance portal enables the company's business managers worldwide to collaborate in developing internal and external business reports. Relevant departments have access to a complete overview and status of the certification processes at all times. All related processes have been automated and simplified, expediting the certification process.

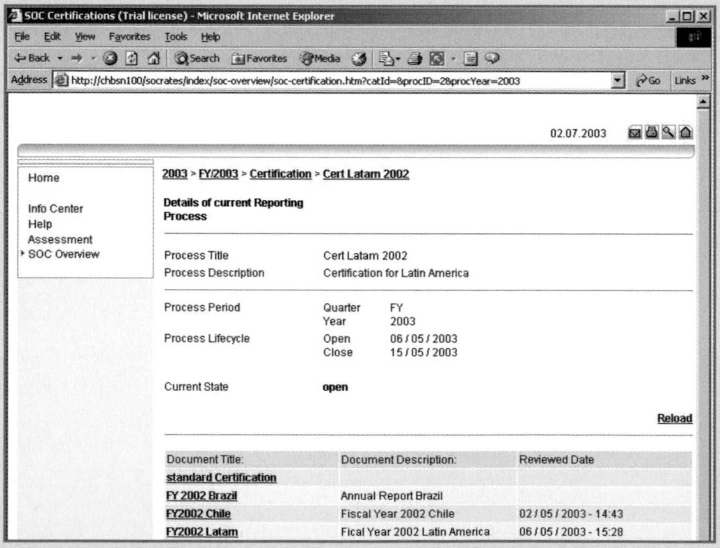

Figure 3.7: Certification Processes at UBS

ECM technologies provide archiving capabilities that interface with many content sources, including email systems, collaboration and document management systems, ERP systems, and locations where information is stored, such as file shares. The administration of an archiving tool enables companies to determine when and how information should be extracted. For instance, email messages may be archived if they are older than 90 days, or larger than 1 MB.

Archiving is perhaps the most under-rated technology in any IT department's arsenal. Its heritage in facilitating long-term and cost-effective storage tends to relegate archiving to storage facilities like filing cabinets and tape warehouses. Archiving information allows organizations to capture electronic information and make it much more accessible in the event of discovery or audit. Content becomes searchable from a single system of record and eases the cost and effort associated with litigation. Archiving delivers the basis for ensuring suitable retention of information and is explained in more detail in Chapters 5 and 6.

Retention Management

Many compliance and information governance initiatives, while grounded in the practice of archiving, are underscored by retention management. Retention management ensures that information is not retained indefinitely, and that a general "lifecycle" can be attached to all content. It is typically characterized by the application of a retention policy to an object – be it a document, an email, an instant message conversation, or otherwise – and the subsequent enforcement of that policy. Generally, a retention policy will dictate how long to keep an object and what to do when that duration has elapsed. Given the sheer volume of information at hand, retention management is typically handled across a broad set of information. Retention control may be based on criteria such as a user's group membership or geographic location – for instance, retaining emails within an IT department for 3 years.

Records Management (RM)

With the daily pressures to comply with regulations, changes to legislation, and the pace of today's global market, being able to manage the lifecycle of content by applying a Records Management discipline is a business-critical capability. When content such as emails, documents, and paper files are classified as business records and managed from creation to deletion, organizations need to assure compliance with information governance requirements. A corporate RM program ensures a consistent record policy and practice that spans all electronically stored information and physical information. These policies are applied to all content according to their business value to an organization.

Search

Although the technologies outlined above help organizations to comply with standards and regulations, they do not prevent litigation or audits. FOIA legislation can force organizations to produce information within very short periods of time. Search technology as part of an integrated ECM solution can help auditors or legal staff locate relevant information. An RM system can be used to group this information into a consolidated list, where "holds" can be applied to suspend the information's lifecycle. Holds can be applied to entire categories of information using classifications and taxonomies. A workflow is then implemented to automate the review of all collected information. On completion of the review, export and packaging capabilities allow the information to be produced for delivery to the requesting party.

Business Process Management

Once guidelines around compliance and governance have been communicated, an organization needs to give employees the support they require to implement the defined processes. Business Process Management (BPM) delivers an effective process engine – initiating processes, defining and distributing tasks, recording their completion, and reporting on the outcomes of a given process. A BPM system with a supporting best practices repository not only helps to support compliance and governance; it enables best practices to be followed and documented. BPM is covered in Chapter 11.

Compliance and Information Governance Applications

eDiscovery

With volumes of corporate data increasing in size and complexity, the process of eDiscovery – exploring, collecting, preserving, and processing information – has become a tremendous challenge for enterprises. The ability to assess relevant information where it resides using one central solution, is key to mitigating the risks and costs associated with eDiscovery.

Litigation readiness reduces risks associated with the volume, organization and legal hold of information. It can prevent significant and unplanned costs. A litigation readiness solution is achieved through a comprehensive records, retention, disposition and legal hold management strategy, built using key ECM components that address content lifecycle management, records management, and email management. This is illustrated in the Electronic Discovery Reference Model (EDRM) below, which allocates the eDiscovery process into steps or that can be effectively managed.

> ## Office of the Superintendent of Financial Institutions

The Office of the Superintendent of Financial Institutions (OSFI), the regulator of federally registered financial institutions operating in Canada, needed to implement a system to streamline, standardize and re-design internal processes and improve the management of information across the organization in response to a government legislation, which specifies that certain types of cases are automatically "deemed approved" if OSFI does not render a decision within 30 days.

OSFI deployed ECM technology to create a central repository for managing unstructured content, as well as process workflows and collaborative workspaces. Currently, OSFI's Case Management System makes it easy for case officers and other expert reviewers to find and share case information, ensuring everyone is spending more time focusing on higher-value areas that require their expertise and judgement.

In addition, OSFI's Business Systems Integration Initiative (BSII) provides a new level of automation, so that OSFI employees can quickly and efficiently manage regulatory processes, improve risk management supervision and speed responses to key stakeholders.

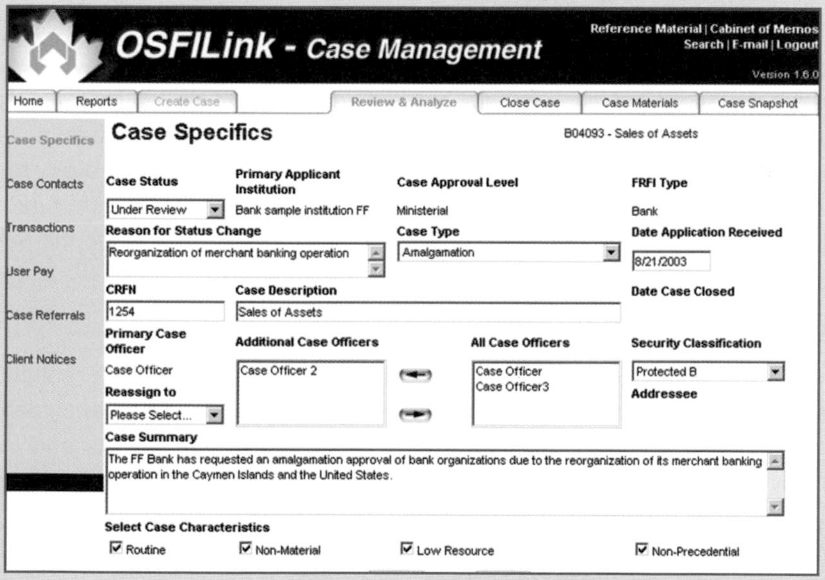

Figure 3.8: OSFI's Case Management

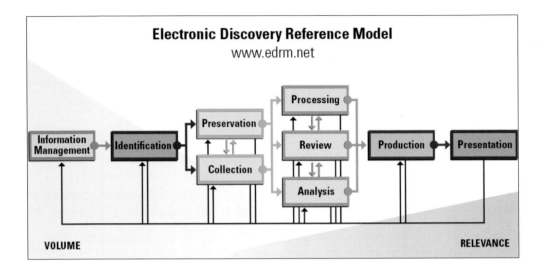

Figure 3.9: The Electronic Discovery Reference Model (EDRM)
©*Socha Consulting LLC and Gelbmann & Associates*

The U.S. Federal Rules of Civil Procedure (FRCP) has implications for an organization's data retention policies. Following revisions to the FRCP and some more recent historic court decisions, companies have begun to take two significant steps toward reducing the costs and mitigating the risks of eDiscovery: establishing and implementing records management within ECM systems and policies, and creating internal eDiscovery teams to manage portions of the process in-house. By developing sound, repeatable processes and working with Litigation Support applications, organizations are lowering both the risks and costs that are associated with eDiscovery.

Pharmaceutical: Clinical Trials

ECM provides the infrastructure, knowledge management and real-time collaborative workspaces that pharmaceutical employees need to share, manage and analyze clinical trial data throughout the clinical trial process. ECM helps to reduce costs and improve quality by providing instant access to CRFs, SAEs, queries, patient diaries and inventory reports. By providing a secure extranet environment where researchers can work together, ECM extends an organization's ability to manage and share clinical data with partnering companies, such as Contract Research Organizations (CROs) and sponsor companies.

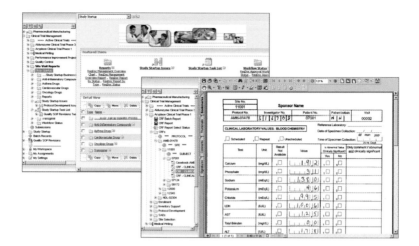

Figure 3.10: Clinical Trials Application

Energy: Change Management

In organizations that process hazardous materials, it is critical to comply with safety and environmental regulations and manage change within their facilities. Management of Change (MOC) is one of the more difficult processes in a plant in terms of downtime, outages, resources, and risks regarding exposure to fines, lawsuits and negative publicity. These risks increase as activities and man-hours increase and generations of knowledgeable employees retire.

An ECM solution helps manage a compliant and documented process for facility change to reduce risk, increase efficiency, safety and reliability, and minimize environmental impact. Through document management and business process automation, it manages all the stages of a MOC lifecycle and related processes and documents, from single-screen initiation to final records management.

Manufacturing: Quality Management

For regulated industries like manufacturing, an organization's quality management system is critical, both for regulatory compliance and for continuous improvement initiatives. Expanding manufacturing companies face the challenge of adjusting to and managing periods of rapid growth. The need to adopt new business practices capable of meeting the demands of large organizations must be reconciled with regulatory requirements that mandate adherence to established procedures and the generation of documentation that proves this adherence. ECM gives manufacturing organizations (including pharmaceutical, medical device, biotechnology, and diagnostic companies) a flexible and expandable solution to manage quality issues and initiatives.

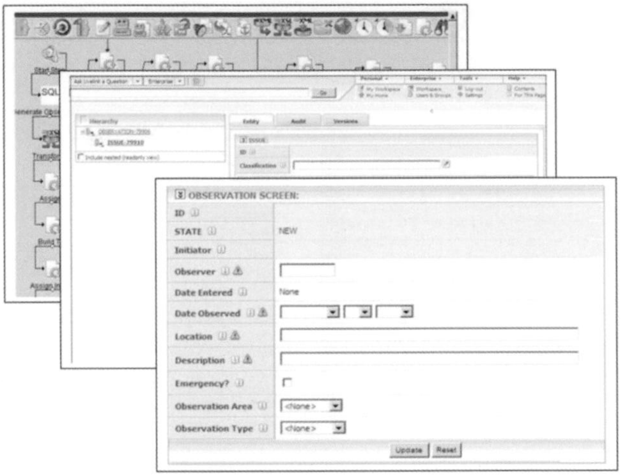

Figure 3.11: A Comprehensive Quality Management Solution

Compliance, Governance and Emerging Technologies

As connectivity improves, bandwidth increases, and devices such as smartphones become more powerful, organizations will be expected to control the flow of information in any format across the enterprise. This includes emerging technologies such as Web 2.0 collaboration tools like wikis, blogs and social networking. As discussed in Chapter 9, these applications are popular because they are accessible and easy to use. The problem this presents for the enterprise is that users are able to set up and use these collaborative tools without the knowledge of a company's IT department or legal counsel.

When content generated using Web 2.0 technologies is hosted outside an organization's IT infrastructure, the threat of exposure of confidential information intensifies. During litigation, for example, an organization must present any materials that might be relevant to a case. eDiscovery requires that legal and IT departments work together to search data stores for relevant content – from file systems and hard drives to Internet services and mobile devices.

Challenges around compliance and governance will increase as digital content grows and people continue to use social software to create and share information. In the public domain, there are obvious data and privacy protection issues, along with security breaches and potential for reputation damage. How do government regulations HIPAA, PIPEDA and the Stored Wire and Electronic Communications Act or industry regulations like EUB and Sarbanes-Oxley impact social media? Is it realistic for organizations to enforce corporate policy outside the work environment?

As the enterprise struggles to balance risk mitigation with individual creativity and productivity gains from Web 2.0 technologies, social media policies must be clearly outlined and communicated so the compliance process itself does not become a source of risk. Inside the firewall, these risks can be mitigated by a fully integrated and secure ECM platform that supports full content storage, archiving, lifecycle and records management functionality.

ECM 2.0: Bringing It All Together

All companies face the difficult challenge of maintaining performance while operating in an increasingly risky and regulated environment. The key to successful compliance with high information governance standards is to ensure that consistent processes are deployed throughout an organization, critical information is managed, and people are fully trained and able to work together within the compliance framework.

A centralized and secure repository, along with content lifecycle, archiving and records management, and search functionality, enables organizations to track and store the necessary evidence to show that their policies, procedures, and processes are being followed – regardless of whether this information is being exchanged via an instant messaging system, a mobile device or via email. With ECM as an infrastructural backbone, organizations can begin to enforce and monitor comprehensive policies for all information sources within the enterprise.

ECM has a proven history for implementing compliant records, document and process management solutions for ISO 9000, the U.S. Patriot Act, SEC, OSHA and the FRCP Act in the U.S. ECM reduces the risks associated with non-compliance by making information governance processes more efficient and transparent. In the chapters that follow, we'll take a closer look at all of the technologies inherent to effective ECM. The concluding section of the book brings all the technologies together and discusses the implementation of an ECM solution in more detail.

Figure 4.1: Information Discovery

This chapter considers the development of search and retrieval technologies and traces their evolution from early online machine-based search services to human-based search and social networks. It explains why information discovery is such an important element of ECM 2.0, especially when methods such as text mining and concept-based search are combined with social media, virtual reality and location awareness. The innovator stories in this chapter illustrate how organizations improve productivity and add value to content by providing quick and easy access to content.

INFORMATION DISCOVERY

Search and retrieval technologies enable people to manage the vast wealth of information available both on the public Web and in the enterprise; it is technology's answer to "finding a needle in a haystack."

Today most people use search services like Google™, Yahoo® and Bing™ to locate information on the Web. Inside the enterprise, search is much more complex than it is on the Internet. When a search is performed against secure data sources across a handful of repositories, permissions must be passed on to each underlying search engine so that appropriate security is maintained. This can be very complicated, especially for compliance applications with additional layers of authorized access. Access to legacy datasets and sources present another challenge for enterprise search administrators. Enterprises can underestimate the costs involved in creating an organizational "Google-like" search experience, especially with regard to scalability, distribution and performance.

Despite the inherent complexities, one of the main benefits that organizations realize from ECM is the cost savings that result from users being able to find information faster. As illustrated in the graph below, more than half of business professionals spend more than two hours a day searching for information. Being able to find relevant information quickly expedites the speed and accuracy of critical decision-making, improves overall productivity and reduces the cost of wasted or duplicated efforts.

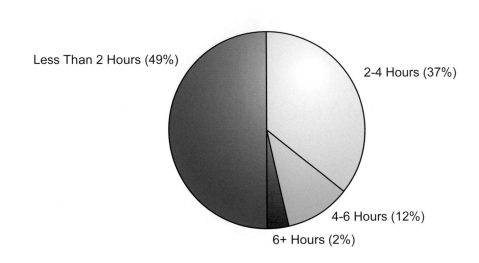

Less Than 2 Hours (49%)

2-4 Hours (37%)

4-6 Hours (12%)

6+ Hours (2%)

Figure 4.2: Time Spent Searching For Information

This chapter discusses the evolution of search technology and its symbiotic relationship with ECM 2.0

Machine-Based Search Fundamentals

Search software first became popular as a means of indexing books and libraries. As the popularity of the Web increased, this technology was re-purposed to index the Web.

An electronic search engine scans the content of a document or Web page and extracts keywords based on specified criteria, including placement, frequency, proximity, concept identification, and so on. An index of these words is compiled into a file that links each entry to the location in the document or Web page where that word is used.

When a user enters a query into a search engine using keywords, the engine examines its index and provides a listing of matching results according to its criteria. When people search the Web, they are actually searching through a previously compiled index of pages. To create an index that allows users to search the Internet requires serious computing power and some very sophisticated algorithms.

Improving Machine-Based Search Results

There are three ways to improve search results: improving the query; improving the index; and improving results. To discuss how machine-based search results are improved, let's examine recall and precision. Recall is the ability to index and retrieve all information that a user is searching for, while precision is the ability to retrieve only information relevant to the user's query. Both of these are measured using percentages. The goal is to retrieve information that is relevant while ignoring information that is not.

There are a number of features that search engines use to increase precision and recall. These include Boolean operators, wildcarding, proximity and parametric searches.

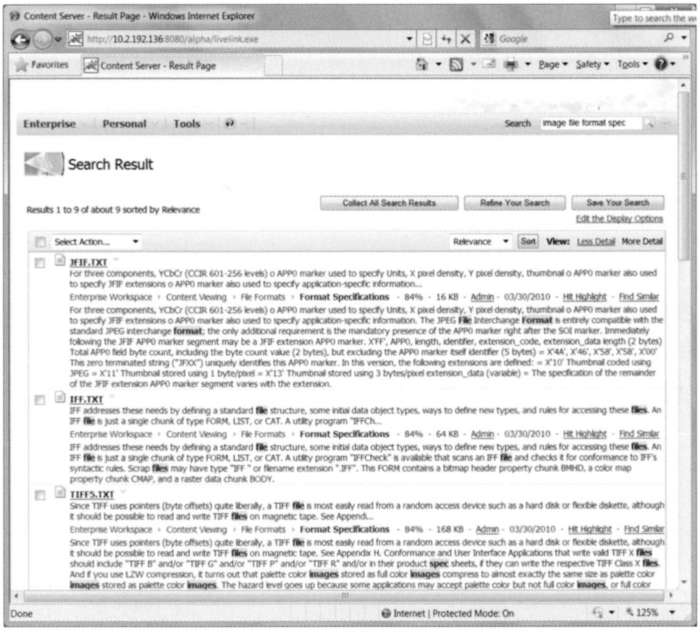

Figure 4.3: Search Results with Hit-to-Hit Highlighting

These and other techniques, such as thesauri, synonyms and base word forms, are ways that search tools can improve search results through the balance of recall versus precision, delivering what is termed improved search fidelity. While is important to keep recall high, it should be balanced with precision so that results are not too overwhelming.

> Global Public Health Intelligence Network (GPHIN)

The Global Public Health Intelligence Network (GPHIN) Centre for Emergency Preparedness and Response Public Health Agency of Canada uses the latest technology to spot threats to human life. The GPHIN system uses translingual text mining to assign relevancy scores to numerous articles coming from worldwide sources, helping analysts count and track instances of possible threats.

A recent National Post article cited GPHIN's importance to detecting global threats. Unlike its American counterpart ProMed, GPHIN does not just track diseases. The group monitors any threat to human life – natural or man-made, for example bush fires in California, pestilence outbreaks in Africa, even theft of nuclear material. As such, the Canadian team and its technology are continuously monitoring over 1000 potential threats around the globe. The team publishes eight different reports, three times a day. It is precisely this monitoring by organizations like GPHIN that triggers responses – such as the WHO declaring H1N1 a pandemic, which in turn accelerates the development of vaccines.

Processing up to 20,000 articles a day, it would be impossible to track this volume without the search technology.

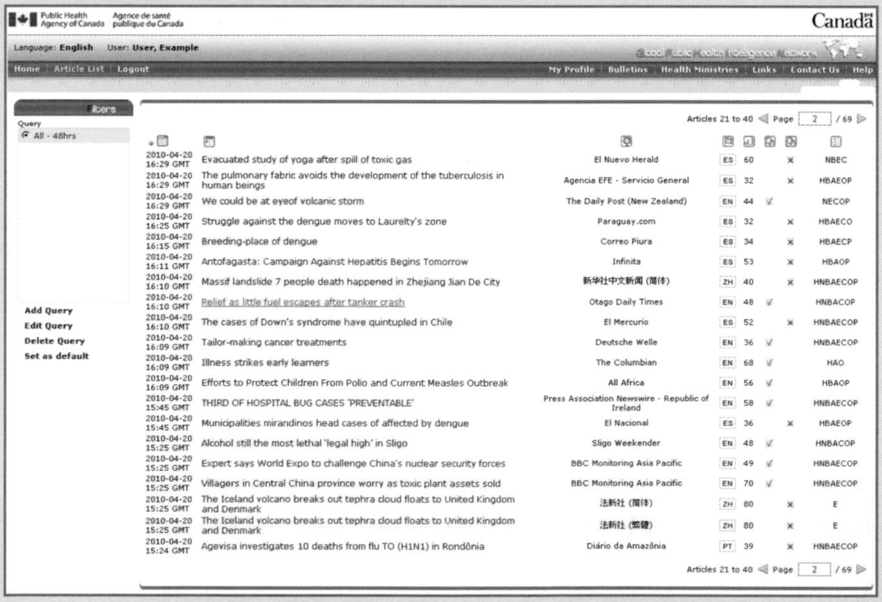
Public Health Agency of Canada / Agence de santé publique du Canada — Canada

Language: English   User: User, Example

Home | Article List | Logout   My Profile | Bulletins | Health Ministries | Links | Contact Us | Help

Filters
Query
All - 48hrs

Add Query
Edit Query
Delete Query
Set as default

Articles 21 to 40 Page 2 / 69

2010-04-20 16:29 GMT	Evacuated study of yoga after spill of toxic gas	El Nuevo Herald	ES	60		×	NBEC
2010-04-20 16:29 GMT	The pulmonary fabric avoids the development of the tuberculosis in human beings	Agencia EFE - Servicio General	ES	32		×	HBAEOP
2010-04-20 16:29 GMT	We could be at eyeof volcanic storm	The Daily Post (New Zealand)	EN	44	√		NECOP
2010-04-20 16:25 GMT	Struggle against the dengue moves to Laurelty's zone	Paraguay.com	ES	32		×	HBAECO
2010-04-20 16:15 GMT	Breeding-place of dengue	Correo Piura	ES	34		×	HBAECP
2010-04-20 16:11 GMT	Antofagasta: Campaign Against Hepatitis Begins Tomorrow	Infinita	ES	53		×	HBAOP
2010-04-20 16:10 GMT	Massif landslide 7 people death happened in Zhejiang Jian De City	新华社中文新闻 (簡体)	ZH	40		×	HNBAECOP
2010-04-20 16:10 GMT	Relief as little fuel escapes after tanker crash	Otago Daily Times	EN	48	√		HNBACOP
2010-04-20 16:10 GMT	The cases of Down's syndrome have quintupled in Chile	El Mercurio	ES	52		×	HNBAECOP
2010-04-20 16:09 GMT	Tailor-making cancer treatments	Deutsche Welle	EN	36	√		HNBAECOP
2010-04-20 16:09 GMT	Illness strikes early learners	The Columbian	EN	68	√		HAO
2010-04-20 16:09 GMT	Efforts to Protect Children From Polio and Current Measles Outbreak	All Africa	EN	56	√		HBAOP
2010-04-20 15:45 GMT	THIRD OF HOSPITAL BUG CASES 'PREVENTABLE'	Press Association Newswire - Republic of Ireland	EN	58	√		HNBAECOP
2010-04-20 15:45 GMT	Municipalities mirandinos head cases of affected by dengue	El Nacional	ES	36		×	HBAEOP
2010-04-20 15:25 GMT	Alcohol still the most lethal 'legal high' in Sligo	Sligo Weekender	EN	48	√		HNBACOP
2010-04-20 15:25 GMT	Expert says World Expo to challenge China's nuclear security forces	BBC Monitoring Asia Pacific	EN	49	√		HNBAECOP
2010-04-20 15:25 GMT	Villagers in Central China province worry as toxic plant assets sold	BBC Monitoring Asia Pacific	EN	70	√		HNBAECOP
2010-04-20 15:25 GMT	The Iceland volcano breaks out tephra cloud floats to United Kingdom and Denmark	法新社 (簡体)	ZH	80		×	E
2010-04-20 15:25 GMT	The Iceland volcano breaks out tephra cloud floats to United Kingdom and Denmark	法新社 (繁體)	ZH	80		×	E
2010-04-20 15:24 GMT	Agevisa investigates 10 deaths from flu TO (H1N1) in Rondônia	Diário da Amazônia	PT	39		×	HNBAECOP

Articles 21 to 40 Page 2 / 69

Figure 4.4: Translingual Text Mining Results

Making Sense of Search Results

Search tools generate search results. These are presented as Web pages containing a list of documents or pages that satisfy a search query. The software attempts to order search results by placing the closest matches highest in the results list. This is known as ranking results by relevance.

To establish relevance, machine-based search technologies relate the frequency of the query in the document to the frequency of the query in the index. This allows for the evaluation of the importance of a term. Most Web-based search engines return results ordered in the most relevant order. The relevance score is calculated based on a statistical analysis of search terms and document results, to identify the documents most likely to be the ones the user was looking for. Sophisticated search tools enable administrators to fine tune the mechanisms that determine relevance ranking.

Search results are presented as a long list of links to the "found" Web pages and documents. Many documents are filled with hyperlinks that reference other documents. These embedded references provide a powerful means to determine relevance. Google's search engine exploits this method of ranking for sorting search results. Each document retrieved by the search engine is assigned a relevance score, which is then modified according to the relevance scores of each document hyperlinked within that document. This enables the search engine to base the value of a document on the value of all documents within its context.

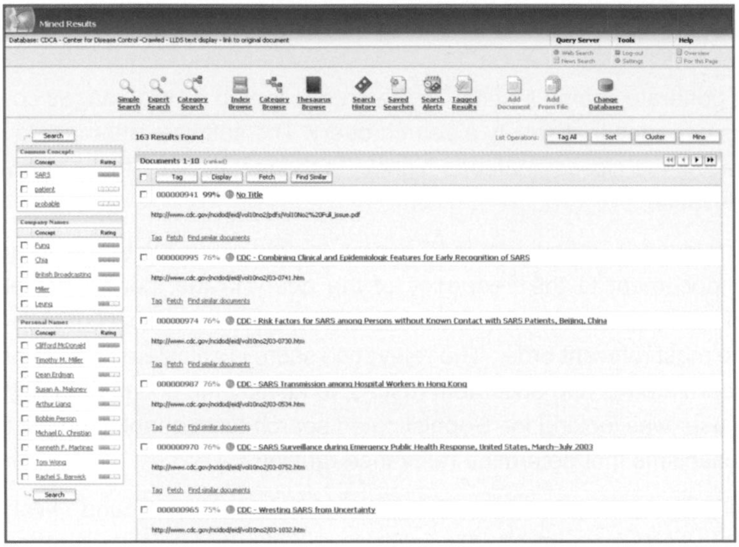

Figure 4.5: Search With Extracted Context of Organizations, Places, Topics

Today's search tools provide a summary under each title that helps to distinguish the relevant hits from the unwanted hits. Search results may also offer hit highlighting, a useful feature that highlights and displays search terms. This can be especially useful if the term being searched for is located on the last page of a 1,000-page thesis. Similarly, hit-to-hit navigation allows users to quickly move from a page containing one or more search terms to the next page in the document containing the search term. User-requested result ordering is another feature that enables users to view the most recently modified documents, or documents sorted by author or title.

Information in Context – Meta-data, Classifications and Taxonomies

Search technologists believed that if content was more effectively structured *before* it was indexed by an engine, better results would follow. So systems were developed to intelligently "tag" every piece of information with relevant contextual information. Meta-tagging and classification is the process of applying identifying labels, category codes, titles, and descriptions to documents. Once systems were capable of gathering and retaining information about information, it became possible to use that context to categorize and organize a content repository.

Adding information to content in the form of meta-data makes search tools much more selective. Meta-data is data about data that can be used to describe the contents of information. When a document, image or other type of data is created, certain elements and attributes such as a name, size or type can be added to the file. Being able to add extra criteria yields better search results.

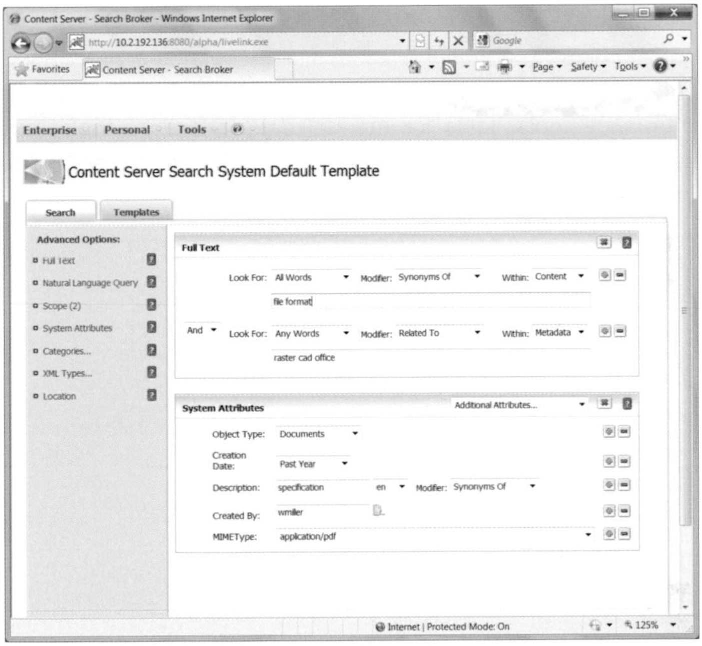

Figure 4.6: Meta-data

Organizations that house large volumes of content have implemented meta-data and classification best practices, creating predefined tags that users can apply to relate and organize their information. Meta-data is organized according to a pre-defined taxonomy. Taxonomy is the hierarchical classification used to categorize documents, digital assets and other enterprise information.

Taxonomies bring a certain consistency to the way content is organized within the enterprise, remaining consistent over time. As an extension of traditional thesauri and classifications, a taxonomy can be developed from scratch or an existing taxonomy can be adapted to correspond to a corporate standard.

The development and refinement of a taxonomy can take years, which usually means that once it is implemented, years of accumulated content requires categorization. In this case, manual tagging can be used, but it has its limits. Manual tagging is time-consuming and subjective, large quantities of archived content may not be processed and valuable information can be lost. For these reasons, organizations are turning to text analytics technologies, and more specifically, to automatic/semi-automatic document categorization.

Today's search technologies provide the ability to tag content against both custom and standardized taxonomies. The majority of available solutions are based on a mix of categorization rules and machine learning algorithms. Usually these solutions come with taxonomy maintenance tools, tools for manual categorization, triple stores, taxonomy based search tools, and other technologies relevant to the structured and semi-structured management of information.

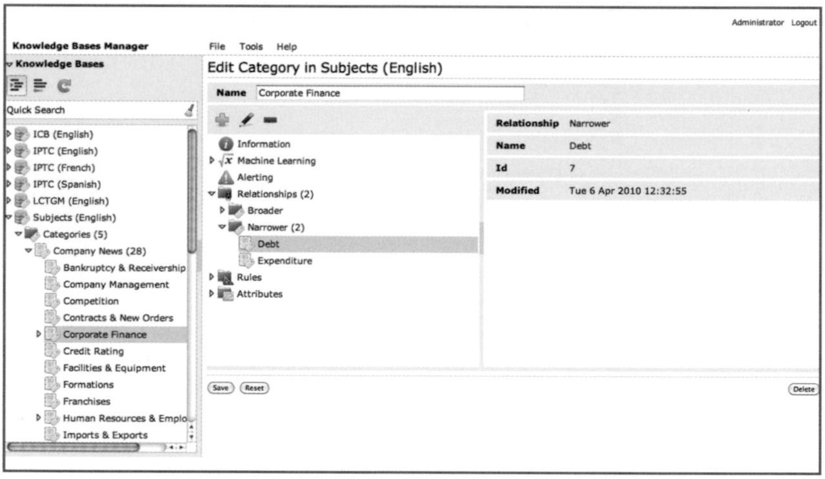

Figure 4.7: Taxonomy Management Tool

Human-Based, "Social" Search

We have examined how enterprise search technologies introduced tools which allowed experts to fine tune the search algorithm for more meaningful results. More recently, Web-based user actions and emerging technologies have added a human element to search.

User-based models have garnered attention because they focus on incorporating behaviors of Web site visitors. By monitoring feedback and behavior, user-centric models can tap into a well of human experience that reflects a range of subjective opinions and judgment related to the usefulness of selected material. Because the feedback is dynamic, social search results are often more current than static rules or meta-data.

As an example of human-based search, social networking gives people in an organization the ability to use conversations, comments and personal profiles to locate expertise, resources and information. In essence, colleagues help other colleagues find pertinent information. Web 2.0 technologies facilitate dialogue, providing avenues for generating peer-to-peer influence. People prefer human reference over machine-based results. This is why searching on Facebook is well positioned to outpace Google's machine-based algorithms. When used in combination with search, the content found on social networks – in profiles, blogs, blog comments and ratings – presents powerful, referential and trusted information. On the consumer Web, social networking influences social behavior and converts prospects into customers. Within the enterprise the effect is the ability to add new dimensions to search with user generated content (UGC).

Figure 4.8: Users Search Across Tags, Communities, Documents and People

Organizations are adopting UGC, including tagging, folksonomy and ratings as additional meta-data to augment search. This kind of meta-data helps users find information more effectively by adding relational value to content within context. An increasing number of organizations are realizing that meta-data can be unlimited, and when applied in social context, it prescribes new ways of relating and organizing information.

Tagging enables users to assign keywords to content types without following predefined terms (or "controlled vocabularies"). Users represent tags in relation to their importance within a tag cloud – a visual depiction of user-generated tags. Searches can be based on tag clouds or member-created tags. Tag clouds have been popularized by sites where there are millions of photos or objects with multiple tags.

A folksonomy is a system of classification based on collaboratively creating and managing tags to annotate content. This is also referred to as social tagging, which has been made popular by Web 2.0 sites. Models of collaborative tagging are used to highlight emerging properties in knowledge structures or networks. Global organizations are using social tagging to organize, share and find corporate information in new and innovative ways.

Ratings also provide direct feedback on the quality and relevance of content. The five-star rating systems on major retail and movie sites are good examples of rating mechanisms.

The Wisdom of Crowds

Although most social search techniques observe explicit user action and feedback, they frequently ignore a key element in determining a visitor's true intent: the context of behavior. Context refers not only to a visitor's individual actions on a Web site, but how these actions compare and relate to the actions of other visitors.

Listening platforms and text analysis enable organizations to "listen" to millions of discrete pieces of social content created to understand the customer sentiment and issues. As this data is distilled, virtual communities of like-minded users begin to emerge. Actions, patterns and tendencies associated with these communities form the basis of a collective perspective.

The exponential growth of content and dynamic nature of today's Web sites require a fundamental rethinking of how to determine intent and match this with the most appropriate content. Enterprise search technologists have begun asking these questions, but the industry is still in transition from an expert-centric to a user-centric mentality.

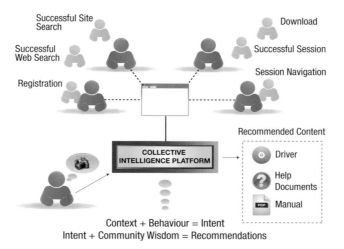

Figure 4.9: Social Search Combines Results and Community Wisdom

> # Cyberpresse

cyberpresse.ca

Cyberpresse (www.cyberpresse.ca) is one of Canada's leading news Web sites covering current events in Canada and around the world as well as sports, arts, business and lifestyle. Fueled by the newsrooms of the largest network of French-language newspapers in Canada, it has more than 1,835,000 unique visitors each month. Cyberpresse is owned by Gesca, a subsidiary of Power Corporation of Canada specializing in newspaper publication and news Web sites.

Cyberpresse wished to improve the user experience of its archive section, as well as render it appealing to its advertisers, which could drive online revenues. The challenge was taking millions of assets and allowing these to be navigated through more than classical means – they needed a powerful search engine.

Deployed through Cyberpresse, semantic site search allows visitors to smoothly navigate through current and archived content – an intuitive and relevant search experience that is enhanced by facets of semantic meta-data. What's more, the search bundles historical and new content together to create highly relevant topic pages with content spanning over 25 years. Cyberpresse has seen an increase in SEO that was triggered by packaging highly relevant keywords in their dynamic topic pages – an additional side effect that was unexpected.

Figure 4.10: Semantic Navigation

Portals and Personalization

To enhance productivity, portals provide a personalized environment that enables users to control information that is delivered to their workspaces. Search agents are commonly used in portals to register topics of interest. Sophisticated underlying technology sends alerts when these topics are found and results are aggregated. Portals also provide brokered search technology – a meta search ability for use in the portal. Enterprise portals deliver a unified interface to collaborative environments and repositories, combining portlets (pluggable software components) into a single Web page. When combined with search, portals improve access to relevant information.

Figure 4.11: Social Search Combines Results and Community Wisdom

The Semantic Web or Web 3.0

The Semantic Web describes the ability of Internet technologies to "understand" the meaning of information, and based on this, to find, combine and act on information on the Web. It was established by inventor of the Internet Tim Berners-Lee and is his vision of the Web as a universal medium for knowledge exchange.

The Semantic Web includes concepts like the linked data cloud; interconnected data available through public Web APIs where users can freely access information. These databases contain information about people, products, entities and more, and this information can be used to complement search results through contextual mashups. There is an opportunity here for text analytics capabilities to act as a "proxy" between unstructured and structured content. For example, text analytics can be used by organizations to help establish critical links, such as the connections made between scientific articles and drug databases in the Drug Bank.

Core Semantic Web technologies differ from text analytics and natural language processing capabilities. They support the vision behind Web 3.0 and consist of technologies like OWL, SPARQL, RDF, etc. Text analytics and natural language processing delivers an efficient and automated way to make use of the core Semantic Web technologies. From a broader standpoint, these technologies help organizations to tap into Web 3.0, especially in an ECM context.

Semantic Web technologies optimize content by understanding its meaning and extracting its full value. Entity extraction, for example, is a powerful way to sort, visualize and organize information like places, people and organizations. Controlled vocabularies and linguistic rules are used to identify and extract all occurrences of an "entity type". Entity types include product names, company names, proper names, geographic locations, dates, times, etc.

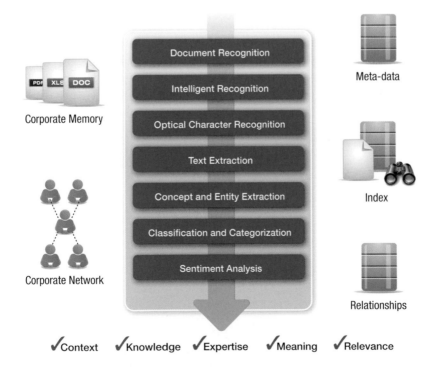

Figure 4.12: Semantic Content is Analyzed, Annotated and Related

Sentiment analysis detects the tone of content in a document, phrase, sentence or entity based on a positive or negative connotation. Organizations can use sentiment analysis to monitor sentiment around their brands in blogs, social networks, customer support emails, phone transcripts, surveys and more. Based on analysis, organizations can improve customer relationships to build trust, deliver more effective products and services, and release effective contextually-based advertising programs.

Leveraging text mining abilities, the Semantic Web alters the search paradigm by delivering a valuable analytic layer on top of search results. Web 3.0 technologies enable people to look beyond content for facts and relationships between objects or things and their properties.

ECM 2.0 and Federated Search

Search performance has come a long way. Today's search and retrieval systems provide a number of state-of-the-art capabilities to aid in the searching, filtering, organization and extraction of information. Features such as federated search deliver unprecedented capabilities to organize and analyze the unstructured information in any organization.

The ability to conduct federated search queries is essential to the effectiveness of an ECM system. Federated search enables users to search across an enterprise repository, other company repositories, legacy applications, and external sources including such resources as search portals like Google and Yahoo – all from a pre-configured interface.

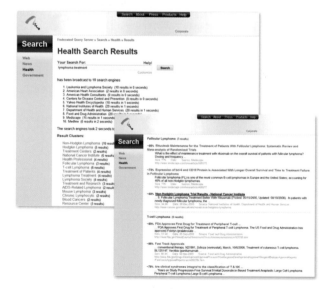

Figure 4.13: Federated Search

evolve24

evolve24 analyzes traditional and social media to determine businesses' overall information landscape and provides quantitative metrics around perception, reputation and risk that let clients understand the key areas of impact in their marketing, communications and management efforts. Because of its ability to correlate perception to key performance indicators, evolve24's services are highly sought by Fortune 500 companies.

"Reputations are built over time and are the response to actions taken by a corporation," explained Scot Wheeler, VP Business Development for evolve24. "For example, reputation can be hurt by unaddressed negative responses to products and services, including poor customer support, regulatory or legislative issues, insensitive ad campaigns, or any perceived affront to an audience, while a new product announcement, a viral campaign or launch of user groups may create highly positive coverage in influential publications and blogs which will help build reputation."

Sentiment analysis allows evolve24 to quickly determine the tone of an article, which offers a key insight into the firm's representation through media. "We have estimated that a person at peak performance can 'tone' 200 articles a day – or 25 an hour," Wheeler said. "With this technology, we can literally score tens of thousands of pieces of content a day for each of our clients – all of them broken down by brand or topic – using a single person to manually test and verify results."

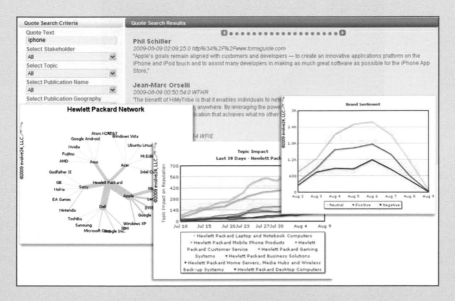

Figure 4.14: Sentiment Analysis at evolve24

The federated search paradigm is the result of online databases and Web resources that populate what is called the "Deep Web". The Deep Web refers to content that is not indexed by standard search engines due to limitations in crawler technology. The surface or public Web is made up of approximately 21 billion pages; less than 1% of what is currently online. Federated search makes searching the massive volumes of Deep Web documents possible, providing a single search interface to various Deep Web data sources.

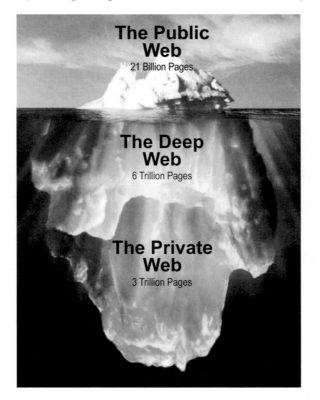

Figure 4.15: The Web is Like an Iceberg

As the quantity of information grows exponentially both inside and outside of global enterprises, the research and development of search-related technologies continues to evolve. Machine-based search technologies are being enhanced by human-based search functionality, providing invaluable context for content to give it more meaning. Enterprise mobility and immersive collaboration deepen the human dimension as users are able to search using physical location or a location-based metaphor as a powerful referential tool. Web 2.0 technologies are paving the way for Web 3.0 and the Semantic Web, with smarter, more connected and analytical search abilities. The potential for access to content is unlimited as the division between Deep Web and search engine content diminishes and technologies are being developed to deliver access to all content.

Figure 5.1: Content Lifecycle Management

Content Lifecycle Management (CLM) addresses the fundamental building blocks of an ECM strategy, combining document management, records management, workflow, archiving and imaging into a fully integrated solution to effectively manage the flow of content. This chapter traces the lifecycle of content, from creation through to archiving and eventual deletion. Innovator stories illustrate how organizations use ECM as a solution to manage content lifecycles across multiple repositories to create new business opportunities, reduce cost and risk, and achieve regulatory compliance.

CONTENT LIFECYCLE MANAGEMENT

In today's workplace, content lies at the core of every process across every industry, from financial services and government to utilities such as oil and gas. Content Lifecycle Management (CLM) is designed to address the real issues that global enterprises are facing today as they struggle to manage large quantities of information. CLM helps organizations manage all types of business content – from initial creation through to final disposition – with the most comprehensive, end-to-end content lifecycle management solutions. This chapter describes the stages of a document's lifecycle and explains how technologies such as records management and archiving help organizations deal with growing volumes of business content, while meeting increasingly complex compliance and eDiscovery requirements.

An employee sends an email through the corporate email system; a project team collaboratively edits a document in real time; the accounts payable department scans and OCR's an invoice into PDF; a customer fills out an electronic order form on the Web – these are a few examples of how content comes to life within an organization. What happens after this point varies across content types, but the lifecycle of each one includes these phases: creation or capture, collaborative review, management and approvals, integration and process optimization, retention and storing (archiving) and destruction.

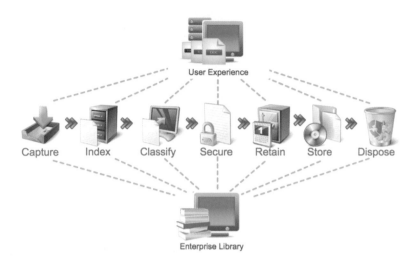

Figure 5.2: The Anatomy of Lifecycle Applications

Without an effective means of managing content, the flow of knowledge itself becomes stagnant. Valuable data must be preserved and obsolete records destroyed to minimize risk and enhance corporate accountability. Within the context of an ECM system, CLM empowers knowledge workers to capture and categorize content according to organizational policies to ensure regulatory compliance, reduce risk and increase the efficiency and cost effectiveness of necessary tasks.

Structured Versus Unstructured Information

To introduce the technologies that underpin CLM, it is necessary to understand the difference between structured and unstructured information and why managing unstructured information is such a challenge.

Structured data is based on numbers organized into tables. These database tables can be quickly manipulated to find data that refers to the numbers in the table. Unstructured data is not as easy to organize and retrieve. Words, an example of unstructured data, are organized into tables similar to an index found at the back of a book. Because the data model for words (unstructured data) is fundamentally different from the data model for numbers (structured data), the technologies that support each must differ.

With estimates of a 60 percent annual growth rate in the amount of enterprise content created and managed – including wikis, blogs, and other emerging formats (see Chapter 9), an organization managing 10 terabytes of unstructured content today can expect that total to grow to nearly 200 terabytes in just seven years.

> City of Atlanta, Department of Watershed Management

The Department of Watershed Management (DWM) is dedicated to providing the highest quality drinking water and wastewater services to City of Atlanta businesses and residents and to its wholesale customers at the lowest possible cost. In addition to managing documents created in support of the Clean Water Atlanta Program, DWM is responsible for managing more than 1.35 million paper documents annually, which exceeds five million sheets of paper per year.

Under consent decrees negotiated in 1998 and 1999 with the United States Environmental Protection Agency (EPA) and the Georgia Environmental Protection Division (EPD), the City of Atlanta was mandated to complete an aggressive Capital Improvement Program (CIP) by 2014. The consent decrees require a document repository in which all documents resulting from the Clean Water Atlanta initiative would be stored and retained based on the State of Georgia's Records Retention Schedule.

ECM enables the DWM to gain departmental efficiencies, enhance customer service, better comply with government regulations, manage risk and improve records management of all its vital client documents. Seven bureaus with a total of more than 1,400 employees are benefiting from full lifecycle document management through automated workflows, routing, and version control of all document types. DWM is expected to enable more than 200 workflows annually and streamline its diverse business processes. To date, the department has over one million documents stored in the repository. Inventory records and other documents are filed, retrieved, shared and processed with ease.

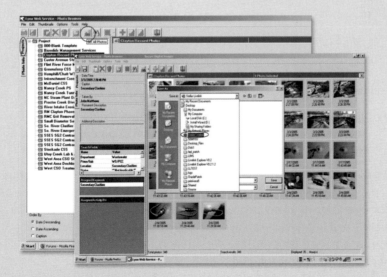

Figure 5.3: Full Lifecycle Content Management

Document Management

Document Management (DM) is the cornerstone of CLM. By definition, document management is a set of technologies that helps to create, track and store electronic documents and/or images of paper documents. Designed to offer a secure and centrally managed repository for both work-in-progress and final output content, DM is related to document imaging and capture, workflow systems and records management systems.

Figure 5.4: DM - Organizing the Storage, Control and Retrieval of Business Documents

Core DM Services

The core services of DM give users the ability to create documents in familiar desktop applications and apply version control and audit trails (or document history) to documents and compound documents when they are added to the repository.

Document management systems were originally developed to help organizations manage the paper-based processes that drive their business more efficiently. Drug companies, for example, regularly produce thousands of pages of research and rely on these to develop and manufacture medication. One common denominator that links companies across many industries is their dependence on compound technical documents to support their business operations.

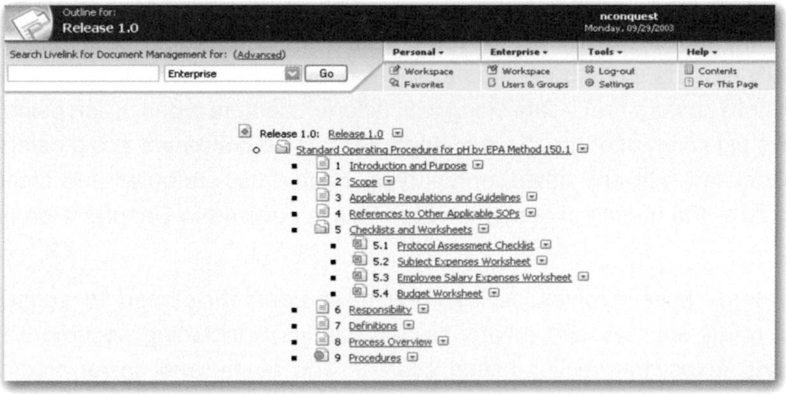

Figure 5.5: Outline View of a Compound Document

Large, complex documents are often authored in chapters or sections with different organizations, departments or individuals responsible for each component. This is especially true of technical publications and regulatory submissions. To streamline processes and allow for effective publication, compound documents can be created from multiple files in different formats. Sophisticated document management functionality allows people to place access rights on components and assemble these into a single document for review, publication or submission.

Version control and revision management gives users the ability to manage the history of complex compound documents. Documents can be "checked-out" of the repository before they are modified. When an author is finished making changes, the modified document can be "checked-in" and the system marks the changes as a new document version. Other DM tools provide auditing capabilities that allow people to examine the document's history.

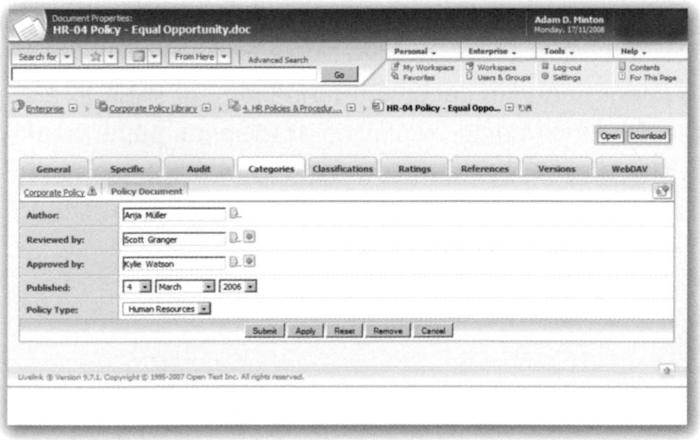

Figure 5.6: Attributes Applied when Adding a Document

When a content file is added to the ECM repository, any additional information that is stored in the repository with the document is meta-data. Upon creation, the system automatically records system meta-data, such as date and time, user name, and so on. Users can store custom meta-data along with different content types. Each piece of custom meta-data is called an attribute. A set of attributes can be combined into a category, which is then associated with any other content type. Meta-data, attributes and categories are used to improve the quality of search results. This is covered in Chapter 4 on Information Discovery.

As DM systems have evolved, repositories have been developed to support content types from many sources and enterprise applications – including document fragments, Web content, faxes, transaction-based content, and digital and social media. As Web applications are becoming more widespread, version control is being replaced by a much more open concept of collaborative authoring. Collaborative authoring allows multiple authors to edit documents without being disrupted by multiple versions or getting "locked-out" of a document. Multiple authors are able to edit document fragments, review comments, track changes and review edits. Collaborative authoring reduces the need to compile revision after revision, and minimizes authors working on a document in isolation. Because authors are given visibility into changes made within document fragments in real time, the editing process is more collaborative and dynamic.

Linking Documents and Business Processes

Document management enables organizations to automate business processes. Consider the development of a technical manual. Like other business processes, developing a manual consists of numerous document reviews typically carried out by several subject matter experts. Different individuals review different documents types, often using a workflow to route a document through an approval cycle. A workflow can replace a paper-based process by electronically routing documents from one person to the next, bringing efficiency and manageability to cumbersome manual processes.

Workflow tools are integrated with document management tools to automate review and approval processes for documents, replacing traditional paper-shuffling practices. To illustrate, let's look at a very simple workflow used to manage the review and approval of a purchase order (PO).

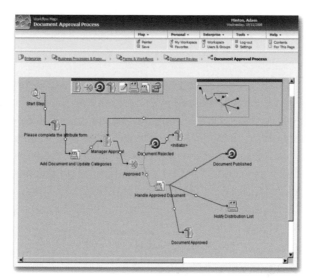

Figure 5.7: Document Review Process

The process is initiated by a staff member completing a purchase order form. Next, the form is routed to a peer group for first level approval. If it receives approval, it proceeds to the next step. Otherwise it is returned to the originator with comments. If the PO exceeds the sign-off limit of the department head, it is routed to the next highest sign-off authority for authorization, and so on. This kind of business logic can be built into a workflow using electronic signatures to automate the process, saving time and eliminating error. When all the correct approvals have been granted, the PO form is routed to the finance and accounting department and a PO number is added to the purchase ledger. The originator is granted approval to proceed and a form is sent to the vendor.

Electronic and Digital Signing

For critical business documents, organizations or regulations may require authentication of a user at the time that approval is granted during a document review process. Electronic signature technology can be implemented in many different forms, but the underlying concept requires that the user authenticate themselves with the system using a password or one-time key at the time that their signature or approval is being granted. Electronic signatures do not require a significant supporting infrastructure to be deployed. Digital signatures are generally based on a public key infrastructure (PKI) and involve encryption technology.

Publication

Once a document is approved, it is ready for publication and distribution. ECM facilitates this by transforming and rendering documents into many formats. By integrating with a Web content management system, ECM enables organizations to publish authorized content to PDF for distribution at trade shows or XML for presentation on internal and external Web sites. Search technology, along with mobile and Cloud-based access, makes this content accessible.

Security and Permissions

The flexibility of the permission structures in ECM suites allows users and administrators to closely emulate their desired physical security. Access permissions can be assigned by role and group. Every object, including documents, folders, workflow and images, must have a unique set of permissions for every user and group in the system. In some cases, where the volume of users exceeds 100,000, the number of permissions models managed by the system expands quickly into the billions and beyond. Complex as it may seem, without the ability to apply unique permissions structures at the most granular level of the system, an ECM system is not truly secure.

Image Management

Thanks to laser printers and copiers, today's businesses create even more paper than ever. Far from disappearing, the problem of managing paper documents is still around.

Document imaging is the conversion of a paper document into electronic format. Imaging technology has been widely deployed by insurance, health management and managed care organizations that process tens of thousands of transactional content every week, such as claims, enrollment forms, referrals and reports.

Transactional content includes not only scanned images but other incoming information from e-forms and faxes, print streams generated from back-office applications and electronic records. Much of this content originates outside an organization from external parties – customers or partners – and relies on workflow or BPM to drive transactional, back-office business processes.

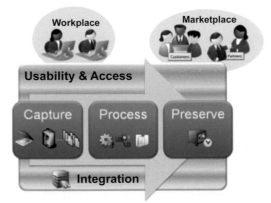

Figure 5.8: Document Review Process

Image management vendors have tried to compensate for scanning limitations by allowing users to add meta-data to images, such as annotations to instruct readers about the document's content. Additional meta-data might include information more specific to the application, for instance, policy number, underwriter or account name.

Scanning represents a critical step in managing paper documents by importing and consolidating huge volumes of paper documents into an electronic system. Scanning eliminates cumbersome paper files but remains an ineffective solution unless integrated with technology that can "file" each document in context and efficiently store it for designated periods while making it accessible upon demand.

As illustrated in the following innovator story, fax machines can be used to scan documents into an ECM system, where content can be indexed and stored to reduce administrative costs and increase accuracy by eliminating manual processes.

Active Processing

As the creation of a document changes according document type, the lifecycle phases of a document also vary. For example, the active phase of an email message is relatively short and involves reading, responding and classifying the message as a business record to be retained or deleted. On the other hand, the active processing phase of an invoice can be a much more involved process, consisting of automatic field identification and data extraction, automatic business rules processing, manual approval, exception triggering, marking up and final approval using an electronic signature.

Redaction, Review and Markup

These three technologies facilitate the document review process, whether for the purposes of improving the quality of a CAD diagram during the design process, supporting customer billing inquiries in a call center or approving a purchase order.

Redaction technologies allow an ECM application to provide differentiated and selective access to portions of a single electronic document. Redaction capabilities are generally integrated into ECM viewers, PDF viewers or document authoring tools.

Review and markup technologies enable different stakeholders to review and mark up a document. This capability is generally supported by workflow technology, which guides the document through all the steps required in the approval process.

A good ECM platform allows multiple reviewers to mark up a document in parallel and supports the markup of many different document formats. Tightly integrated workflow and document management functionality is required to manage multiple iterations of a document and maintain an audit trail of all actions completed during the approval process.

> Mumbai International Airport

Mumbai International Airport Limited (MIAL) is a joint venture company owned by a GVK Industries-led consortium and Airports Authority of India working under the Ministry of Civil Aviation. The company manages India's busiest airport, the Chhatrapati Shivaji International Airport (CSIA). MIAL employees send and receive hundreds of faxes every month to and from vendors and government agencies. Previous paper-based faxing methods did not uphold timely turnaround or essential privacy. MIAL relied on close to 50 fax machines that required consistent and costly maintenance as well as constant supply refills. Additionally, sensitive documents were not private or secure.

MIAL has eliminated fax machine queues and gained reliable security for all faxed documents with a document delivery and fax software. MIAL employees now send and receive documents without leaving their workstations. Instead of printing pages to feed through fax machines, employees can fax documents right at their desktop computers. Integration with email allows any sent or received fax to appear alongside emails for secure and easy reference, forwarding, or storage.

The company expects to eliminate close to 40 fax machines, with the remainder as backup devices in case of email failure. Expenses associated with maintaining dozens of fax machines are now designated as cost-savings. Faxes that used to take 15-20 minutes to process are now delivered and tracked electronically within seconds. Employees who link to the office via mobile devices when they are traveling also stay on top of urgent faxes and staff members have increased efficiency because the solution has optimized their time.

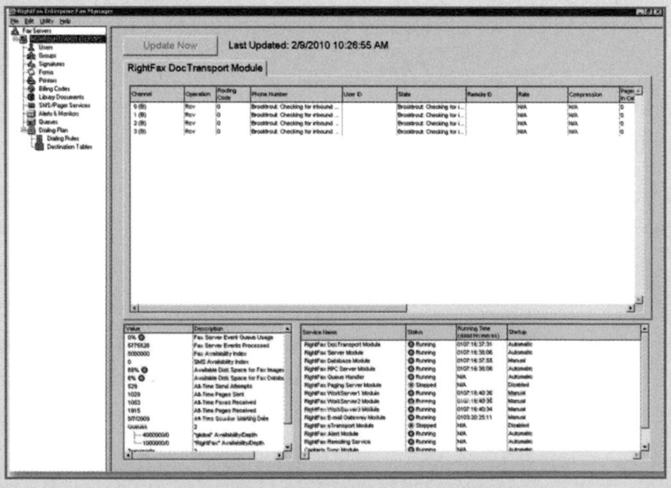

Figure 5.9: Fax Management at MIAL

Records Management

With the daily pressures to comply with regulations, changes to legislation, and the pace of today's global market, being able to manage the logical lifecycle of content by applying a Records Management (RM) discipline is a business-critical capability. When content such as emails, documents, and paper files are classified as business records and managed from creation to deletion, organizations need to assure compliance with corporate governance requirements.

RM is by definition the process of identifying, classifying, storing/retaining, preserving and destroying records. By classifying enterprise content as business records, organizations also identify the business context and value of corporate information. The complete records management process gives organizations a much clearer understanding of what enterprise content represents. Effective enterprise records management helps to extract maximum value from documents; making the most of business content.

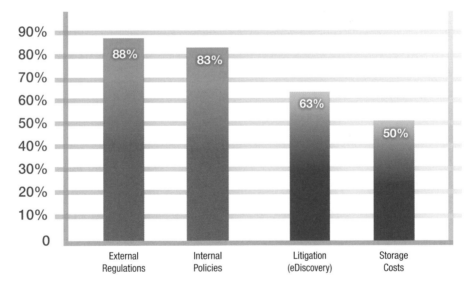

Figure 5.10: Top Motivators for Deploying RM

Records management is a logical extension of document management: enriching the meta-data on content, enhancing security, extending the corporate repository, and allowing scheduled archiving, movement or destruction of content based on corporately approved rules and event triggers.

Along with an organization's business requirements, it is important to also note that RM practice is also defined by the discipline prevalent in different jurisdictions, such as:

- The Department of Defense's: DoD 5015.2-STD

- The Model Requirements for the Management of Electronic Records (MoReq2) in the EU

- Evaluation and Approval by The National Archives (TNA)

- Australia's Victorian Electronic Records Strategy (VERS)

- DOMEA for eGovernment document management and electronic archiving

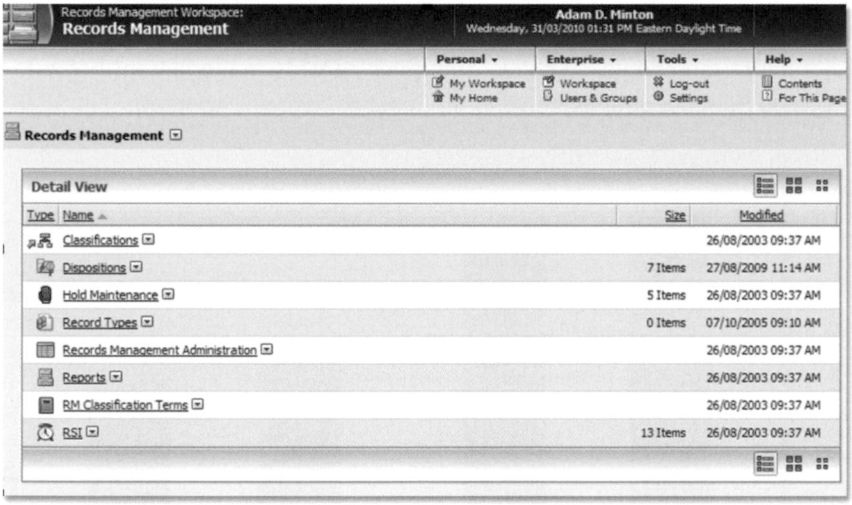

Figure 5.11: Records Management Workspace

Retention Schedules

How long should the records be saved and when can they be safely destroyed? It is common for companies to have written policies and retention schedules. Organizations define and document policies for records management and ensure that the policies are implemented and maintained. The retention schedule includes how long the records should be kept, where the records are kept, who can access the records, who can file them and who has the authority to dispose of them.

One would think that, since almost all documents are now electronic, control and access would be straightforward. But this is not the case. Electronic records exist in many different locations; employees access and store records electronically at home and on mobile devices.

> Canadian Heritage: 2010 Winter Games

To prepare for the Vancouver 2010 Olympic and Paralympic Winter Games, the Department of Canadian Heritage turned to ECM to ensure safe, secure and easily accessible records, documents and collaboration. With numerous departments, and committees heavily involved (including the Vancouver Organizing Committee for the 2010 Olympic and Paralympic Winter Games [VANOC], the government of British Columbia, the city of Vancouver and the resort municipality of Whistler), it was imperative that the latest documents were easily accessible, collaboration was safe and secure, and records of all the processes and documents were kept to ensure order and to share lessons learned and best practices with the team the next time the country hosts the Games.

The Government of Canada (GC) created a shared system initiative called Records, Documents and Information Management System (RDIMS). This includes document management, records management, imaging, workflow, reporting and email integration products. Mobility was also important for the project to enable access to documents via the Web.

One of the more attractive features RDIMS offers the GC is that the system is fully bilingual and allows people to work in either English or French seamlessly. A Francophone employee is presented with a French environment and an Anglophone is presented with an English environment. All employees can submit documentation or search in either language. Another advantage is that the system has created a framework for how to manage information, whether it's by email, hard copy, or electronic documents. One of the greatest benefits, however, is the assurance that content is secure.

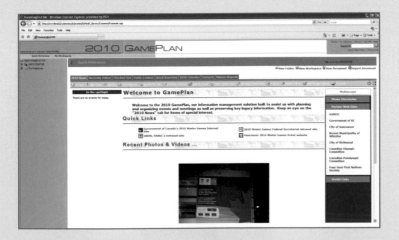

Figure 5.12: Integrated Records, Documents and Information Management System (RDIMS)

> Patrimoine Canadien: Jeux d'hiver de 2010

Pour se préparer en vue des Jeux olympiques et paralympiques d'hiver de 2010 à Vancouver, le ministère du Patrimoine canadien a eu recours à la gestion de contenu pour assurer un accès facile aux dossiers, aux documents et à la collaboration, en toute sécurité. Étant donné la participation importante de nombreux ministères et comités (dont le Comité d'organisation des Jeux olympiques et paralympiques d'hiver de 2010 à Vancouver [COVAN], le gouvernement de la Colombie-Britannique, la ville de Vancouver et la Municipalité de villégiature de Whistler), il était impératif que les documents les plus récents soient facilement accessibles, que la collaboration soit sécuritaire et que les dossiers de tous les processus et documents soient conservés de façon ordonnée, afin de diffuser les leçons apprises et les pratiques exemplaires à l'équipe, la prochaine fois que le pays sera l'hôte des Jeux.

Le gouvernement du Canada a mis sur pied une mesure de systèmes partagés appelée Système de gestion des dossiers, des documents et de l'information (SGDDI). Il comprend des produits de gestion de documents, de gestion de dossiers, d'imagerie, de flux de travaux, de production de rapports et d'intégration de messagerie électronique. La mobilité était aussi un élément important du projet, qui devait permettre d'accéder aux documents via le Web.

Pour le gouvernement du Canada, l'une des caractéristiques les plus attrayantes du SGDDI est qu'il est entièrement bilingue et qu'il permet de travailler en anglais ou en français de façon homogène. Ainsi, un employé francophone a accès à un environnement en français et, inversement, un employé anglophone se fait présenter un environnement en anglais. Tous les employés peuvent soumettre de la documentation ou faire des recherches dans l'une ou l'autre des langues officielles. Le système possède une autre caractéristique utile : il comprend un cadriciel précisant comment gérer l'information, qu'elle se présente sous forme de courriel, de copie papier ou de documents électroniques. L'un de ses principaux avantages, toutefois, est l'assurance que le contenu est protégé

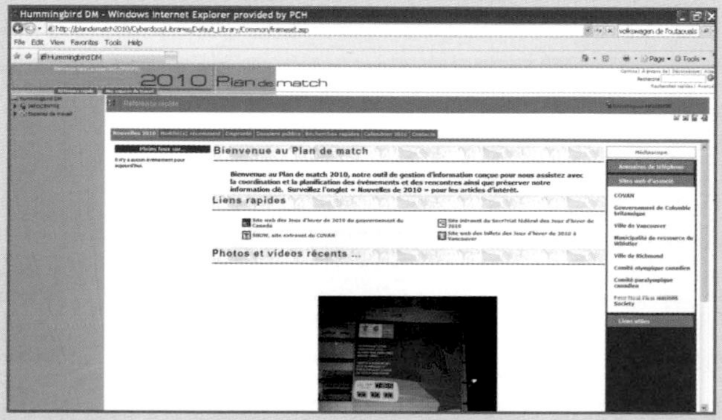

Figure 5.13: Système de gestion des dossiers, des documents et de l'information (SGDDI)

www.opentext.com/ecmbook/innovator/canheritage

Classification and Taxonomies

When users add documents to an ECM repository the object can be classified and managed as a record based on applied meta-data. Classification schemes, or file plans, provide a representation of the organization's business functions, activities and transactions. When classifications are linked to a retention schedule, the full lifecycle of a document can be automatically and securely managed.

Most regulations and corporate policies stipulate that a document's lifecycle is dependent on what type of document it is, how relevant this type of document is to the business or the regulators, events that happen in the business itself and the jurisdictions under which the document falls. For example, if the documents in question are HR records for an employee working in the U.S., then regulations stipulate that these records must be kept for a certain period of time after the employment relationship terminates. In order to be able to describe various document types, an organization needs to be able to apply various classifications according to predefined taxonomies.

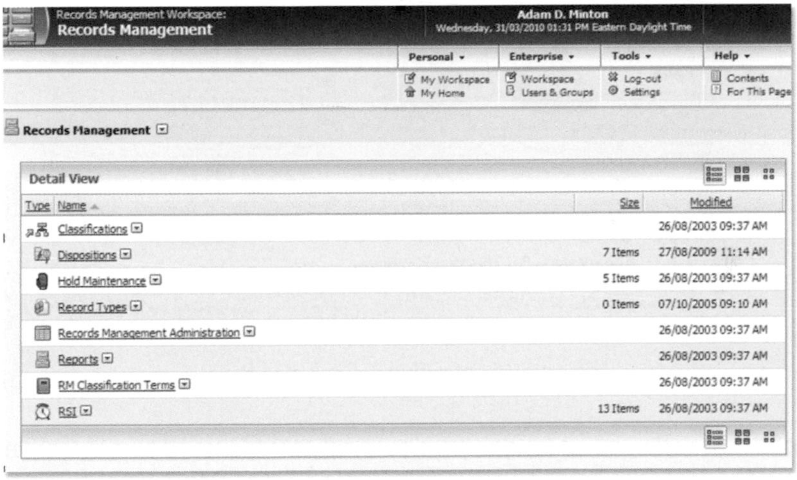

Figure 5.14: Declaring a Document as a Record

Records management, when combined with retention management, delivers a comprehensive CLM solution by providing context – allowing organizations to combine retention with context and to use this context to determine how content is stored, how policies are used and why.

RM and the Impact of Emerging Content Types

The expansion of RM beyond the scope of physical records includes adapting principles for emerging content types such as blogs, IMs or wikis. Organizations are increasingly empowering end users to take ownership of their content and manage it in a system without feeling confined by file plans. At the same time, organizations need to ensure that their content is protected by an RM system to prevent deletion and adhere to regulations.

New forms of content can be securely managed within a fully integrated ECM system that delivers RM capabilities in the background. Collaboration, search and a Web-based system with desktop accessibility gives users a common interface to content, making records management processes transparent to the end user.

Figure 5.15: Mashups Inherit RM Rules

Mashups of content, for instance, can be displayed to support separate working groups and communities within an organization. Content does not need to move or change for RM classifications to be presented in new and innovative ways. Recent versions of blogs and chats can be highlighted or surfaced in an organization's intranet, and can automatically inherit or be assigned RM rules.

Disposition, Storage and Archiving

Once a document's active processing phase is complete, its policies determine the rest of its lifecycle. At this point, the technologies that automate storage management, document archiving and destruction come into play.

Storage Management

Regulations or the threat of litigation often force organizations to maintain information for longer than their business would otherwise require. The extra storage space alone, whether virtual or physical, creates costly business overhead. ECM's storage management capabilities enable organizations to migrate content from high-cost storage to lower-cost storage over the lifecycle of content. This allows two-year-old emails, which have outlived their business use, to be stored on low-cost disk, optical storage or tape. While this content is securely stored, it remains fully accessible from within the system, where it can be searched for, retrieved and viewed.

ECM helps bring storage expenses and operations under control by integrating CLM with a layer of intelligent storage virtualization. Storage is driven by business context, harnessing the rich meta-data of applications to optimize storage – automating data migration across multiple storage tiers, leveraging less expensive media for less critical content and ensuring high availability of premium storage services for essential business content.

An effective ECM system supports a breadth of storage management capabilities, lowering total cost of ownership by providing a platform for storage, archiving and managing content.

Archiving

While some regulations and governance guidelines require content to be stored in an indexed, accessible manner (SEC 17a 4, for example), some require that information be secured and easily restored upon request. Archiving provides organizations with the ability to achieve this.

Archiving allows for the quick and easy research, retrieval, sharing, forwarding and reuse of data. An organization can electronically archive its content permanently in auditable form. Documents can be selected for archiving from the system, optionally converted to a long-term format such as PDF and removed from the originating system. In some cases, the information may still be accessible from the originating systems.

Archiving works hand-in-hand with a records management solution and other ECM suite components to ensure that content can be retained or destroyed according to policy. By disposing of content – deleting and removing it completely from the storage environment at the appropriate time – archiving helps an organization meets official regulations, while significantly reducing storage requirements.

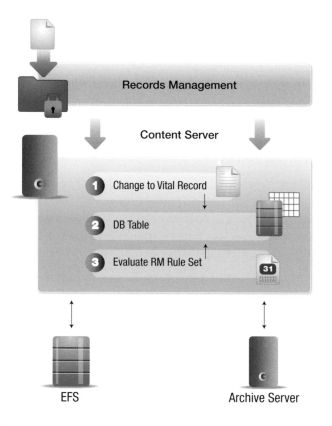

Figure 5.16: RM and Archiving for Comprehensive CLM

In the event of litigation or regulatory audit, organizations must determine which content has legal value and preserve it by placing a litigation hold on it. But they must also be sure that the email and electronic documents they are holding meet admissibility standards and requirements. Following accepted guidelines for electronic documents retention, including using a records management and archiving system within an ECM suite, helps ensure that electronic documents can be used as legal evidence in a court of law.

Disposition and Holds

Disposition is about disposing of content. CLM actively manages the lifecycle of content, enabling records managers to track and report on all necessary disposition activities. Disposition approvals can be routed via workflow to the appropriate authorities requesting approval for particular activities, such as deletion of records.

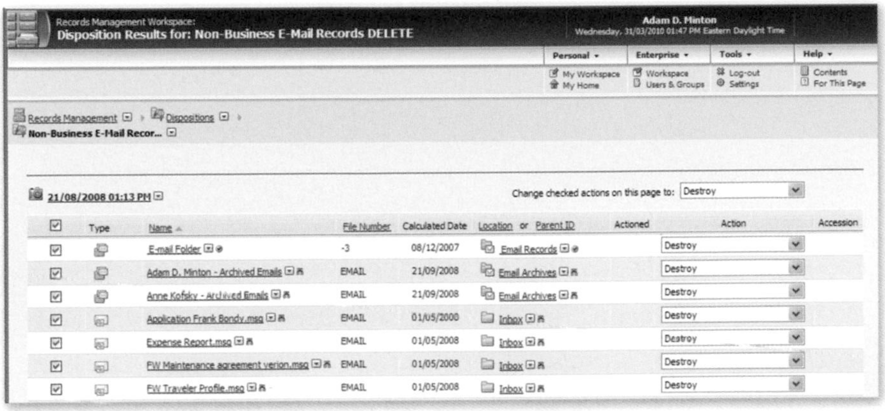

Figure 5.17: Disposition Listing

If an object or document is on "hold" or has multiple holds applied to it, it is typically frozen and cannot be deleted until all holds are removed. Holds are generally used for specific purposes, such as distinct audits or specific legal cases.

Often, there are hidden costs associated with keeping old content around. Storage costs are minor when compared to the costs incurred when companies are required to provide insight into their content. It is these hidden costs an organization eliminates by automating the disposition of content at the end of its lifecycle.

CLM and ECM

When integrated as a core component to a comprehensive ECM 2.0 solution, CLM enables organizations to manage the complete lifecycle of all types of corporate records and information holdings, in electronic or physical format. ECM offers CLM solutions that are tightly integrated with email and document and records management systems to ensure content integrity and to minimize risk and litigation.

Fully integrated CLM delivers an automated system that removes the complexities of document management, records management, workflow and archiving. Cross-repository functionality such as federated records management and enterprise search, along with collection tools are important components for mitigating legal risk. This approach not only covers the logical life of a piece of content, but also spans across the underlying hardware storage platforms. The benefits of ECM move beyond minimizing risk and ensuring compliance. Because it can be extended to support full content lifecycle management, ECM improves total cost of ownership, eliminating the need to invest in new hardware to address content growth and lifecycle issues.

Figure 6.1: Email Management

Email has become an integral business tool used to maximize productivity. Along with improving collaboration and communication, email presents significant risk for organizations if it is not managed. In this chapter, we discuss email as a prevalent form of communication, the risks it presents and how organizations can integrate email management with ECM 2.0 to maximize lifecycle management and minimize risk. Innovator stories demonstrate how global organizations are archiving and managing email effectively to decrease litigation expenses in eDiscovery, improve efficiencies and achieve compliance.

CHAPTER 6

EMAIL MANAGEMENT

There are more emails sent in one day than the entire historical repository of major search sites. Considering the metrics of usage alone, email management is a daunting task – one that requires an easily adopted solution and close adherence to email management policy.

Despite innovative advancements in collaborative technologies, email remains the primary de facto mode of business communication for companies around the world. As the technology has developed, the content of email has also changed, maturing from the exchange of simple textual messages into the primary means for sharing of unstructured content, including documents, image and digital media files. For many organizations, email continues to function as not just a method for sharing information and documents, but also for document storage, as users repurpose their mailboxes into electronic filing cabinets.

According to the Radicati Group, the typical corporate user now processes 156 email messages per day. Running simple math yields staggering results: by such measures, an organization of 10,000 employees would generate approximately 400 million emails over the course of a single year. From a storage perspective, that much email consumes roughly 20 terabytes of new storage space every year. And over the course of seven years the company could expect to accumulate nearly two billion messages, consuming as much as 80 terabytes of storage space. The majority of email storage space consumption is due to file attachments, and with the advent of rich media, these files are growing in size.

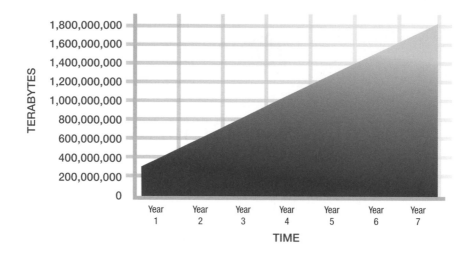

Figure 6.2: Email Storage Depletes IT Resources

Email Archiving

Traditionally, the resolution of email-related issues has fallen under the responsibility of the IT department. And with a volume of email on such a large scale, IT's main concerns include the server and storage hardware required to keep the application up and running, the ability to backup (and occasionally restore) the environment in a timely manner and ensuring the healthy operation of the messaging system.

Email archiving technology as a component of a comprehensive ECM 2.0 solution enables large amounts of email to be quickly and transparently offloaded from the mail environment and stored in one more suitable for long-term retention. Although email messages are extracted from user mailboxes, email archiving technologies often employ a technique called "stubbing" which replaces the extracted emails with a corresponding shortcut, or pointer. This means that while a message is no longer physically stored in a user's mailbox, it is still readily accessible by the user in the same manner that they are accustomed to.

Emails are commonly archived according to rules that a service runs against corresponding user mailboxes. These rules dictate which messages should be extracted, and when. Common rules may include age or size of message, mailbox volume, custom folders, and content or meta-data.

Email archiving is an effective way to reduce the cost and complexity of the email environment. It enables messages to be offloaded from the mail server, where they are costly to retain and intensify the complexity of processes such as backing up the email environment. Once stored in the centralized archive, messages are much more readily accessible via enterprise search, in the event of an audit or legal discovery exercise.

Founded in 1919, Halliburton is one of the world's largest providers of products and services to the energy industry. With more than 50,000 employees in approximately 70 countries, the company serves the upstream oil and gas industry throughout the lifecycle of reservoirs.

Like many large corporations today, most business records at Halliburton are created and maintained using email. Due to different methods of email storage throughout the company, many users did not make the connection between emails and official business records, and may not even have been aware of what exactly qualified an email as a vital record. As a result, Halliburton was spending millions of dollars on eDiscovery due to the retention of mass amounts of unnecessary employee email.

Halliburton chose a combination of Email Management and Records Management to establish control over their email records. Emails designated as business records are stored in the ECM archive, where retention is based on Halliburton's corporate record retention schedule, applied using Records Management. The company's email management system allows people to protect and save their business records for the retention period required by law, while allowing the Records Management team to follow the entire lifecycle of the business record contained in email.

All employees with access to Halliburton's email network will be placed on the new email management system. Halliburton's potential long-term successes include decreased litigation expenses in eDiscovery, an increase in Business Record compliance, and a considerable decrease in unnecessary email storage and associated costs. However, perhaps the most significant business benefit so far is the increased knowledge of what a business record is, and how long it must be retained.

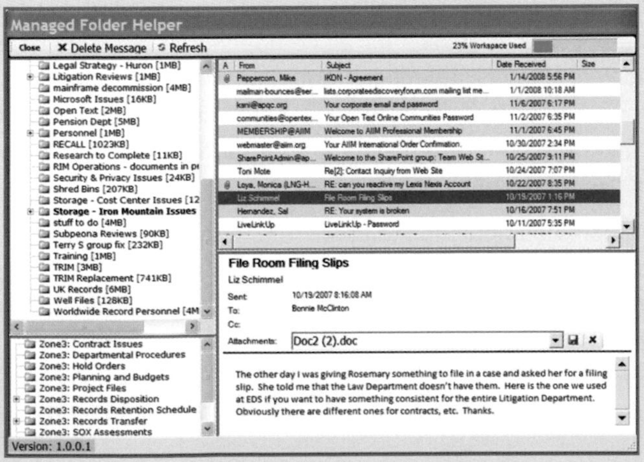

Figure 6.3: Integrated Email and Records Management at Halliburton

Minimizing Litigation Cost and Risk

Archiving email invariably provides many IT cost-related benefits. However, without a systematic, logical, business-based plan for storing legally required email and disposing of unimportant, non-business relevant email, an organization may still expose itself to unnecessary legal risks and costs.

The legal woes of many companies have been underscored by an inability to produce potentially relevant email during the course of electronic discovery or eDiscovery. During corporate civil and criminal litigation it is not uncommon for companies to be compelled to produce relevant documents and messages associated with individuals within a given time period. The inability to do so result in fines, sanctions, and otherwise incurs the ire of uncompromising trial judges.

While it is important to archive email to reduce the IT cost of the messaging environment, it is vital to truly manage the email that is being captured in accordance with a consistent and standardized policy – such that in the event of litigation, a company can be confident that it has retained what is necessary, and can demonstrate good faith and policy adherence in the event that information has been disposed of.

Email management technologies often complement the principals of email archiving. They allow policies to be applied against the ingested emails that dictate, for instance, how long the message is retained for, who has access to it and how it is actually physically retained. Such technologies enforce policy by applying what is called a "classification" to captured email. A classification is more or less a category that describes what the message represents. And each classification has an associated retention policy, access control designations, and so forth.

Such classifications may be applied based on a user's role, on the country a user is employed in or the actual content and relevance of the message. There is no single approach to email retention that applies for all companies. A privately held firm with few clients has vastly different email retention requirements when compared to a global company operating in an industry associated with serial class action litigations. The main consideration an organization should make is whether the application of policy should be automated or interactive, or a combination of both.

The most common automated approach to email retention is based on an individual's role within the company. For instance, depending on the department an individual is associated with, a corresponding retention policy is applied against all email. The primary attraction to such automated approaches is two-fold: it is relatively simple to implement and maintain, as there is little complexity to the policy and its application; and it is also applied in a very consistent manner – all email messages are saved for the same length of time, for the same employee.

For many organizations the eventual act of disposing of archived email can be fraught with concern. The threat of legal sanctions compels organizations to be very measured in enforcing email retention and disposition decisions. Many companies question the legal appropriateness of deleting email arbitrarily after a certain time period just because, for instance, it was associated with a particular employee. A much sounder approach is to dispose of email based on content and according to formal policy for content or records management. For this reason, a contextual approach to retention is often preferable. But what is the most effective way to determine business relevance?

Email Classification

To manage email in a responsible and legally defensible way, a good starting point is to develop policies around varying treatments of different types of email. Different kinds of emails need to be retained for different periods of time; the challenge is in identifying the important emails, separating them from the unimportant ones and determining an appropriate retention period. Email content can be classified into categories that identify which messages are critical business records, which content has immediate business relevance but the organization is not legally required to save it; and email that is transitory or has no long-term business or legal value.

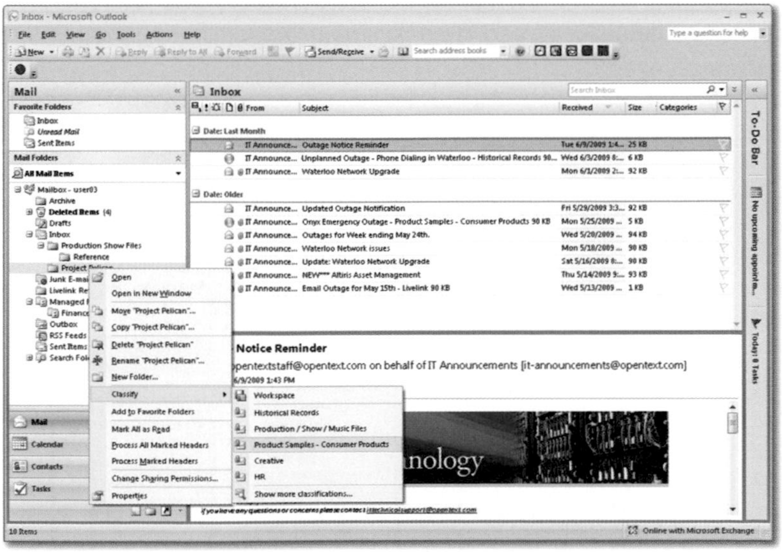

Figure 6.4: Users Apply Appropriate Classification to Folders

Companies may adopt an approach that dictates users should identify the messages that are business-relevant and important to save. The employee who creates a message, after all, often has the best sense of what it represents. To simplify email management for end users, it is critical to embed such decisions into the tasks users are already doing as a part of their daily jobs.

One approach to email management is to leverage the user-defined folder structure within inboxes, allowing users to continue using the folder structure they have already created and simply indicate which folders contain messages that are critical to the business and which contain messages that the user wants to save for reference purposes. IT, working with Legal, defines the classification schema and retention policy for each category and then pushes this classification "picklist" to every inbox. Each user's view of classification options is tailored to, and derived from his or her role in the organization – a user in a customer support department might see entirely different options than a user working in engineering.

Some organizations prefer to define records-enabled folders centrally and push them out to users. This strategy helps the enterprise ensure that the right kind of information is being saved by providing general guidance to users about the types of messages that are important to the business. For instance, the organization might create project-based folders to capture all information pertinent to each project or, as in the example below, folders related to areas of the business, such as Finance or HR. These folders are then propagated in each user's inbox automatically, and the next time users log in they will see the new list of folders in their mailboxes.

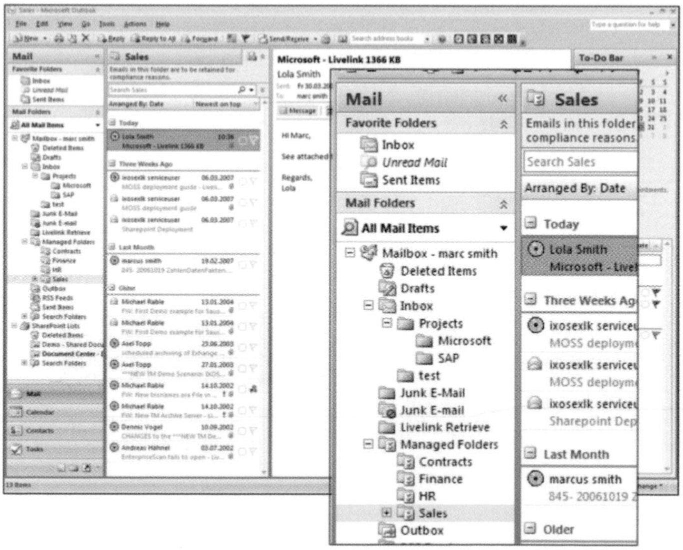

Figure 6.5: Email Classification by Department Folder

The folders themselves have defined records management characteristics, including re-tention schedules and other meta-data.

Similarly, classify-on-send capabilities enable users to assign a descriptive "tag" to an email as it is being composed. The act of classification becomes a simple step alongside the usual process of selecting recipients and typing the subject line. Email management solutions may also expose the classification selected by the sender to internal recipients of that message – meaning that when employees receive an email that has already been classified by a co-worker, it saves them the time and effort.

A properly designed email management solution provides simple mechanisms that allow users to embed classification actions into the normal tasks they perform on a daily basis. Messages are extracted from the email environment and stored in the centralized, long-term ECM repository, and are easily and readily accessible to users.

Email Disposition

While taking a very generous approach to email retention certainly helps companies avoid the risks and fines associated with spoliation and non-compliance, they are still tasked with being able to find information when required to.

Many organizations' legal departments are primarily interested in deleting irrelevant, non-business value email to avoid the high cost of sifting through information in response to a legal discovery requests and early case assessment. The costs incurred throughout the eDiscovery processes can often be directly correlated to the volume of information retained in an organization. In fact, one GB of data could potentially cost $20 million per terabyte. In a recent case involving a computer chip manufacturer, for example, projections estimated that six to eight terabytes of subpoenaed content would require 100 lawyers working for several months to review the messages. Invariably, not all of this content was business-relevant and could have been disposed of without legal impact, saving considerable amounts of money in attorney and other fees.

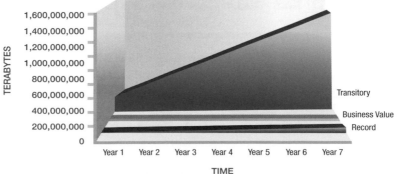

Figure 6.6: Deleting Transitory Messages Reduces Total Volume by 85%

> Deichmann

The Deichmann Group is Europe's largest shoe retailer, generating annual sales of 3.2 billion Euros. Engaged in businesses in 19 European countries and the USA, the company supports 28,000 employees in over 2,700 stores worldwide.

The construction department plays an important role in Deichmann's growth strategy. To enable efficiencies around content in this department, the organization needed an archiving solution to store, manage and securely share all construction-relevant information, building plans, correspondence, and more. Part of this requirement also called for an email archiving system to satisfy the needs of growing amounts of legal regulations in this field.

Deichmann implemented an email archiving solution as part of an integrated company-wide infrastructure for electronic files, workflow and archiving – a comprehensive ECM solution that integrates with Deichmann's existing ERP infrastructure and offers multi-client capabilities for supporting various subsidiaries from each country. Today, emails from about 1,000 users at Deichmann can be archived in an audit-proof format to ensure regulatory compliance. Their approach to implement a company-wide infrastructure for ECM at the outset and then expand and adjust it in accordance with the needs of each department proved to be a complete success.

Figure 6.7: Deichmann's Web Site

Email management tools provide the capacity for organizations to dispose of unimportant, transitory email. They may provide rules which run against mailboxes and purge email after a particular length of time if it has not been classified or otherwise identified as important by end users. In order to ensure that users have a final chance to review and save any information that is valuable, an email management system informs users about which messages are pending deletion and provides simple means to classify and consequently save them.

In the event of litigation, or the perception that litigation is imminent, it often becomes necessary to implement special measures that ensure all email associated with particular individuals or custodians within a corporation is preserved and readily accessible. But during the course of normal business operations, benefit may be derived from disposing of transitory email in a timely, but responsible manner.

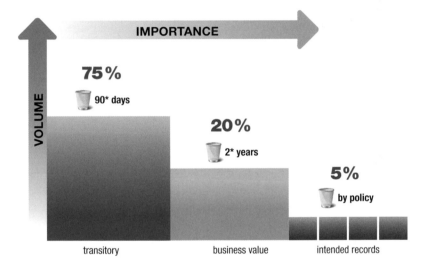

Figure 6.8: Corporate Records are Comprised of a Small Portion of Emails

Integrated Records Management

Email management provides various mechanisms that allow messages to be interactively or automatically classified in accordance with their business relevance. The act of classification also associates an appropriate retention policy, and other records management characteristics with the messages. As a function of an ECM system, email management may be fully integrated with a corporate records management program.

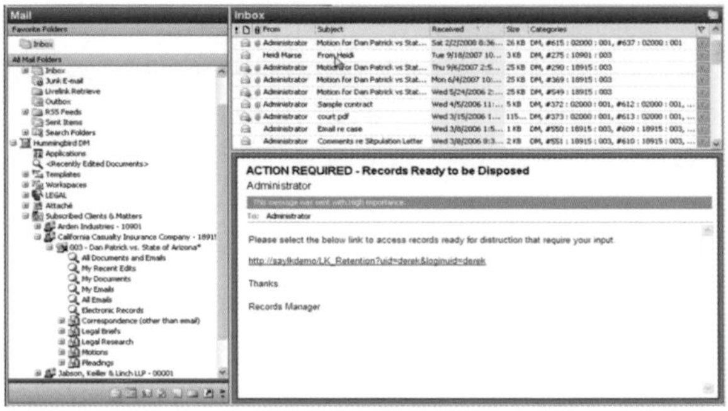

Figure 6.9: Email Management Integrated with Records Management

By integrating email management with an underlying records management engines, the trappings of an RM program become immediately applicable to email as well. For instance, organizations may quickly and consistently apply litigation holds to potentially relevant email, ensuring that they cannot be deleted under any circumstances and that they are preserved for use in litigation and discovery. Records management is discussed in detail in Chapter 5, Content Lifecycle Management.

Email Management in a Secure Repository

A central repository is a key requirement for any true, enterprise-scale email management system. A records-enabled central repository is where email messages themselves are stored and managed. This repository provides the ability to apply disposition and retention rules that automatically archive content and then dispose of it at the right time. By ensuring business continuity and recovery in the event of disaster, a central repository also protects the business against accidental loss of critical email messages and other business records.

Email management based on a central and secure enterprise repository ensures that business users collaborate and share content across departmental and geographical boundaries. The ability to use email as a collaboration tool is much stronger when business email messages are stored centrally and accessible by more than just a sender and recipient. Email is a notoriously "siloed" application. Storing business-relevant messages in a repository allows users to search for and take advantage of information that would otherwise be inaccessible.

Using email management to allow users to classify emails and consequently move their business-relevant messages into the managed repository makes the messages instantly searchable by other users who may benefit from this information. This aids in delivering tangible business value to users and increasing overall user adoption across an organization.

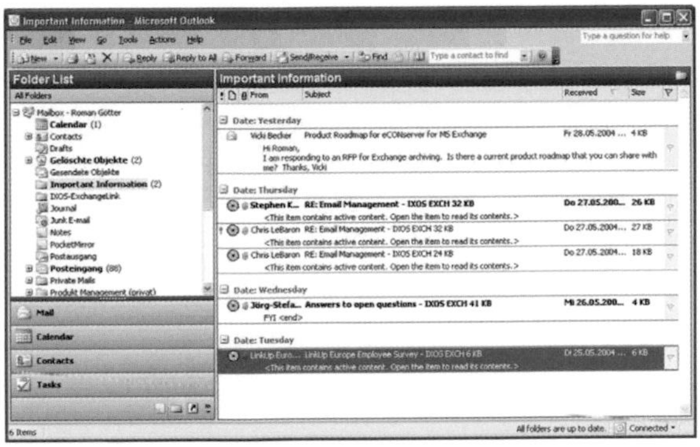

Figure 6.10: Records Management and Search Provides Access to Archived Mail

ECM 2.0 and Email Management

While user engagement and adoption are ultimately both the means and measure of a successful email management project, it is the bad publicity and financial hardships associated with poor practices that are often the primary catalysts for an email management initiative.

Email management is a critical component in any ECM strategy for the benefits it delivers. Beyond the security, compliance and productivity gains it delivers, a managed email environment provides important additional benefits. Integrated records management and search delivers access to corporate knowledge, improving productivity and the accuracy of information. Integration with ERP and business process management systems also leads to higher levels of productivity, as business processes triggered by an email can be effectively managed.

In any organization, email systems present risk and opportunity. A company is at risk if its email systems are unmanaged. If steps are taken to bring email into the sphere of ECM, opportunities are created for improving business operations. By deploying management tools for email systems, organizations can experience significant returns on investment, including increased compliance, expanded knowledge management and improved productivity. The investment in integrated email management typically pays off as cost savings are compared to the cost of running the disparate, dated single-function messaging solutions in place in most organizations today.

Now that we have reviewed the principals of email management, these same techniques can be applied to other collaborative content types within the context of ECM 2.0, including social media types like blogs and wikis, to achieve the same results.

Figure 7.1: Web Content Management

Today, the Web plays a key role in the way organizations do business. For this reason, Web Content Management (WCM) is a critical corporate requirement and a key technology in an ECM suite. As part of a comprehensive ECM 2.0 solution, WCM has synergies with digital media management, social media, collaboration, and records and document management. The benefits of implementing WCM within an ECM solution are explored and illustrated by the organizations profiled in this chapter.

CHAPTER 7

WEB CONTENT MANAGEMENT

Many businesses support a number of Web sites which are integral to their business operations, from the corporate Web site and employee intranets to ecommerce sites and partner extranets. The need for effective Web content management (WCM) comes with the proliferation of content in all formats and the rise of the Web browser as a universal means for access to information. WCM describes the management, assembly and delivery of content utilizing the Internet as the distribution mechanism and Web browsers as universally available client infrastructures. In order to do this, WCM systems dynamically package available content and presentation information in browser interpretable markup code, generating useful and meaningful information to the consumer within a browser experience.

Web content management incorporates the capability of contextual delivery to deliver the right content to the right people at the exact time they need it. By delivering content across applications and devices, WCM moves beyond basic content management needs to deliver dynamic content in context according to a user's personal and changing needs in real time.

While the rapid distribution of information yields distinct competitive advantages, it simultaneously increases the risks associated with releasing this information – including the potential to misplace confidential information or publish inaccurate information. When integrated with ECM technologies, such as workflow and document and records management, WCM delivers a robust and secure solution for managing and distributing content across the enterprise.

> BEHR

BEHR Process Corporation is largest provider of premium paints and stains to the North American Do-It-Yourself (DIY) home improvement market.

Using Web Content Management, BEHR has evolved its online presence from a static HTML site to a cinematic experience designed for homeowners and do-it-yourselfers alike. Visitors to the site have a vast array of tools to help them pick, compare and test-drive colors. Features include a Virtual Color Center that replicates BEHR color centers found in The Home Depot stores, an Inspiration Gallery with wide-format, magazine-quality images to spark ideas and an online Workbook where users can save and track their home projects and color choices.

Web Content Management provides advanced rich media management capabilities and a high-performance foundation for behr.com, enabling deep interactivity and an easier, immersive Web site experience. Behind the scenes, WCM enables BEHR to minimize IT involvement in Web site updates, putting the ownership of behr.com directly into the hands of the eBusiness and marketing professionals who drive its online initiatives.

Figure 7.2: BEHR's DIY Web Site Experience

Web Publishing

WCM systems manage Web pages and all elements that make up Web pages, typically assembling these pages to form an overall Web site. A Web site is a collection of related pages with supporting images, videos and other digital media that share a common domain name or address in an Internet Protocol-based network. These pages are developed using other Web objects such as graphics, other pages, or dynamic components such as Web applications (Java applets or Ajax controls, for example).

The content on a Web site can be static, dynamic, or a combination of both. A static Web site is rendered to a Web server at the time of publication and all elements remain constant after publication. Dynamic pages are HTML pages that are created at the time of access. Examples include a Web page that dynamically assembles its navigation and content according to a visitor's access rights or role.

WCM System Functionality

Independent of content source, a WCM system must provide a way to edit and integrate content into a Web site in an easy-to-use, consistent manner. To maximize efficiency, editors should only be required to develop and publish content. WCM interfaces are simple, intuitive and easy to use, allowing non-technical users and periodical contributors to publish content quickly and easily.

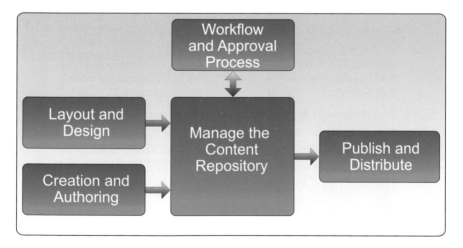

Figure 7.3: Simplified Content Management Lifecycle

> # RBS 6 Nations Rugby

The RBS 6 Nations Championship is the world's foremost annual international rugby event. Rugby teams from England, France, Ireland, Italy, Scotland and Wales compete each year in a series of fiercely-contested matches. Each game is followed by tens of millions of rugby fans all over the world via television, radio, mobile devices and the Web.

The existing RBS 6 Nations Championship Web site was unable to meet the demands of the high-speed download environment. With so many Italian and French supporters visiting the site, there was also a need to extend its language capabilities and provide information to the international media in their own languages. The tournament organizers, Six Nations Rugby Ltd., decided to revamp the site.

Using a WCM system, the site was completely rebuilt to reflect the prestigious image of the RBS 6 Nations Championship. The system delivers ease of use, Web 2.0 capabilities and content integration, linking massive amounts of material within the actual site structure. RBS plans to take the new site forward with new media plus dynamic content, such as video footage, photo galleries, and material from press conferences. Importantly, the site is now delivered in French and Italian, as well as English, increasing its appeal across mainland Europe. Since the site was launched, the number of visitors has increased substantially. When the tournament was in full swing, visitor numbers were up from 1.58 million to 1.78 million year over year, and numbers are expected to rise as more French and Italian visitors use the site.

Figure 7.4: RBS 6 Nations Championship Web site

With a WCM system, the editor creates new content or integrates existing content using a decentralized, tailored and browser-based user interface. The new content is then stored in the WCM content repository and published to the Internet, intranet or extranet by the WCM system. To safeguard corporate design standards and ensure professional integration across an organization's Web sites, WCM offers various ways to separate layout and content. Each page in a Web site can be defined by a template (often called a Cascading Style Sheet or CSS). Templates contain layout information for each page type, managing how content is assembled. Changing a page template results in subsequent changes to the appearance of all pages based on that template. The ability to change layout information is centralized through the template structure in a WCM system. This makes it easier to implement style changes and ensures content integrity.

Figure 7.5: In-Context Editing Experience

Combining workflow capabilities with WCM allows for a more controlled publishing process. For many organizations, including Mercedes in the example that follows, a workflow is used to enforce brand consistency or ensure regulatory compliance when publishing various content types across multiple channels in the enterprise. Workflow adds the additional controls required.

By separating content from layout, Web authors are able to manage text and the integration of digital media. An important capability of a WCM system is the management of the appropriate rendition of a media object such as an audio, video, podcast or Flash file for presentation on the Web. To achieve this, WCM systems offer lightweight media asset management functionality or integrate with media management systems.

WCM systems are increasingly providing non-technical users with easy to use system components. Authors can use in-line and in-context editing to edit content directly in the page leveraging Microsoft® Word®-like tools to provide a familiar editing context. On the administrative side, editors can create Web page layouts using a set of pre-configured, drag and drop widgets. Widgets are portable Web applications which allow non-technical users to add dynamic design, content or functionality to Web pages. Widgets and in-line editing are part of an array of easy to use modular functionalities that WCM solutions present.

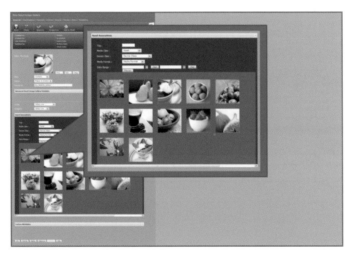

Figure 7.6: Simplified Content Management Lifecycle

Web sites are increasing their use of widgets to simplify and enhance end user experience by proving more relevant, accessible and contextual content. Examples include delivering data syndication to high traffic sites and implementing maps, notifications, feeds or search functionality into a page. Dynamic WCM systems allow editors to define both the layout and content of a page based on its target audience. This means that the system can deliver the five latest sports headlines on a page that is regularly accessed by a sports enthusiast.

Most professional Web sites include search functionality that allows users to find specific data within the site. Some WCM systems include out-of-the-box search tools to add search capabilities to a site. The search tools manage the indexing of content changes and ensure that only active content is being returned through search results.

> # Mercedes-Benz

Mercedes-Benz

With more than 500 separate Web sites within the Mercedes-Benz USA umbrella, including 350 dealer sites, Mercedes uses Web Content Management to maintain brand consistency across this highly complex series of interlocking sites – all on a single platform.

Over a million distinct, reusable content items, such as vehicle features and specs, parts and services information, and promotional offers, are stored in a single content management system and shared by more than one thousand contributors across many sites. The sites support digital media formats, including video, sound, and photography to engage visitors on multiple levels. Approval and workflow processes ensure consistent branding and messaging, supported by over one hundred non-technical content approvers.

When it comes to marketing prowess, Mercedes sets the pace – demonstrating what can be done when advanced technology is designed to support non-technical users. Mercedes knows that delivering brand and message consistency across such a highly complex series of sites would not be possible without an enterprise-scale foundation like WCM.

Figure 7.7: Mercedes Uses WCM to Deliver a Seamless and Rich Web Experience

Distributed Content and Collaboration

A WCM system should support a large number of editors working simultaneously from any location. An integral feature of WCM systems is the ability to allow any number of objects and files to be worked on by different people. Editors use a browser with Web access to check out content for edits, similar in function to a document management system (see Chapter 5). When editing is complete, the object is checked back in and the changes become visible to other system users. This mechanism ensures effective content management and consistency.

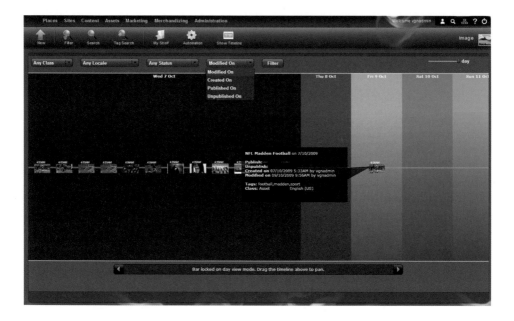

Figure 7.8: Content Events and Operations along a Timeline

Global organizations that offer multilingual Web sites rely on editors from different countries. For this reason, WCM systems provide a multilingual user interface capable of handling the different character sets associated with diverse countries, such as Japan or Korea. WCM systems also support the generation of multilingual and unicode content in a Web-viewable format. This is especially challenging, considering that the output provided by Web servers is interpreted by a variety of Web browsers which render content according to their own specifications. Further to the ability of managing the representation of multilingual content, WCM systems also manage the translation process for the content itself, ensuring that a multilingual Web site offers the content consistently in supported languages.

Figure 7.9: WCM Systems Support Internationalization

WCM systems use sophisticated access control systems for Web objects. In addition to defining groups, users and roles, it is possible to assign specific access rights to object trees or individual objects. In addition to the basic capabilities of reading and writing, it is also possible to impose restrictions on the ability to change object attributes. The right to rename, move or copy Web objects may be individually assigned.

One major problem with Web sites is checking consistency of references and links. WCM systems can automatically ensure that there are no inconsistent links in the Web sites they publish.

> ## Junta de Andalucia

The Junta de Andalucia is the Regional Government of Andalucia, Spain. The Web site of the Ministry of Environment of the Regional Government of Andalucia has established itself as one of the most advanced sites within the entire administration of Andalucia, both internally and externally.

To power the site, the Ministry selected a CMS solution based on its stability for the management of volumes of content, flexible and dynamic design of the navigation trees which helps to maintain consistency and homogeneity within the site, and the extensive functionalities for role management, user permissions and the design of specific workflows. Internally, the content manager enables editors to perform complex content management, including the tools and widgets that enable users to design text fields, texts in WYSIWYG format, dates, drop-down lists supplied from databases and the assignment of taxonomies and meta-data to content groups.

Using the CMS system, over 10,200 cataloged pieces of content and 11,500 static files can be managed and interrelated without duplications. Externally, this freshness and modernity and the constant development of the Web site has resulted in an exponential growth in the number of users visiting the portal daily, now amounting to 2 million visits per month.

Figure 7.10: Junta de Andalucia Ministry of Environment Web Site

Content Delivery

As Web sites play a larger role in business operations, global organizations are increasingly delivering content that is defined by user preferences in real time to deliver a relevant and more personalized Web experience. To offset information overload, content that is more targeted is much more useful to a Web site visitor. If an organization can deliver relevant content at the exact moment of need, it will be more effective at influencing or assisting the visitor. Web content of value delivers a much higher return on the investment in its creation. For this reason, WCM solutions have been designed to automatically deliver content based on user profiles, actions and behaviors.

The Value of Content

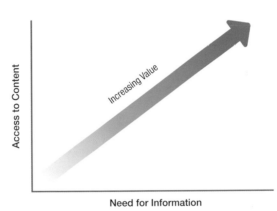

Figure 7.11: WCM Systems Support Internationalization

A major aspect of WCM is the ability to deliver content in context, or in other words, manage the end user experience. Experience management refers to the tailoring of content to the end user above and beyond personalization. It is as much about managing delivery as it is about managing content.

Experience management works most effectively when it is integrated with content authoring. During content authoring, the content developer can tag content and specify who needs to view each piece of content and in what order. This content sequencing enables authors to script the user experience for maximum benefit and predictable results.

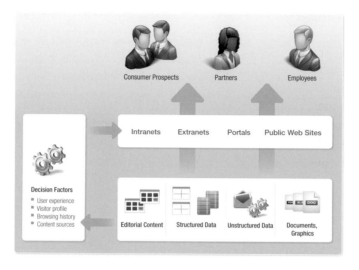

Figure 7.12: The Experience Management Process

Consider the scenario in which a group of new employees is starting their first week at a company. To become acclimated, these employees need to learn about the company in a logical, predictable manner. Content authors can leverage WCM to develop a step-by-step, content-driven guide to the company that employees can access online. Authors simply tag each piece of employee orientation material to read, "View this piece first, followed by this piece, and so on." Following this sequence, all new employees gain access to exactly the information the company believes they should see, when they need to see it.

Along with dynamic delivery of content, personalization and Web feeds are giving Web sites the ability to deliver more gratifying experiences to Web users. As discussed, personalized pages generate content based on a person's role, preferred language or industry. Portals typically permit this type of customized access to content.

Web feeds such as Really Simple Syndication (RSS) give organizations the ability to add context to existing content. RSS describes Web feed formats used to publish frequently updated content in blogs, news headlines, audio and video in a format that allows publishers to syndicate content automatically. Users are then able to subscribe to timely updates from favorite Web sites or aggregate feeds from many sites into one location on the Web, their PC or a mobile device.

WCM has evolved from the management of content to presenting new opportunities for revenue generation from Web sites. Through the dynamic delivery of content, organizations can create user friendly, customer-centric Web sites. Marketing organizations, for example, are able to leverage Web sites to deliver highly targeted campaigns, increase lead generation and improve customer loyalty. Dynamic sites can be augmented by ecommerce capabilities, search engine optimization, social media and Web analytic tools.

The effectiveness of user experience can be measured using Web analytic tools. Web analytics is the collection, measurement, analysis and reporting of Internet data for purposes of understanding and optimizing Web usage. A whole discipline in itself, Web analytics includes tools to measure tracking, site usage, traffic sources, content overview and site visitor conversions. These tools are often presented by a dynamic Web page that provides statistical analysis. Either built-in or integrated with a third-party solution, these dynamic Web pages allow organizations to obtain valuable statistics on usage patterns.

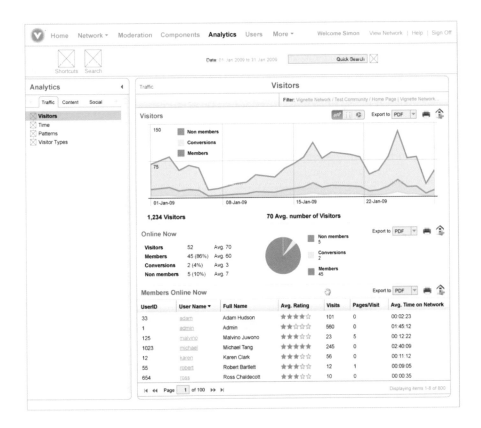

Figure 7.13: An Example of Web Analytics

Combined with Web analytic tools and recommendations features such as social tagging (discussed in more detail in Chapter 4), WCM systems are delivering a comprehensive solution for the effective provision of highly relevant and personalized Web experiences.

Suffolk University is located in downtown Boston, Massachusetts. Established in 1906, the university offers degrees in more than 70 areas of study, and has additional campuses in Dakar, Senegal and Madrid, Spain.

To celebrate their centennial year, Suffolk University launched a redesigned and expanded version of their Web site using a CMS system. The new Web site features an improved and easily-maintainable site structure with thousands of pages of information for staff and students alike, including an online course catalog. There are now over 200 users across campus involved in maintaining the information that is posted on the Web site. This has created a much more dynamic system where people from all areas of the university are actively creating and editing their own, self-relevant content.

Brand identity is maintained throughout the site because the technology ensures that users only have the ability to edit content and not the appearance or layout of the site. This is achieved using templates that lock in the appearance of the Web pages and only give users the power to make content edits, ensuring a consistent look and brand identity. The result is a comprehensive online presence that drives more visitors to the site and offers an optimized experience for those who want to learn about the university's programs and course offerings.

Figure 7.14: Suffolk University – Improving the Quality of Dynamic Information with CMS

WCM and Emerging Technologies

WCM was a production tool that laid the way for social networking and emerging Web 2.0 technologies. Today these technologies are allowing organizations to engage with their stakeholders to provide rich and interactive experiences. User generated content (UGC) can be managed by a WCM system, integrating this content into a larger repository where it is securely stored, managed and delivered in a disciplined manner. Workflow, tagging and meta-data can be applied, along with access rights according to a permissions model in a shared enterprise repository.

Web 2.0 technologies are presenting opportunities for organizations to monetize user generated content on their Web sites. As customers visit product-focused communities, for example, organizations can modify products and services to directly meet consumer needs or direct promotions to a highly targeted audience. More information on UGC and social computing is available in Chapter 9 on Social Media.

An increasing number of companies are also considering open source software for WCM and delivery in the cloud. Open source online communities are available as corporate Web sites from vendors delivering software solutions as a service. Chapter 13 provides more detailed discussions around open source software and "cloud" services.

ECM and WCM

Content is the primary driver for organizational productivity in today's business world. As nearly all business processes move online, organizations have a tremendous opportunity to move beyond basic WCM to derive greater value from their content.

Web technologies and the overall Web experience will continue to develop. To support dynamic pages, WCM systems will have to be flexible to accommodate external applications, products or interfaces. WCM integrates with other ECM 2.0 applications allowing authors to use customer information from across the enterprise ecosystem, publish documents from shared repository or CRM system and transform digital media from a media management system for presentation on a Web site.

Content gains more value when it is published to a wider audience. Consider a document that is shared in a knowledge repository. As the document is downloaded, viewed, shared and edited, it is assigned meta-data and readership is tracked. This content can then be associated with a business process managed by other enterprise applications. The ability to interface with Web content management systems and use social media tools gives organizations the ability to socialize content and obtain immediate feedback. An integrated ECM system that supports WCM gives organizations the ability to publish content through Web properties for Web and mobile access and maintain a link back into the core ECM store for valuable meta-data and audit information.

A WCM system offers organizations many benefits. It helps global organizations meet increasing demands placed on both internal and external Web sites to deliver business-critical information to stakeholders. The technology controls Web site content proliferation while enhancing communication, improving productivity and minimizing corporate risk.

WCM helps organizations achieve compliance by managing the archiving of all Web pages, along with transactions that occur on each Web page – an ability that is critical for financial institutions, for example, who may be required to reproduce archived versions of their Web site.

Web content management enables organizations to effectively manage Web site content from conception through to publication across all channels – online, print and mobile – enabling tight controls that dovetail into the core services of a comprehensive ECM system.

Figure 8.1: Collaboration and E2.0

Collaboration lies at the heart of organizational teams and the way they work together. In this chapter, we show how integral collaborative technologies are to ECM and how they form the basis for Web technology developments to follow, including online communities and the emergence of Enterprise 2.0 or E2.0. Innovator stories are profiled to illustrate how collaborative technologies help people make critical connections to the resources they need to be more productive and innovative.

As Web 2.0 and social media technologies dramatically reshape the landscape of collaborative technologies, Chapter 9 provides a follow on to this chapter with its focus on Social Media.

COLLABORATION AND E2.0

ECM is about understanding the relationship between people, processes, and content within an organization. People are a critical component in the ECM equation. The reality of business is that organizations are run by people, not technology. When people work together, they share knowledge, ideas and expertise to identify and resolve issues, discover solutions and develop new products and services.

Collaboration technologies were developed to present effective ways for people to work together. Performance and productivity gains are critical drivers behind the evolution of collaborative and virtual team applications. By allowing people to collaborate according to individual schedules across different time zones and geographies, Web-based collaborative tools have evolved into Web 2.0 technologies like social networks, blog and wikis. These new technologies will change the collaboration landscape forever. Social networking, Web mashups and cloud computing are becoming household terms. Higher bandwidth and ubiquitous computing have transformed the knowledge worker into the mobile worker. The promise of immersive collaboration has pushed the limits of collaboration tools by creating a seamless experience for people working together.

This chapter will examine three generations of collaborative offerings within global enterprises.

The first generation of collaboration tools includes email, virtual team applications, intranets and extranets, virtual meetings and instant messaging. These tools laid the groundwork for collaborative applications to follow – and interact with newer technologies to present compelling solutions.

Second generation applications evolve from repository-based collaboration to fully integrated ECM and Enterprise 2.0 or E2.0.

Finally, we focus on the future of enterprise collaboration as it applies the human element to technology. Immersive collaboration describes how fully integrated virtual environments can enrich collaboration in the workplace and enable new and exciting ways for people to work together.

First Generation Collaboration Applications

Early collaboration applications were Web-based software programs that enabled project teams to work together from dispersed locations. These applications ranged from shared "workspaces" to messaging and conferencing applications. Collaborative software evolved to incorporate third-party, real-time applications like instant messaging, application sharing, whiteboarding and online meetings. Integrating these capabilities enabled people to collaborate using one interface without having to move between different applications. Early virtual project team applications paved the way for future developments in ECM, including online communities and the incorporation of emerging Web 2.0 technologies.

Figure 8.2: Project Work Spaces

Email-Based Collaboration

The majority of enterprise collaboration takes place through email. The statistics around the number of emails sent every day are impressive. In fact, obtaining the total number of emails sent each day is comparable to establishing how many people in the world drive cars every day.

Email is an example of asynchronous collaboration. Asynchronous collaborative software allows teams to collaborate remotely, but each person works in isolation, communicating with other members using file sharing applications or email messages. By comparison, synchronous collaborative software allows geographically distributed teams to work together in real time by transferring files, chatting, sharing a whiteboard and using voice or video technology. The benefit of synchronous (real time) collaboration is that it provides immediate interactions and allows everyone to be more responsive.

The first generation of enterprise collaborative tools emerged in response to the popularity of email, which has exposed the challenges associated with asynchronous collaboration in an enterprise context. To illustrate this development, let's examine the problems inherent with email as an effective collaboration tool.

Repository-Based Collaboration as the Alternative

Email-based collaboration is an ineffectual way to work because it is fundamentally disorganized and limited. By its very nature, email encourages people to work together in an ad hoc and isolated way.

Word Attachment

Returned Document

Figure 8.3: Email Collaboration Between Individuals

Consider a knowledge worker who needs to have a document approved by a group of colleagues. While it is possible to email a document to a group of people simultaneously, problems occur when modifications are made to the document, which is then emailed back to the author. Depending on the size of the group, the author could end up with multiple versions of the same document and consolidating these is a time consuming task. Because the rest of an organization is not aware of the interaction or changes made to content within the email thread, the value of knowledge exchange is limited.

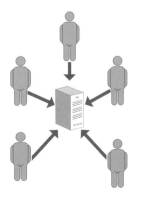

Figure 8.4: Document Collaboration Among Groups

Repository-based collaboration is much more effective than email because of its ability to build and sustain a central library or repository. Group members can be given secure access to documents where they can share in updating the document based on read, write and edit permissions and even collaborate in real time to edit documents. Repository-based collaboration delivers a structured method for teams to work together and access knowledge. Duplicated efforts and confusion are eliminated by document management features such as version control and audit history. People can be more productive because their work is organized according to a defined process. The flow of information can be outlined and mapped to a workflow which is fully integrated with content and collaboration applications on an ECM platform.

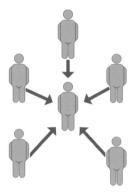

Figure 8.5: Support for Multiple Users

A secure, central repository enables people to follow the policies and procedures for governance established by an organization. As content that needs to be managed, email presents significant corporate risk and liability. Enforced policy, an email management system and end user training are all key elements of successful email management. This is discussed in detail in Chapter 6.

Intranets

An intranet is a private network inside an organization, essentially an internal application of the Internet. The development of intranets was a giant step forward in the evolution of collaborative applications and of the ECM market as a whole.

Intranets provide secure access to corporate information, including policies and procedures, human resources forms and sales and marketing collateral. Intranets eliminate the barriers that keep people from collaborating on projects effectively. Regardless of the number of team members and their locations, intranets erase time zones and geographic boundaries.

> # Hyatt

HYATT™

Hyatt, one of the world's premier hotel companies, and its subsidiaries and affiliates (collectively, "Hyatt") provide management services for 424 hotels and resorts throughout the world to deliver hospitality to guests in 45 countries. With a commitment to personalized service and cultural relevance, Hyatt is focused on providing authentic hospitality to its guests.

To keep a global hotel company like Hyatt delivering the type of customer service that it is known for requires the engagement of many individuals. This is particularly challenging considering that these individuals span continents, time zones, cultures and languages.

Hyatt implemented an intranet solution to move the company from multiple information silos to a more connected and seamless community. Called Hyattconnect, the portal gives Hyatt associates access to an easy-to-use content management interface where they can find up-to-date information on policies, procedures, best practices and internal articles through a secure connection from any computer with a Web browser. Using the portal, individuals can collaborate on projects and tasks, reducing project timelines. The Web Content Management and Media Services components ensure efficient distribution of appropriate content and media types across multiple devices, as well as improved search capabilities.

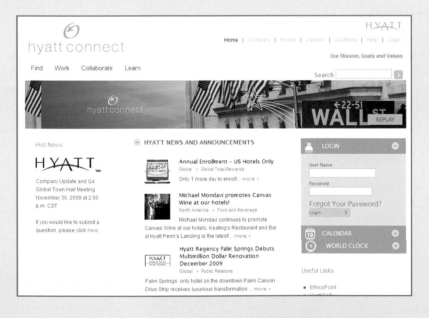

Figure 8.6: Hyattconnect – Facilitating Internal Collaboration

Unlike client-server environments, intranets provide a server-centric approach to project collaboration. Intranets create universally available, cross-platform networks that enable working groups to communicate, share tools and information, assign and track tasks, and manage complex projects. Consequently, companies find it cost effective to enhance their infrastructure using intranets because they can easily extend the reach of their business processes to remote users.

Intranets are being increasingly enriched with online meetings, instant messaging, calendaring, blogs, wikis and other technologies to improve communications and collaboration.

Online Meetings

While intranets introduced a consolidated workplace, they did not provide an effective means for users to collaborate in real time. The most effective collaborative applications incorporate a real-time meeting tool that lets users set up and attend meetings quickly and easily. Bringing together team members from multiple locations and times zones gives them a sense of proximity and ensures that projects stay on track. By hosting meetings online, organizations can significantly reduce travel costs. Attendees are able to whiteboard, chat, share documents and applications, and mark up documents in real time. Immersive collaboration, gaming and simulation technologies are driving the development of meeting capabilities to facilitate complex collaboration using 3-dimensional environments within the enterprise.

Instant Messaging

Organizations have become flooded with consumer instant messaging (IM) services. The ability for users to initiate collaborative exchanges with one another, or to host public conference rooms, delivers a new level of spontaneity. When integrated with ECM, enterprise IM enables users to save the contents of their collaborative exchanges into a shared repository, building the corporate knowledge base as a by-product of collaboration.

Figure 8.7: An IM Session Featuring Application Sharing

CARE Canada is a non-profit and non-religious charitable organization. For over half a century, CARE has been bringing emergency relief to those in need around the world.

CARE's community-based programs in approximately 70 countries place a special focus on working with women because they are disproportionately affected by poverty and are crucial to fighting it. Based on this, CARE Canada has successfully initiated the I Am Powerful campaign to promote the empowerment of women internationally. Having trusted ECM since 1998 as the foundation for their intranet, CARE Canada revisited the solution, which they named Minerva, as their main tool for knowledge sharing and distribution to help support the campaign.

Comprised of women responsible for spreading the I Am Powerful message, users champion the repository. The reference group works in different departments in numerous sectors. Many of CARE's contributors are not highly technical, so the solution has to be user friendly, interactive, and easily accessible. The system contains documents for distribution, information for their personal use and in-depth knowledge that is restricted to their view only. Minerva has proven to be a secure repository that encourages knowledge sharing and informational consistency within the reference group and throughout the CARE organization.

Figure 8.8: CARE Canada – Promoting the Empowerment of Women Internationally

In regulated industries such as financial services and healthcare, SEC and HIPAA regulations are compelling organizations to archive the contents of IM sessions in addition to the contents of emails. For example, a developer and project manager may have an important conversation about software architecture using IM. Two months later, when patent litigation demands that the company produce all records of interaction concerning this same architecture, the conversation can be easily accessed from a central repository, where it has been stored and indexed. To provide this degree of control over content, it is most effective to integrate IM with ECM.

Extranets

Extranets extend the enterprise outside the firewall to include partners, suppliers, and customers in business projects and processes.

Collaboration with partners and suppliers poses an ongoing challenge as people work from remote locations and across time zones, often using disparate resources. Just as intranets have enabled companies to share information and collaborate across the enterprise, Web-based extranets empower companies to strengthen external communications and increase efficiency by facilitating secure information exchange with partners and associates outside of the firewall. By involving partners in their business processes, organizations can access domain knowledge and expertise, implement best practices with every process, reduce product development cycles and create new services to improve competitive position.

From supply-chain management to regulatory compliance, manufacturing and engineering, an integrated extranet platform allows organizations to maximize their investment in diverse technologies and improve operational efficiency. Organizations can use extranets to create, sustain and manage online communities or e-marketplaces – global trading communities that function across diverse computing environments, business transactions, resources, knowledge and expertise.

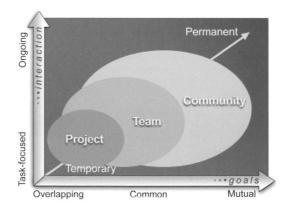

Figure 8.9: Collaborating Across Project Teams and Online Communities

> ## International Organization for Standardization Central Secretariat (ISO)

The International Organization for Standardization Central Secretariat (ISO) is a world-wide federation of national standards bodies from 156 countries. Complying with ISO standards, such as ISO 9000 for quality management is a must for any organization before it can compete in the global economy. Companies in every kind of industry – from chemical to information technology – are required to comply with particular ISO standards as a prerequisite to doing business. Maintaining and publishing content on more than 15,000 ISO standards is no simple task. The very success of the ISO program depends on making sure that the most up-to-date, valid standards are made easily available to worldwide users.

The ISO's Central Secretariat uses ECM to effectively manage the entire standardization process – from development to distribution. ECM provides a long-term foundation for capturing knowledge and is Web-based, so it can ease the process of distributing information over the ISO extranet. This means customers have instant access to information directly from their Web browser, along with print-on-demand capability, which reduces operational costs. With ECM as its strategic underpinning, ISO uses ECM to manage content for its bilingual Web site – www.iso.org – and also to manage content for its Web store.

ISO has greatly reduced the time required to publish international standards and can now manage all official documents and reports electronically. It was one of the first virtual Internet communities and is one of the largest virtual organizations in the world today.

Figure 8.10: ISO's Web Store

Online Communities of Practice

Communities of practice (CoP) have become popular as technologies have allowed organizations to bring together dispersed expertise and resources across global operations to become more responsive to an evolving marketplace. A community of practice is a self-organizing collection of people who collaborate and share resources to support work in a specific field. Members of communities of practices form relationships, establish trust and exchange knowledge. Organizations develop communities of practice to facilitate knowledge transfer and collaboration amongst employees, promoting produc-tivity and fostering innovation through the act of sharing, refining and distributing best prac-tices.

Communities are based on trusted relationships. Within any community, the connections between people are what matter; the tools used to facilitate the community are secondary. A community offers its members a variety of ways to interact with other members. Mem-bers need to be able to establish a sense of identity within the community. Facebook does an excellent job of this, allowing its members to interact using Web 2.0 tools like profiles, messaging, rating, tagging, sharing and more. These tools do not define the community; rather they help the members build a great sense of community. We discuss specific Web 2.0 applications like social networks in detail in Chapter 9.

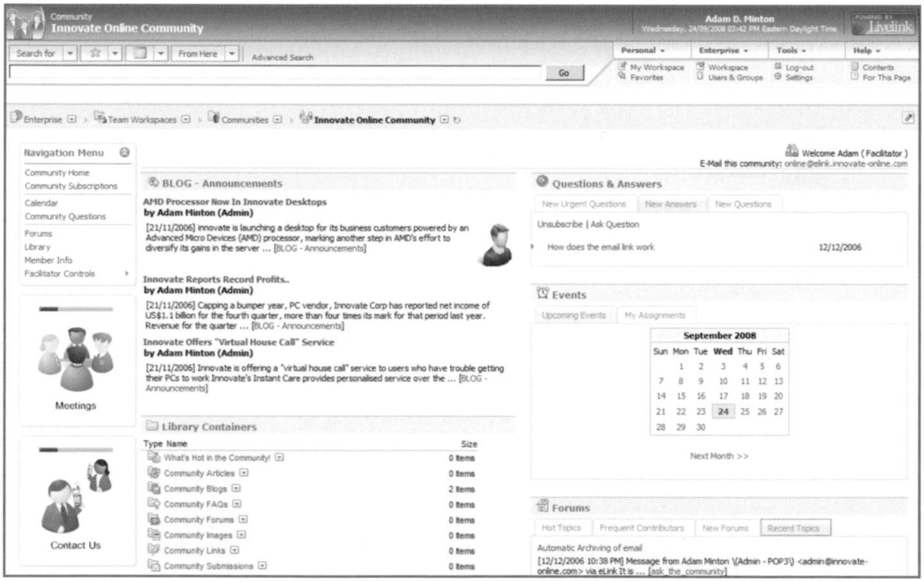

Figure 8.11: CoPs Capture Collective Knowledge

Web 2.0 technologies are transforming how organizations collaborate and share knowledge. Interactive online communities give organizations the opportunity to capture, share and manage ad hoc collaboration to improve productivity, foster innovation and gain competitive edge. CoPs provide a platform for knowledge sharing and collaboration. This kind of knowledge exchange incites a process that raises awareness, encourages interaction, identifies experts and captures collective wisdom to establish best practices. Using emerging technologies to facilitate improved communications has given rise to the notion of Enterprise 2.0 as a new business model that leverages Web 2.0 technologies to give organizations competitive advantage in a global economy.

Enterprise 2.0

Enterprise 2.0 (E2.0) refers to the application of Web 2.0 technologies to deliver content management and collaboration solutions inside the firewall, within a business context. Most global organizations already support an arsenal of tools to facilitate communication, including email, instant messaging, intranets, content management solutions, mobile phones and more. What is new and exciting about Web 2.0 technologies is that their focus is on the *ways* that people interact to share knowledge. E2.0 technologies immerse the knowledge worker within the sharing structure of the enterprise in fast and easy to use ways, providing a seamless and rich collaborative experience. The benefits are higher levels of productivity as knowledge workers can connect immediately to exchange information in real time.

E2.0 describes a movement that weaves together the content fabric in an enterprise. Wikis, blogs and IM have the ability to transform a corporate intranet into a dynamic and highly interactive structure built by distributed peers. As more people engage in authoring, linking and tagging, an organization's content becomes more searchable, analyzable and manageable. When the processes around content are seamless and visible, it becomes easier for organizations to manage content and meet regulatory requirements. For this reason, along with improved efficiencies and productivity gains, ECM platforms are integrating social media with current product offerings.

> SNCF

The French rail group found a way to manage documents and help staff collaborate to better serve 1 billion customers every year. SNCF has successfully restructured its electronic content management system and is now energizing its professional communities via a single portal.

Internal challenges faced by SNCF included: amalgamating and using all available information, capitalizing on and sharing best practices, setting up spaces dedicated to professional communities and consistent presentation of information on the intranet. Since the 2005 launch, communities structured around the professions within the infrastructure division have evolved, enabling genuine cooperation through sharing best practices and using IT tools developed on a local level. In fact the community was so successful that deployment has expanded to include three out of four divisions at SNCF.

The online professional communities are simple to use and highly innovative; they constitute a rapid and pragmatic exchange system that guarantees confidentiality based on profiles. Anyone can post useful information about SNCF activities here, and it can then be accessed and used by everyone. Today, sharing best practices is a reality, and the response to information has improved significantly.

Figure 8.12: SNCF's Community of Practice

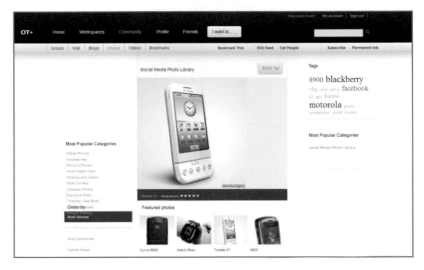

Figure 8.13: Engaging Employees with Social Computing

Enterprise 2.0 moves the conversation from the water cooler directly to a secure corporate network, creating a historical knowledge base of ideas, opinions, experiences and content. Employees no longer have to rely on email, conference calls or meetings to share ideas and stay informed. E2.0 defines a new era of community-based environments where people meet, network and improve collective knowledge.

Mobile Collaboration

The digital economy has created a shift in the way that we work together. With increased connectivity and accessibility, people are relying more on mobile devices to work remotely. Yesterday's knowledge workers are becoming today's mobile workers as people are no longer limited by location to be productive.

With mobile collaboration, a distributed workforce is productive wherever it works. A salesperson is a good example of a remote employee who needs to stay connected to people and information in a persistent way to work effectively. Mobile collaboration allows remote users to contribute to collaborative instances in ways that non-mobile employees are not able to. ECM technologies are enabling this by linking physical devices with virtual and mobile environments to facilitate the transparent exchange of media types and information. Consider a virtual meeting. A mobile worker should be able to "walk" into a virtual meeting room, join the meeting, invite other attendees to join the meeting and watch a live streaming video together or collaborate to edit a document in real time. Mobile ECM connects mobile professionals with content and resources in their preferred environment. Mobile ECM is explored in Chapter 14.

All trademarks found above are owned by the respective trademark owners and the authors of this book
do not intent to imply that any such trademark owners are endorsing any specific ECM software product.

Figure 8.14: Mobile Community-Based Collaboration

Immersive Collaboration

ECM transparently connects people, processes and information, uniting the back office with the front office of an enterprise to improve productivity and cost-effectiveness. A shared virtual workspace can be used for shared document editing, remote collaboration, teleconferencing, and linking real-world data into a virtual space for collaboration.

Real-time collaboration gives people a much more visceral sense of the patterns of data and processes that exist in an organization. As Web 2.0 technologies enter the business environment, organizations are beginning to realize the potential of immersive collaboration. Immersive collaboration describes how online virtual environments can enrich collaboration in the workplace. In an ideal work environment, people have access to all the content they need: documents in all formats, the status and tasks of all colleagues, digital media via audio, video, mobile and virtual communication channels, as well as links to physical content where possible. As immersive collaboration emulates the human capacity to receive many messages simultaneously, technology will become an extension of the human sensory system.

Collaboration is already reflecting the multi-channel interfaces of computer gaming and simulation environments. The ECM landscape is encompassing rich, interactive and contextual collaboration. Emulating Second Life as a working model, organizations are experimenting with virtual events. Imagine attending an event where users establish a professional identity using an avatar, attend various presentations, chat with other attendees, and call virtual meetings on the spot. The business benefits are as multifaceted as the platforms that enable immersive collaboration – increased productivity and workforce engagement, costs savings and innovation.

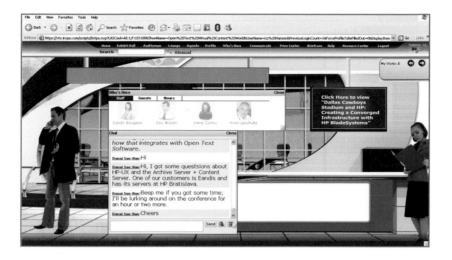

Figure 8.15: A Virtual Tradeshow Booth

While recent developments in digital media, mobility and interactive immersive environments will form the basis for the development of next generation ECM platforms, many questions remain unanswered. How should workplace systems reflect the expectations around personal devices, physical environments and social online spaces? How will these workplaces support differing generations, values and cultures? How will organizations make these spaces secure? We will examine these questions in more depth in the following chapter on Social Media.

Figure 9.1: Social Media

This chapter is about social media and social collaboration. It serves as an extension to the previous chapter on collaboration, which introduced the concept of Enterprise 2.0, or E2.0. E2.0 describes how knowledge workers use Web 2.0 technologies to participate, interact and collaborate with one another within a business context. While individuals use Web 2.0 technologies to interact on the Internet, use of social media in the enterprise is subject to rules of governance and compliance, along with the requirement to transparently demonstrate that processes and interactions around content are secure. E2.0 differs from Web 2.0 around these issues of security and privacy. This chapter explains how to make social collaboration secure within the context of ECM – what we refer to as ECM 2.0. Innovator stories demonstrate how social media is being used effectively to engage with customers in new ways, inspire innovation and increase business opportunities in an emerging social marketplace.

CHAPTER 9

SOCIAL MEDIA

The Internet has experienced a paradigm shift with the introduction of new interactive Web 2.0 technologies and communication models. Web sites have transformed from static pages to dynamic sites, online communities and social networks supporting a rich culture of user participation and contribution. Social media refers to the dissemination of content and media through a social network. Social media is content (often called user generated content or UGC) that can be shared easily with the use of Web 2.0 technologies. While social media is about the content and information; Web 2.0 is a term that describes the technology as an enabler.

Social media is media that is produced by social interaction and distributed on the Internet in highly accessible and scalable ways. Social media uses Web-based technologies to transform media monologues (one-to-many) into social media dialogues (many-to-many). It supports the free exchange of knowledge and information, where people are producers as well as consumers of media.

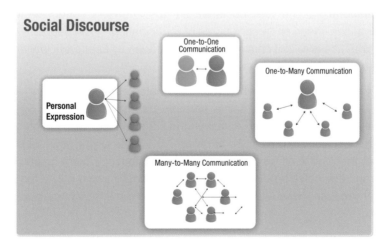

Figure 9.2: Many-to-Many Social Media Dialogues

UGC can include ratings for an article on a news site, comments left for a product on a Web site and personal information posted on a social network. Social media is powerful because it shifts power back to the consumers. While this has been possible before with online letters to the editor and moderated newsgroups, what sets social media apart is the proliferation of capabilities that empowers users to be editors.

There are numerous technical and sociological changes that are supporting the widespread use of social computing. More powerful technology, faster connection times and lower costs are bringing more people online. Along with improvements in accessibility, demographics are playing their part in introducing social collaboration to the enterprise. As boomers retire, organizations are rethinking their models of knowledge transfer. Gen-Xers are adopting social computing tools to find the knowledge and exposure they need to do their jobs effectively. Their successors, Millennials, as "digital natives" will expect to use the same social collaboration tools in the office that they use at home.

From a business perspective, organizations are just starting to incorporate the principles of UGC into their Web strategies to create new business models for driving revenue. Social media is being regarded as an area of potential investment as businesses progressively regard social networks, online communities and the Web as effective channels of communications.

A Brief History

Web 2.0 was coined at a conference in 2004 hosted by O'Reilly and CMP Media. According to Tim O'Reilly, founder of O'Reilly®, Web 2.0 is a trend that moves away from traditional client-server based applications to technologies that rely on the Web as a platform for collaboration. The Web becomes an open network conducive to facilitating emergent applications based on "architectures of participation"[1]. The popularity of sites like Wikipedia and YouTube is reliant on a network effect driven by user participation. The focus is on people; the technology is their enabler.

Besides being participatory in nature, Web 2.0 technologies are lightweight, easy to use, fast to deploy and available as an online service. Examples of Web 2.0 technologies include Web-based communities, social networking sites, video-sharing sites, wikis, blogs, forums, mashups and folksonomies. Some Web 2.0 tools are not new but date back to the beginning of the Web itself. In the early days of computing, users helped other users learn about computers, solve problems or share experiences using online forums, bulletin boards and user groups. These were the early forms of Web 2.0 technologies.

---

[1] http://tim.oreilly.com/

While developments for enabling interactive applications in a Web 2.0 environment are based on standard technologies, new languages are being created to facilitate Web 2.0 interactions. These key development technologies include AJAX, Web Services and Service Oriented Architecture (SOA).

ECM 2.0 Creates the Social Workplace

Within an enterprise context, social collaboration creates a knowledge sharing culture, enriching intellectual capital in the process. The "social workplace" connects people with their peers, critical content and information. Culturally, it breaks down hierarchical and administrative barriers to innovation and idea exchange among employees. Technologically, the social workplace combines ECM technologies with social collaboration to bridge geographical, organizational and generational gaps. ECM 2.0 refers to managing content from Web 2.0 social networks, blogs, wikis and other Web 2.0 technologies.

Unlike an intranet, which is typically organized according to function or role, the social workplace facilitates knowledge exchange from the bottom up according to areas of expertise or by project. The social workplace fosters the natural formation of communities around topics of interest. These communities are built on corporate networks that disseminate knowledge to all employees. Within these communities, tools like forums, wikis, and blogs are used in a variety of ways to provide employees with a platform for exchanging and managing the information used to accomplish everyday tasks.

Figure 9.3: Consumerization of the Enterprise – Facebook for Organizations

ECM 2.0 Technologies

Blogs are an extremely popular Web 2.0 technology. This is because people can create and publish blogs, adding content and images quickly and easily. Editorial in nature,

STA Travel has approximately six million customers in over 90 countries and more than 2,000 staff worldwide. Over 80 percent of STA Travel's customers begin their relationship with STA Travel online. As a result, the STA Travel Web site is a crucial component of its marketing strategy for gaining new business.

STA Travel makes extensive use of blogs to engage with customers and ultimately, increase retention and customer sales. On a self-service basis, each STA Travel customer can create their own travel blog to keep friends, family, and other STA travelers aware of the status of their trip. Travelers have the ability to provide Web visitors with a full picture of their travel experiences, complete with digital photos and video. Travel fans are able to share experiences, recommendations and lessons learned by reading other peoples' blogs and information related to their travel destinations through the STA Travel network. Social tagging makes important user-generated content easy to find, with rankings based on popularity.

Thousands of blogs were posted shortly after the launch of STA Travel's blog feature, generating more than 100,000 visits and over one million hits for STA Travel. The close link between editorial content, travel offers, user generated content and recommendations creates a significant increase in the attractiveness and credibility of the STA Travel Web site. According to the Chief Executive Officer at STA Travel, "The survival of STA Travel depends on having a successful online presence – it keeps us relevant. Our new solution is meeting all our required business objectives such as revenue generation, improved online sales conversion rates and increased referral income."

Figure 9.4: STA Travel's Blog Feature

blogs communicate an author's point of view and solicit feedback in the form of comments. Thought leaders use blogs to communicate their insights and expertise, often collecting large online followings. In this way blogs are extremely social, associating a personal profile with content. Inside the enterprise, blogs can be used in projects or working documentation to communicate news or share information internally. In effect, blogs can replace emails when information needs to be communicated on a many-to-many basis.

As a form of blogging, micro-blogs or "tweets" are blog posts with a limited character set to keep messages short. Micro-blogs are incredibly viral as followers can subscribe to receive status updates or streams of alerts – which can all be accessed using Web sites, mobile devices or desktop software. As a real-time replacement for email, micro-blogging has the potential to become a new informal communication medium, especially for collaborative work within organizations.

Figure 9.5: An Enterprise Wiki

Like blogs, wikis are popular because they are easy to use. A wiki is a collection of articles that can be edited, linked, and expanded by any authorized user. Wikis facilitate the open sharing of knowledge on a designated Web page. In true Web 2.0 form, wikis combine ease of use, access and coordination that more complicated collaborative tools lack. Their ability to offer users easy access to contextual collaborative tools has given wikis strong footing with early adopters in the enterprise market. Organizations use wikis to collect enterprise knowledge and insights for best practices or to collaboratively write online documentation. When used effectively, these tools can have a very positive impact on worker productivity by reducing the number of incoming emails that need to be read, managed and stored. The social workplace is Facebook for the enterprise, offering employees a virtual place to access and share rich profiles, a contacts list with status updates, and the ability to post their own status or write on someone else's "wall."

Enterprise social networks facilitate connections based on self-generated user profiles. Typical social networks are profile-driven. Profiles deliver access to personal and professional information, pictures, relevant links, blog sites and more. Within an organization, the member directory is a dynamic version of the employee directory, where employees can connect with others based on skills, expertise or interest.

Figure 9.6: Users Can Search for Resources by Profile

With ECM 2.0, value is added to content that is tagged, rated and commented on in context. Social bookmarks can be used in the workplace to generate a common set of links that members of a project team might share around topics of interest. Models of collaborative tagging are currently being adopted by large organizations because they prescribe new and innovative ways to relate knowledge and can reveal emerging knowledge structures.

The ability to assemble and personalize Web presentations of people and information within changing contexts is a distinguishing feature of Web 2.0. Mashups combine multiple, disparate data sources into new and unique applications, services or dashboards. Mashups are fast and easy to deploy, use open Application Programming Interfaces (APIs) and enable non-technical users to produce customized Internet applications. Mashups can be used to connect to critical data sources within the enterprise. As shown in the figure below, accounts payable clerks can access relevant information to resolve payment process exceptions via a familiar Outlook-style user interface, from a number of different sources. As described in Chapter 10, digital media can be syndicated and mashups used to enhance the overall digital media experience.

Figure 9.7: Using Mashups to Streamline the Accounts Payable Process

As social collaboration attains new heights with Web 2.0 sharing and maintaining quality content within an organization becomes increasingly important to achieving productivity. The organizations that are adopting social computing are seeing a new workplace culture develop in which collective personal information and experiences are part of its intellectual capital. Employees who actively share their knowledge are regarded as experts and achieve a high level of recognition within their organizations. A "sharing expertise" culture is cultivated and practiced throughout the entire user community.

Offering more ways to collaborate and access resources than an intranet, the social workplace gives users a variety of ways to access an organization: personal, by group or department or by enterprise. The social enterprise gives organizations the ability to promote knowledge exchange, help employees find experts or information and create a sense of belonging that fosters personal relationships to improve teamwork, employee retention and productivity.

In large organizations, social media is generally not part of a company-wide strategic effort. Instead, efforts are focused around tactical, departmental and initiative-based deployments. Examples include a product manager launching a social micro-site to support a new product, a brand manager creating a social site for a specific promotion, or technical support using a wiki for documentation. In many cases, marketing departments have been leading social media deployments within the enterprise.

Sources of economic value	Firms that *do not* adopt Social Computing	Firms that *do* adopt Social Computing	Industries most affected
Community	No user content or interaction	User content, forums, add value to brand	Media, retail, telecom
Customer service	No follow-up to user suggestions	Community self-help reduces service costs	High-tech, automotive
Sales	Lower loyalty erodes prices	Community loyalty reduces commissions	CPG, finance, telecom, travel
Marketing	Bad targeting and no use of WOM	WOM and better targeting raise ROI	CPG, automotive
Production	Products don't meet user demand	Co-design reduces waste	CPG, media, high-tech
R&D	No use of user intelligence	Community input raises success rate	Healthcare, high-tech

Figure 9.8: Organizational Approaches to Social Computing

But how can the enterprise expect to benefit from creating a social workplace? The McKinsey consultancy firm has conducted three annual surveys to answer this question. In the most recent, participants revealed that they had better access to knowledge and expertise, experienced higher levels of satisfaction and were able to innovate at higher rates. Innovations that result from social software are probably the most tangible return on investment for the social workplace. In this study, in fact, innovation rates rose by as much as 20 percent and knowledge workers experienced a 35 percent increase in access to expertise – all through using social computing tools[2].

Companies will have different objectives for using social media depending on the positioning of their products and services, and the industries they sell to. Without an enterprise strategy for the management, integration and secure support of social computing technologies, many social media sites are being used by departments without the proper overarching governance, brand consistency, user experience integration or content strategy in place. As these sites become more visible and increase their requirements for resources and integration, IT departments will be increasingly asked to participate in strategic discussions around social computing solutions.

---

[2] McAfee, Andrew. *Enterprise 2.0 is vital for business*, FT.com, 2009

Hatch's value system includes the pursuit of technical excellence and continuous improvement by providing high-quality, innovative, technically advanced, and comprehensive services to its clients and workforce. When it saw a need for social networking and Web 2.0 technologies, Hatch chose Communities to help unite its 8,700 employees in the global mining, metallurgical, energy, and infrastructure sectors.

Hatch saw social networking and Web 2.0 technology as essential in addressing two critical concerns: the capability to exchange information within a dispersed work force, and Generation Y employees want to pursue ways to communicate beyond traditional email or formal document and data repositories. This new generation of workers has grown up using these technologies and they want to continue to use them at work.

Web 2.0 technology allows a free-flowing, unstructured way to communicate. Up until recently, the majority of knowledge sharing was fairly structured through document repositories. Hatch wanted to look at alternative ways in which they could encourage the exchange of knowledge within the company. Because of that, they became very interested in Communities of Practice (CoPs) and decided to move forward with some trials. Hatch started with 12 communities, but there are now over 100 and the numbers are increasing exponentially as the technology catches on. Employee membership rose rapidly from a few users to several hundred in only six months. With its ECM solution, Hatch can benefit from the growing opportunities provided by social computing to support advanced collaboration while at the same time provide a secure and managed Enterprise 2.0 environment for their content and intellectual property.

9.9: CoPs Provide a Free-flowing and Unstructured Way to Communicate

ECM – A Context for Risk Management

Social media is often linked to the risk of exposing protected data, such as the intellectual property found in a corporate intranet. Transparency is required as both litigators and regulators seek to expose employee communications and decisions, and social media based communications are no exception.

Web 2.0 tools generate a myriad of risks for the enterprise. End users are responsible for generating social media content and managers may not be able to fully control the content. IT departments may not be suitably organized to manage social media technologies securely. Social media can conceal security risks posed by the unmonitored use of content by third party applications. Using tools available outside of the firewall puts corporate information at risk.

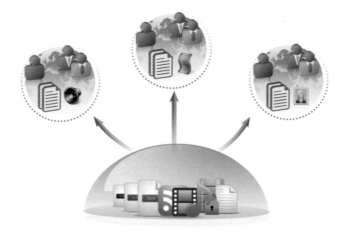

Figure 9.10: A Trusted ECM Repository Supports a Trusted Network

Enterprise content management practices can reduce exposure to the security risks emerging from flaws in Web 2.0 technology infrastructures. With the proper benchmarks in place, social media benefits companies by improving communication to support business processes, increasing visibility and speed of content through a broad author base and increased productivity by connecting people to relevant content and expertise.

> Cohn & Wolfe

cohn&wolfe

Cohn & Wolfe is a strategic marketing and public relations agency with core areas of expertise in consumer, digital, healthcare, technology and corporate communications. Known for creating and implementing powerful communications programs, Cohn & Wolfe's client roster includes Hilton, Dell, Nike, Whole Foods Market and American Express.

When WPP public relations agencies GCI Group and Cohn & Wolfe merged, they were faced with the task of creating a unified global agency and working environment that would enable it and its people to succeed. Cohn & Wolfe understood it was crucial to build a system to share expertise and interact with ideas.

Cohn & Wolfe developed a new kind of portal that is not so much an Intranet as an internal social network – a site with the familiar look and feel of social media sites such as Facebook. The site embraces the overarching idea of social media: let any-one create content and let anyone engage and respond to that content to generate a snowball effect of conversation and idea development. The goal: let self-directed talent thrive. The agency's Web 2.0 tools (including blogs, wikis, forums, profiles, communities, social bookmarks, tagging and subscriptions) not only deliver on their original purpose of unity and collaboration, but also fuel business productivity. Cohn & Wolfe was able to develop a platform that connects everyone and at the same time provides a valuable source of ideas and expertise to sustain the agency's fo-cus on thought leadership. The platform generates its own momentum; growing and improving the more people use it.

Figure 9.11: Cohn & Wolfe's "Den" – An Internal Facebook for the Organization

The Social Marketplace

A "social marketplace" is created when organizations use social computing technologies to collaborate and connect with customers, partners and other stakeholders to build communities around products, services and overall brand experience.

Social marketplaces and the strategies that guide them are developed by organizations to gain trust from customers, prospects and partners. Closing the gap between business objectives for customer satisfaction and customers' actual experiences and perceptions requires metrics that account for engagement and influence. Analytics, digital footprints, and online monitoring are part of the benefits of investing in digital content and interactive media. Converting awareness, engagement and online interaction into leads and pipeline is a core objective.

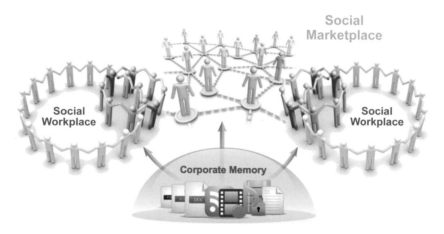

Figure 9.12: The Social Workplace and Marketplace Enriched by Corporate Memory

As social marketplaces grow into a new phase of online interactivity, customers and prospects will share information, seek feedback and create content pertinent to the business cycle. Organizations that see the value of Web and mobile interaction with their external stakeholders can preserve market share, accelerate pipelines, cultivate customer loyalty and reduce the costs of frontline customer service. Customer engagement and proactive peer-to-peer support and recommendations; development and solidification of communication and recommendation channels; the ability to spot and react to new opportunities for markets; and community engagement with brand to build loyalty and customer commitment – these are the fundamental values the Social Marketplace delivers to business.

The dialogues that create and define market demand occur within the social marketplace. Marketers can use social media to engage and aggregate loyal consumers to identify key influencers and deliver targeted programs for inexpensive word of mouth (WOM) marketing campaigns. Tapping into communities of consumers enables organizations to monitor sentiment about products and services and measure the influence of user generated content on buying behavior by tracking the actions that encourage or discourage repeat purchase.

Organizations can use social media to capitalize on the "long tail" effect. The long tail as it pertains to retail involves the niche strategy of selling a large number of unique items in small quantities along with selling fewer popular items in large quantities. Whereas Web 1.0 technologies supported the distribution of content limited to experts and expert opinion, social media allows organizations to segment customers and encourage them to participate in contributing long tail content to increase the exposure and sales of low volume products.

Finally, organizations are discovering that they can monetize the content created by the members of consumer communities to increase revenue or decrease operating expenses. Media giants Fox News and CNN, for example, have implemented community news reporting capabilities (u-Report and iReport respectfully) to extend their global reporting capability without increasing costs associated with putting additional reporters in the field or paying for stories from other media companies. It is now common to see member photos and videos included within these companies' news stories on their Web sites as well as in their televised broadcasts.

Making Social Media Safe

To determine if content is at risk, an organization needs to determine how its Web 2.0 content is stored, how the content is managed and whether management and storage methods comply with relevant external regulations and internal governance policies. Social media shares many of the same issues around regulatory compliance with email because it involves a similar sharing of unstructured content. Through the effective use of ECM, it is possible to create similar governance, risk management and compliance processes for Web 2.0 content and collaboration.

The natural tendency of Web 2.0 applications to operate outside of business departments, cutting across traditional organizational boundaries, creates an interesting challenge for governance and risk management. Because Web 2.0 operates outside of conventional constraints, developing, monitoring and managing content control policies becomes more complicated.

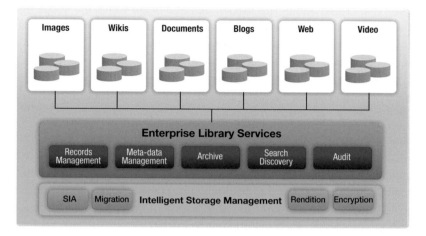

Figure 9.13: An Integrated ECM and Social Computing Architecture

The growing social media risk management problem needs to be addressed fundamentally from the ground up. Part of the core approach is to recognize that not all content is created equally. Different kinds of applied content needs to be retained for different periods of time; the challenge lies in identifying the important content, separating important information from the unimportant and determining an appropriate retention period. The "content life-cycle" concept – what happens to content after it has been processed – introduces another important aspect of social media content management.

For many organizations, it is important to control the complete lifecycle of corporate content. The definition of content lifecycle – from creation through to archive and final disposition – should be a shared view between an organization and its regulators. Once this view is established, content needs to be integrated into an organization's current ECM system of storage and archive repositories, while at the same time made available for regulatory compliance, records disposition plans and access by various business users.

ECM and Social Computing

Social media should integrate seamlessly within an enterprise's information ecosystem. Companies operate with the help of pre-existing information systems and technologies, and social media must be compatible with the existing ERP systems and technology infrastructure. ECM provides an ideal platform for creating content quickly and easily, while also delivering it in a personalized context. Many of the problems and risks associated with social media are minimized or eradicated through the use of an integrated ECM solution, which is beneficial for companies seeking to incorporate social media into their information

> Northrop Grumman

NORTHROP GRUMMAN

Northrop Grumman Corporation is a global defense and technology company whose 120,000 employees provide innovative systems, products, and solutions to government and commercial customers worldwide in four main business areas: information and services, electronics, aerospace and shipbuilding. Northrop Grumman Integrated Systems, based in El Segundo, California, designs, develops, produces and supports network-enabled systems and subsystems for government and civil customers worldwide.

Northrop Grumman is using ECM to support more than 40,000 users from different business sectors enterprise wide. The solution, called "ShareCenter," provides a single and secure repository for knowledge capture and enables employees to search, classify, collect and disseminate corporate knowledge sources. In 2006, Northrop Grumman's Integrated Systems sector brought in Communities of Practice to help facilitate even greater collaboration and knowledge sharing.

Using Communities, employees can take advantage of the blogs, headlines and forums all within one structure. The rich interface enables users to customize the look and feel of their Web site, create their own graphics, bring in data and essentially offer a one-stop shop for members. Giving their employees the opportunity to share information, hold discussions on relevant topics and make their knowledge and expertise known across the different sectors has helped employees to build stronger knowledge networks and gain access to collective intelligence across the business areas.

Figure 9.14: Northrop Grumman Leverages Web 2.0 Technologies

strategy. By deploying social computing across a uniform and secure platform, external systems can be dynamically linked with the support of interfaces. Mashups can then be created to allow enrichment of the content through additional contexts from other data and external applications.

The integration of Web 2.0 applications with ECM delivers a uniform technology platform for Web and user generated content. One central repository can be maintained for company and user data. Search results can be centralized and permission-based. As well, all Web 2.0 tools, such as blogs wikis, forums and other Web Component functions adhere to Web page branding and look-and-feel standards. All of these applications can be extended to mobile users, to deliver access to people, processes and content via social media tools – from any place at any time.

All trademarks found above are owned by the respective trademark owners and the authors of this book do not intend to imply that any such trademark owners are endorsing any specific ECM software product.

Figure 9.15: Mobile Social Computing

Web 2.0 and social media have moved beyond their original definitions as online consumer trends to embrace Enterprise 2.0 or E2.0. Today, blogs, forums and other Web 2.0 tools have become a business communication standard and an essential component for successful Web marketing and communication strategies. The opportunities available to companies that benefit from Web-based internal and external collaboration are both numerous and obvious, as demonstrated by STA Travel, Cohn & Wolfe, Hatch and Northrop Grumman.

Figure 10.1: Digital Media

Digital media is a corporate asset that needs to be managed. Media Management delivers the sophisticated technologies required for the management of digital media. In this chapter, we examine how media management is a critical component of ECM 2.0. Innovator stories feature companies that use digital media management solutions to facilitate training and communications, improve asset management and increase collaboration across the enterprise.

DIGITAL MEDIA

The increasing use of video and the convergence of video and mobile devices are shaping the way people consume information. Low cost digital cameras in cell phones, increased global bandwidth and the popularity of applications like YouTube and Flickr have produced a new type of digital media.

Digital media is most simply defined as any information that is created and shared virtually, rather than physically. This content type will become increasingly important as enterprises start to rely on higher quality collaboration and content shared through video.

Figure 10.2: An Online Manual in Video Format

The popularity of online video in the consumer sphere is easily illustrated by YouTube's massive consumption rate. The 1 billion video streams viewed each day are said to consume as much bandwidth as the entire Internet in the year 2000. As videos make their way into the enterprise, the consumption of digital media will be impacted by increasing demand and the rising cost of bandwidth.

When broken down by byte, we can see how video downloads and transmissions are bandwidth intensive. While one page of HTML requires 10 KB to access, the audio required to "speak" the same words requires thirty times more bytes, or 300KB. The video required to view a person speaking the same words requires 300 times more, or 3MB. The use of video makes significant demands on Internet infrastructure, driving networks to expand their capacity.

The consumption of online video is the result of increases in broadband access forming a reinforcing cycle of capacity increase. The rising demand for online video is driving the demand for high bandwidth services. As the enterprise adopts these services, bandwidth will become a major variable cost. Managing content will be a key factor for bandwidth management, and this will have an environmental impact as improvements in bandwidth efficiency can reduce an organization's overall power consumption and carbon footprint.

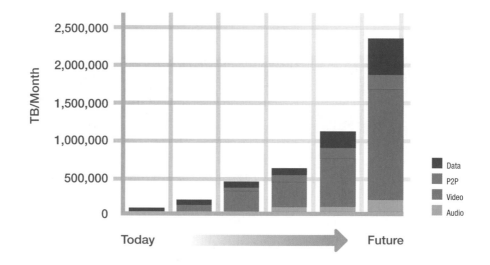

Figure 10.3: Video Will Dominate Internet Traffic

Digital media is becoming as pervasive inside the firewall as it is on the Internet. Organizations will need to manage all aspects of this media, including ingestion, storage, management, retrieval, production and distribution of digital assets. The technology used to manage digital media is referred to as Digital Asset Management or Media Management.

Digital Media Content as Business Assets

As new technologies have joined traditional methods of distribution, the term digital media has grown to encompass Web sites, video games, email, desktop publishing, MP3 players, podcasts, personal video recorders, recordable CDs and DVDs, high-definition TV, GPS systems and 3D modeling. Even the high-resolution digital displays on gas pumps, elevators and billboards have made global distribution of media files part of our everyday lives.

Inside an organization, digital media serves a variety of audiences across departments, including production, marketing, training, human resources, creative services and editorial. With increases in consumption of digital content, the need for organizations across industry verticals to manage and deliver digital media communications has grown dramatically. Manufacturers of products that range from kitchen appliances to toys are discovering that they build communities of users with quality digital media content. With this comes the need to manage the valuable intellectual property invested in this content.

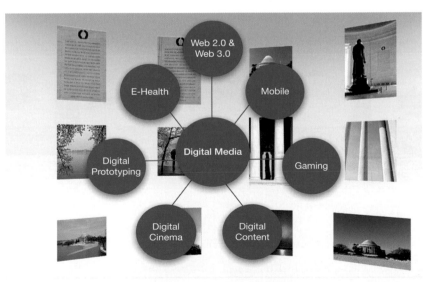

Figure 10.4: Media Management as Hub

Organizations regard digital media elements as true business assets that need to be managed and protected. Global corporations are spending billions of dollars on the acquisition and protection of intellectual and creative property rights and the means to generate intellectual property that includes videos, records, graphics, and more. When we consider that the amount of unstructured data in large corporations makes up almost 90 percent of a company's information, it is fair to assume that digital media makes up a large portion of an organization's unstructured data.

In the business world, as the volume of information increases, decisions have to be made more quickly. Media management, when combined with ECM helps organizations manage the complexity of digital media and provides the speed required to transform information into advantage and business agility.

Media Management

To exploit the value of their assets, organizations must develop a well thought-out strategy for managing their digital content. Strategically, the owners of digital content assets are confronted with two overriding challenges – the desire to make use of digital assets as aggressively as possible, and the need to safeguard the material by enforcing the rights and licensing permissions associated with it.

For all businesses, a media management solution must be evaluated from two perspectives: how it handles digital media across the content lifecycle and how the system fits within an organization's larger IT ecosystem.

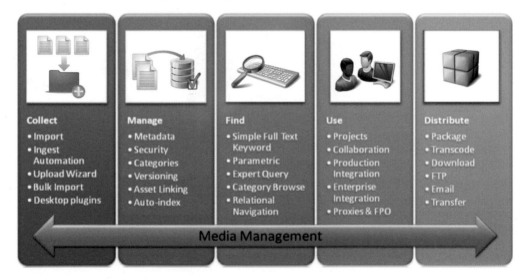

Figure 10.5: Digital Content Lifecycle

> # Electronic Arts

As the leading interactive entertainment software company in the world, Electronic Arts (EA) understands the need to control its brand globally. The company insists on a consistent look, feel, and voice when distributing its products, even within the challenges of localization. Like many companies, EA's marketing content has traditionally been maintained in numerous systems across the enterprise, making it difficult to locate and distribute content.

With the introduction of a media management system, EA established a centralized repository of their valuable digital content, including broadcast commercials, print ads and Web content. The launch of a new title represents a significant investment that requires a highly coordinated, global team effort. Users across the company are able to securely access these assets via the Web as they develop new marketing campaigns. Once created, this marketing content is securely distributed via the Web to regional offices and affiliates across 26 territories and 8,500 employees throughout the world.

Through this enhanced ability to reuse existing content, EA has increased its Web site traffic and revenue, while experiencing significant cost savings, that are based on reductions in production and distribution costs.

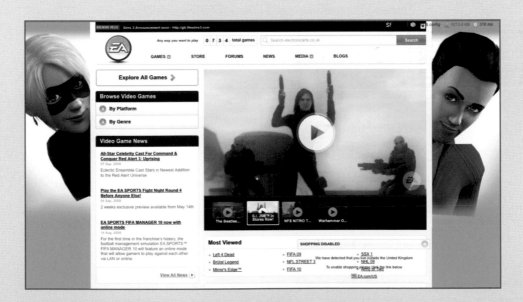

Figure 10.6: Electronic Arts' Digital Content Media Assets

Access and Storage

An effective media management solution relies on a highly scalable and extensible database which can be combined with mass storage for intelligent asset management. Since digital media content comes in many file formats, the system should support a large number of existing formats and accommodate new formats. Some systems are capable of recognizing over 150 formats, including popular image file types, document formats and standard streaming audio/video formats.

The first order of business for any media management solution is collecting these assets into a central repository. A media management system can securely manipulate a wide variety of file formats and provide the tools users need to add intelligence to assets through meta-data and taxonomies.

Meta-data, discussed in greater detail in Chapter 4, is used to apply descriptive information to digital media throughout an asset's lifecycle. For a media company, the ability to apply meta-data is essential. Usage information (where the content element has been used) is critical in calculating the economic value of content and evaluating the potential for reuse. Since the ability to protect and leverage an asset depends on knowing additional information about it, media management makes extensive use of meta-data.

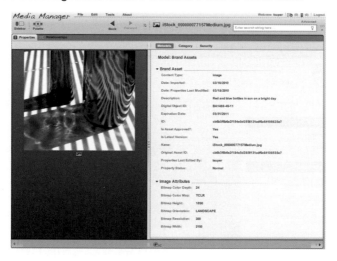

Figure 10.7: Meta-data Input While Uploading Assets

Taxonomies are categories that enable digital assets to be efficiently organized. A media management solution uses meta-data to automatically assign taxonomies to digital media during upload. The definition of a digital asset as content plus meta-data has driven organizations outside of media markets to take a more strategic look at their content inventory.

Media management gives producers, editors, designers, and Web developers the ability to access a central repository of pre-approved digital assets, including logos, photos, storyboards, film, video and animation. This allows companies to dramatically reduce time spent searching for content and increase focus on creative production. Media management goes beyond the ability to locate desired content; it also promotes content reuse which lies at the heart of production management. The cost-savings can be enormous when considering how much is spent to develop new media and the additional costs, both in dollars and human effort, required to prepare content for distribution across diverse media types and platforms.

Production

A media management system allows users to edit, package and transform digital content. Most often, digital assets are used in combination to produce a finished product. For example, the layout of a brochure involves fonts, graphics, illustrations and photos. A media management system maintains the relationships between these assets through various modifications and renditions, allowing users to navigate easily from layout to related assets.

Since any creative endeavor is a team effort, media management should make it easy to share ideas, discuss issues and reach a consensus, review work-in-progress, and keep track of assets. Within a media management system, a workflow delivers defined tasks for production – along with all the tools required to manage participants, assets, notifications, comment threads and project security.

User Interface

A key component to a media management system is the user interface (UI).

Figure 10.8: Media Management User Interface

For most users, the UI consists of a configurable Web browser that supports the different demands of power users, casual users and read-only users. Today's UIs are driven by standard application programming interfaces (APIs) and exposed through Web services. This allows for components to be placed in other applications or portals, presenting a UI that can be personalized by user roles. For example, to support power users like information archivists, media librarians, or production specialists, the UI can be configured to enable complex searches which can be saved and shared with other users.

Multi-Channel Distribution

Distribution allows direct, field and channel marketing to distribute finished brand and promotional media assets. It provides a self-service model for authorized field personnel to request or pull materials from a secure fulfillment system. Within the broadcast industry, distribution management gives personnel the ability to automate the schedule and delivery of finished digital programming materials.

A multi-channel world demands a solution that can dynamically, efficiently, and securely distribute digital media across Web, print, wireless, broadcast, and cable outlets. For a commercial provider of entertainment programming, automated scheduling and distribution via media management saves time and ensures that enforceable business rules govern the distribution process.

Figure 10.9: Distribution Asset Management

Technology trends driving the creation of digital content across an increasing number of channels have impacted media management. So, for example, where it was once sufficient for a book publisher to maintain archived copies of their works, publishers today want a solution that will extend these archives to emerging new channels for online book retailing, audio books and the new generation of eBook readers.

Like publishing companies, television broadcasters are increasingly required to package and format content for potentially hundreds of new distribution channels – and most of them on demand.

These trends represent a shift in basic media management requirements where the focus is on how well the system integrates with other technologies, how fast these integrations can be accomplished and how flexible they are in the face of ongoing market and technology advances.

Brand Asset Management

Companies like Electronic Arts and Timberland have spent millions of dollars developing, promoting and ensuring the integrity of their brand through tangible and non-tangible means, such as public perception and mind share. With so many media types and distribution channels, the challenges and opportunities increase exponentially from both a risk and cost perspective. By bringing media management into an organization to address brand management, departments like marketing, advertising, public relations and creative services can access and collaborate around a central database of approved digital brand assets.

Intellectual Property Management

Intellectual Property (IP) is central to entertainment and media business models, and an important aspect of media management for companies in every industry. Companies must ensure they have the legal right to use media and the tools to protect it from inappropriate use, duplication or distribution.

Media management protects an organization's intellectual property. Assets reside in a secure and centralized repository where content can only be accessed by users with assigned access rights. Typically, IP rights exist with the media as a set of meta-data or as a separate asset, such as a contract. Once an asset has been properly licensed, a secondary policy can be triggered that allows the asset to be exported, published, or downloaded.

Increases in bandwidth have spurred the growth of online video services and peer-to-peer file sharing, causing organizations to develop and deploy digital rights management solutions in order to control the distribution of digital media.

> ## Timberland

Timberland is a global leader in the design, engineering, and marketing of premium-quality footwear, apparel, and accessories for consumers who value the outdoors and their time in it. Timberland markets products under the Timberland®, Timberland PRO®, Mountain Athletics®, SmartWool®, Timberland Boot Company™, Howies®, and IPATH® brands. With headquarters in the United States, Timberland offices span North America, the United Kingdom, and Asia.

Timberland implements media management software to manage their digital assets and all types of rich media, including brand and company logos, digital photos, promotional images, catalogs, photographs, video, ad layouts, concept designs, and more. The system enables Timberland to centralize their collection in a secure repository for global use. It satisfied the key requirements of not only marketing, but of the broader enterprise – product development, licensing, apparel, corporate communications, and e-commerce.

What do Timberland users like most about the media management system? One-touch, one-click downloads. Quick keyword search. Contact Sheet. Simple navigation. Sets and Collections – all via the Internet. Overall, Timberland's media management solution has improved productivity and collaboration across the enterprise. In the future, there are plans to implement the workflow function to further enhance these benefits.

Figure 10.10: Media Management at Timberland

Digital Rights Management

The combination of digital media, conversion technologies and PCs has made the unauthorized duplication of copyrighted digital media accessible and easy to do. As a result, organizations in the music and movie industries have developed Digital Rights Management (DRM) technologies to protect their business, which is dependent on the revenue generated from their digital IP.

DRM describes access control technologies that impose limits on the use of digital content and devices. Content scrambling, DVD Region Codes, encryption algorithms and other technologies give owners of content copyright control over their intellectual property. DRM is most commonly used by organizations in the entertainment industry, including music stores and e-book publishers.

As digital media evolves, media management technologies are developing solutions for improving the syndication of digital media, producing powerful new metaphors which enable IP owners to syndicate both content and "experience" while retaining control over the asset and its usage metrics. We look at this in more depth in the following section on Digital Experience Management.[1]

Web 2.0 and the Digital Experience

When Web 2.0 technology trends are combined with the maturation of media management technologies, the result is the application of transformative processes to all types of media.

Figure 10.11: DEM and Tethered Media1

---

[1] Frank, Andrew and Mike McGuire. *Charting the Shift of DRM to Digital Experience Management*, Gartner Group, 2007

Digital experience management (DEM) extends the ECM value proposition from a content repository to an enabler of next-generation immersive collaboration, viral distribution and syndication scenarios.

Internally, organizations are required to find more effective ways of giving knowledge workers the information they need in the various contexts of E2.0 and Web 2.0 solutions. These trends are presenting significant content distribution opportunities for organizations outside the enterprise, along with enabling social collaboration tools within the enterprise.

Content-driven widgets offer a unified content experience across multiple repositories with decentralized, multi-context embed and syndication services. Content widgets are mini applications that extend content from any source into an embeddable experience. Widgets can be used to embed media players to dynamically distribute media to social networks, for instance. In an enterprise context, widgets combine the access, control, distribution and presentation of digital media with ECM technologies.

Figure 10.12: Content Widgets Extend Content into Embeddable Digital Experiences

Tethered content is a form of Internet content syndication that does not require the content owner to give up control of the experience and use of their content as it is shared online. The content owner decides how their content can be shared and used by Internet sites and end-users by delivering the content through widgets. The content owner extends widgets into social networks, Web sites, blogs and across devices, where end-users can take the content and place it in other sites, and video mashups, in a way that can be tracked and managed.

HBO is America's most successful premium television network, offering rich digital media content, blockbuster movies, innovative original programming, provocative documentaries, concert events and championship boxing. HBO sought a solution that would allow them to easily access and share digital content both within HBO and the larger Time Warner family. The requirements for the overall system functionality and user experience entailed the system handling large volumes of content, as well as addressing disparate databases, workflows and use cases for each of the organizations.

HBO's Media Management implementation encompassed all of HBO's digital photographs supporting such areas as marketing, promotions advertising and sales. These assets can range from location shots from HBO Films to a gallery of quality professional photos of HBO celebrities.

Part of their overall strategy was to ensure careful management of meta-data. Assets are tagged with corresponding meta-data, such as contractual information, as early as possible to ensure that meta-data travels with the asset throughout its lifecycle. This meta-tagging process is enforced with an embedded workflow component. The HBO digital asset management system is accessed by all of the Regional Offices and currently holds more than 325,000 assets.

Figure 10.13: HBO's Media Management Solution

Tethered content is a multi-context approach to content distribution and management in a world where sharing in viral ways has been a concern for most content owners. It offers a new way to generate value from more open distribution without losing control of the content, while still maintaining a connection with the end-user.

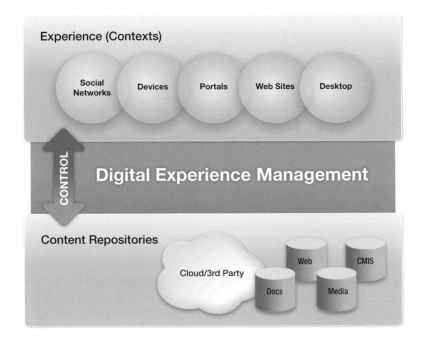

Figure 10.14: Multi Context Syndication

Inside the firewall, DEM integrates content, control, and experience into a social portal by leveraging content from shared repositories in highly differentiated ways. Outside the firewall, DEM enables organizations to participate in wider social networks, balancing the desire to maintain control of their IP with the creation of immersive visual experiences to attract consumers.

Cloud computing offers another delivery channel for digital media. The convergence of video software and infrastructure technologies has enabled the creation and delivery of video content to distributed audiences in a secure and scalable fashion. For more detailed information on content storage and distribution in "the Cloud," see Chapter 13.

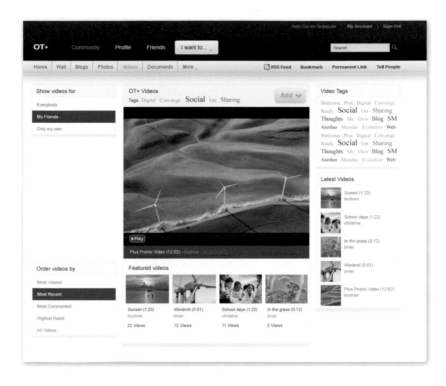

Figure 10.15: Video Delivered in the Cloud

A final example is based on the proliferation of video creation and distribution on the Internet, embodied by the success, capacity and appeal of YouTube®.

YouTube for the Enterprise

With the rise in popularity of the Internet and Web sites, organizations became newspaper publishers. To remain competitive and relevant today, organizations will be required to operate and manage their digital media similarly to a television station.

Many organizations have accumulated large amounts of video content in corporate communications, education and training, HR administration, sales enablement and other departments. The desire to use video to educate and communicate across the enterprise, both internally and externally, has resulted in the need to store and manage these assets in a scalable and secure fashion.

But how does the average Internet consumer use of video differ from a corporate user? Typically, when a consumer downloads a video online, the video is distributed over the

Internet with little concern for control and security. The video is accessed and viewed on demand. Organizations, on the other hand, need to integrate video into their existing business and IT environments.

Within an organization, video is distributed over private networks, connects to the company's technology infrastructure and scales to support an audience of many. Videos are saved, stored, archived and deleted according to an organization's rules for content lifecycle management. Finally, security and publishing control are imperative as organizations are required to mitigate risk and adhere to compliance requirements. Organizations embracing YouTube for the enterprise must have the robust infrastructure required to support the demand for company-wide video creation and viewing.

Figure 10.16: Video Library Management – Streaming Corporate Content

> Ocean Conservancy

Every year, Ocean Conservancy, a non-profit organization and advocate for the ocean, arranges the International Coastal Cleanup, a global shore-cleaning project where hundreds of thousands of volunteers from all over the world collect debris and ocean trash from rivers, lakes and oceans. Participants keep track of every piece of trash they find so they can either mail in their data or submit it through the Web. Ocean Conservancy uses that data to produce the world's only index of the problem of marine debris. The report is shared with the public, industry, and government officials as they work together to find solutions to the problem of marine debris. In 2009, Ocean Conservancy used hosted Media Management to help manage the data and photographs from the 24th annual International Coastal Cleanup.

The pilot project was a great success. Today, Media Management provides a safe, centralized repository that securely manages all of Ocean Conservancy's digital assets, including the ones created all over the world during the 2009 International Coastal Cleanup. Key benefits include:

- Secure and central content repository

- Improved productivity and efficiency

- Enhanced collaboration and creative workflows

- Better response time to news agencies

- Savings of time and costs

Figure 10.17: Ocean Conservancy's Web Site

ECM 2.0 and Media Management

Media management technologies have reached a level of maturity that has moved away from performance to stress modularity and broader system integration. As the Internet continues to grow to support new digital formats and technologies, the business world will follow suit.

ECM, combined with media management, delivers a scalable, component-based asset management and delivery platform that leverages distributed business services. It scales vertically to allow growth in numbers of assets, and horizontally to enable solutions that span functional boundaries. It enables a repository that accommodates many types of storage, including cloud-optimized storage. ECM's combined collaboration and content lifecycle management gives organizations the ability to automate the lifecycle of a digital asset and dramatically expand its use or value.

Figure 10.18: Mobile Access to Digital Media Widgets

The vision of ECM 2.0 is the consolidation of all media into a seamless system that presents new ways to exchange and process knowledge. The integration of video-based collaboration with secure media management delivers new solutions for the creation, distribution and consumption of digital media.

Figure 11.1: Business Process Management

Business Process Management (BPM) governs transaction technologies used in ECM suites to improve efficiencies, shorten cycles, lower costs, and increase product and service quality. This chapter describes BPM; what it is and how it fits into the ECM equation. To demonstrate effective BPM, we profile companies in different industries who are effectively managing processes to run their business more efficiently, achieve compliance and reduce costs.

BUSINESS PROCESS MANAGEMENT

Organizations today are improving business processes to shorten cycle times and bring products and services to market more quickly, reduce operational costs and meet regulatory compliance. To stay competitive, many organizations are re-evaluating their approach to business processes and looking for ways to improve these procedures.

Most organizations are unable to control manual processes. Paper- and manual-based processes have traditionally involved high margins of error caused by processing bottlenecks, delays, duplications and inaccuracies. While computers promised to significantly change the way we work, technology alone has not been enough. Business process management (BPM) defines an approach that utilizes computing technology to automate, streamline and optimize processes by managing the flow of work and information across an organization. BPM encompasses much more than the technologies used to automate processes; it also describes the business discipline that drives process management and the change management required to successfully implement and manage business processes.

As a discipline, BPM involves a strategic approach focused on aligning all processes within an organization to deliver value to the customer. It promotes improved business performance, while striving for innovation, flexibility, and integration with technology. In the past, process optimization focused primarily on efficiency. To reflect rapidly changing market conditions, BPM's focus has shifted to operational excellence and the iterative process that supports continuous process improvement.

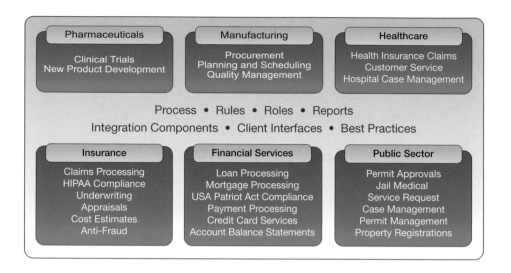

Figure 11.2: Examples of Business Process Management Applications by Industry

Complex BPM solutions have been developed to meet specific sector requirements. Examples of this include loan forms processing, mortgage processing, case management, accounts payable, customer service, procurement, production management and new product development.

The Business Drivers of BPM

As a practice, BPM has been around as long as business has. In fact, processes exist within a network of people and systems in an organization that have evolved over decades, making them difficult to identify, extract and change. It is often a challenge for organizations to understand exactly how their processes work and even harder to determine how to implement better ones.

Business processes refer to any process, ad hoc or structured, that take place within an organization to complete specific jobs or actions. At a basic level, business processes are transaction-based. When technology is added to automate processes, BPM describes how people interact with this technology, information and each other to get their jobs done.

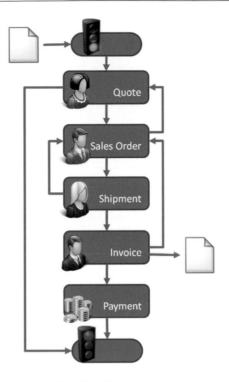

Figure 11.3: The Sales Invoice Process

Both in theory and practice, BPM integrates people and content from multiple applications for the continuous improvement of end-to-end processes. The ease with which this can be accomplished empowers process owners to integrate workflows with enterprise applications (such as Business Intelligence, or BI) and infrastructure (built on a Service Oriented Architecture or SOA, for example) to streamline the flow information and processes across an organization.

BPM is successful because it understands that organizations rather than technologies define business processes. Organizations use BPM technologies to support the processes that drive the success of their business. Furthermore, business processes are not isolated, one-time events within an organization. Each process is a connection of people and content, and as these connections span project teams, departments and entire organizations, BPM is an indispensable component of an ECM solution.

The value that BPM delivers is its ability to define and execute business processes independent of applications and infrastructure. This transforms an organization into a knowledgeable enterprise because it provides a detailed explanation of all activities required to complete a specific business process. An organization "in the know" can better manage the flow of work and content across applications, people and departments.

> European Court of Human Rights

The European Court of Human Rights (ECHR) is part of the Council of Europe, an international intergovernmental organization that was established in 1949. Currently, the Council is made up of 47 member states that have all signed up to the system of human rights protection under the European Convention on Human Rights.

Over the last few years the Court's caseload has exploded, with the number of applications to the Court growing from 14,000 in 1997 to over 54,000 in 2008. Recognizing that it was time to streamline its internal approval processes, the Court's IT Department developed an in-house automated workflow solution. The workflow helps manage the approval process for committee and chamber cases and provides the Court with a mechanism that streamlines its case management processes, further enhancing the productivity of the legal divisions.

Overall user sentiment is that the system saves time, is easy to use, has led to less work for the legal assistants, and is more streamlined than sending the committee notes by paper. Division assistants highlight the fact that the workflow solution automatically tracks the route of the workflow, and that the dynamic reports make it easy for the divisions and sections to find out what stage a workflow is at. With the workflow solution for committee notes successfully underway, the Court now plans to begin piloting its workflow for chamber notes.

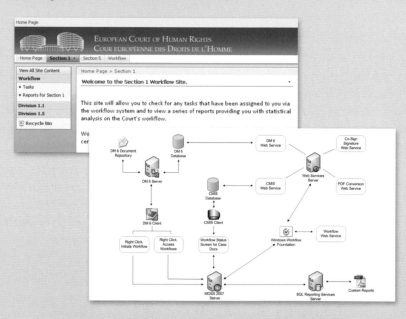

Figure 11.4: A European Court of Human Rights Workflow

Organizations that have not implemented a BPM system suffer from the inefficiencies associated with inconsistent business processes. These inefficiencies result in delays in project cycles and late approvals, which negatively affect time-to-market and competitive advantage. They are exposed to significant legal, corporate governance and regulatory compliance risks due to the inability to route decision-centric information to the right people at the right time.

Workflow and BPM

Workflow is the combination of tasks that define a process; it defines, automates and tracks the flow of tasks between individuals, systems and departments. While BPM helps to auto-mate complex business processes across an organization, workflow helps to standardize the interactions between people and content.

Workflow was initially viewed as an add-on to document management capabilities, map-ping the approval processes that involved the circulation of documents. Based on triggers and rules, workflows route documents in sequence to the right constituents for review and sign-off. Standard workflow features included process modeling and execution.

As the process industry matured, sophisticated workflows were developed to manage more complex, parallel processes. Finally, emphasis shifted from the document and the work it generated to the process that defined how work was generated. This change in focus, along with the growing complexities of processes, led to the growth in importance of BPM. As the need to design and manage more complex processes grew, BPM functionality became integrated with ECM platforms to provide better access to content, tighter controls over content and improved collaboration to execute processes in a timely manner.

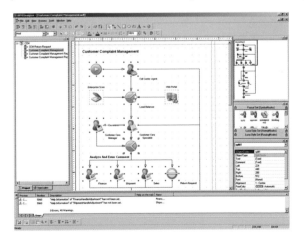

Figure 11.5: An Example of a Workflow

> Genzyme

Ensuring careful management of information for FDA submissions is a major undertaking for life sciences companies such as Genzyme Corporation. To help it achieve this goal, Genzyme needed a solution that would help project teams work together, manage and share information, while providing processes and controls to ensure careful management of that information.

Virtual project areas provide the ideal secure environment to enhance project collaboration, preventing reinvention of the wheel and speeding time-to-market.

Genzyme's information library increases efficiency, while document management capabilities support the company's compliance with the FDA's mandate for electronic records requirements.

"ECM is a fundamental part of the way we work at Genzyme. Developing innovative treatments directly affects the quality of people's lives, so time-to-market is always foremost in our minds in the pharmaceutical industry. Having key information immediately accessible online improves our efficiency and productivity, enabling us to fulfill the commitment we have made to patients that much sooner," says Genzyme Contract Associate.

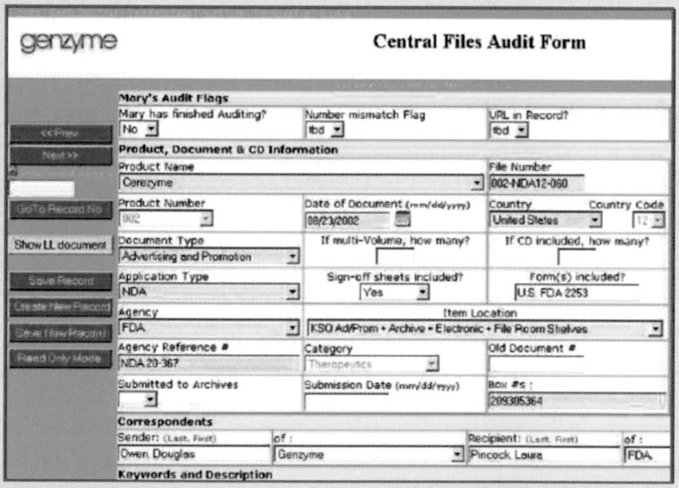

genzyme

Central Files Audit Form

Show LL document

Mary's Audit Flags

Mary has finished Auditing? No | Number mismatch Flag tbd | URL in Record? tbd

Product, Document & CD Information

Product Name: Cerezyme | File Number: 002-NDA12-060

Product Number: 002 | Date of Document (mm/dd/yyyy): 08/23/2002 | Country: United States | Country Code: 12

Document Type: Advertising and Promotion | If multi-Volume, how many? | If CD included, how many?

Application Type: NDA | Sign-off sheets included? Yes | Form(s) included? U.S. FDA 2253

Agency: FDA | Item Location: KSO Ad/Prom • Archive • Electronic • File Room Shelves

Agency Reference #: NDA 20-367 | Category: Therapeutics | Old Document #

Submitted to Archives | Submission Date (mm/dd/yyyy) | Box #s: 209305364

Correspondents

Sender: (Last, First) Owen Douglas | of: Genzyme | Recipient: (Last, First) Pincock Laura | of: FDA

Keywords and Description

Figure 11.6: Genzyme's File Auditing

Content and BPM

Many organizational processes involve managing both structured (invoices, claims forms or tax returns) and unstructured (documents, images, emails, and faxes) content in various formats and across applications. This content needs to be brought together from multiple systems and sources. Examples of these processes include invoice processing, claims management and order fulfillment. These processes require participants to review documents for approval and make decisions based on content found in scanned or digital format. Transactional or collaborative content is typically routed through a process using a workflow. In this way, BPM moves beyond simply automating transaction-based processes to orchestrating all elements of a process in parallel, including human and content-based interactions.

A customer complaint, for example, typically involves an automated response of acknowledgement for the complaint which is followed up by an employee. A single point of access gives users the ability to navigate between all required content such as invoices, contracts, content recorded during a phone call, customer history, and more, alongside the required process. The complaint management process is comprised of steps that need to be executed and each task can be closely monitored by management to ensure resolution of the complaint, good customer relations and ultimately, customer retention.

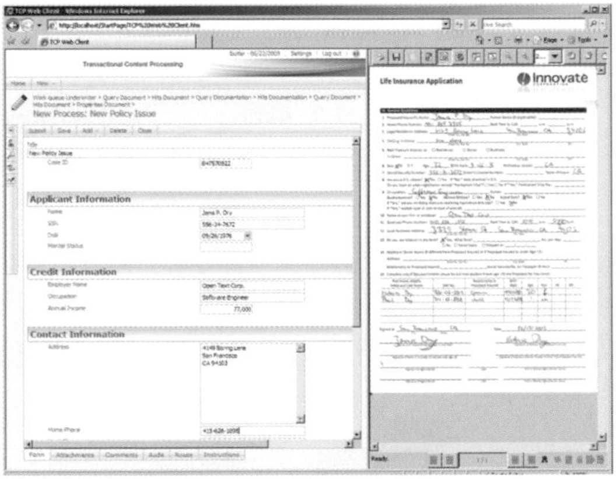

Figure 11.7: Insurance Underwriter Process

Effective BPM interfaces with applications such as ERP, SCM and CRM, enabling organizations to expedite their workflows and conduct transactions across multiple applications. In Chapter 12, we discuss how the Enterprise Ecosystem combines business content with transactional data from enterprise applications to maximize the value of content.

An BPM system enables organizations to eliminate paper-based processes, reducing print and distribution costs. Combining image capture with electronic forms, records and content management applications, BPM accelerates an organization's content-driven processes.

BPM enables organizations to continually improve operational processes and align these processes within the context of laws and regulations, as well as standards and policies. Organizations familiar with Sarbanes-Oxley, Basel II and HIPAA compliance understand the effect that internal and external processes have on corporate integrity. The continual improvement of processes is critical to the long-term success of compliance initiatives. BPM solutions, when combined with an ECM strategy, are well positioned to support compliance initiatives by delivering extensive audit trails, optimizing efficiencies, supporting adherence to process and promoting transparency across the organization.

Managing the Process Lifecycle

How does an organization effectively integrate the way people work together with information and technology?

This is a challenge because business processes are complex, dynamic and often implicit within an organization. To manage cross-functional processes, organizations implement BPM because it enables processes to be modeled, refined and modified as business needs change over time. BPM is both a methodology and a technology that helps organizations examine, understand and manage business processes that interact with people, technology and information.

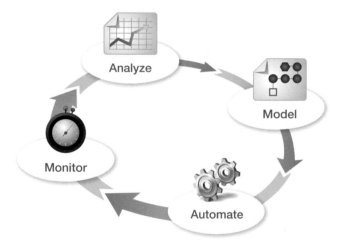

Figure 11.8: A Process Lifecycle

BPM combines technology components into a single and comprehensive solution that manages the entire lifecycle of a process. Prior technology focused around business process modeling and workflow; today it is focused on the process lifecycle – from design and modeling to automation, monitoring, analysis and optimization.

Process design encompasses the identification of existing and future processes. Process models graphically portray business processes within a BPM environment. These components allow business and technical teams to collaborate on a shared model that describes how the business process functions.

Business rules are used by BPM systems to provide definitions for governing behavior, and a rules engine is used to drive process execution.

At execution, BPM coordinates the lifecycle of a process, bringing together all resources involved. The outcome depends on an effective interplay of all the interdependent resources.

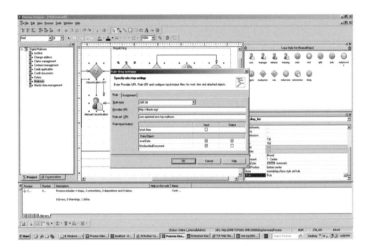

Figure 11.9: Defining Processes with Business Rules

Not only does BPM technology provide the tools required to define, model and execute business processes, it also allows resulting software "objects" to be analyzed from a business perspective for reporting and process optimization. Process monitoring capabilities allow business managers to gain insight from historical business intelligence. Business activity monitoring (BAM) employs dashboards which aggregate and present data about a process as it executes. Part of an effective monitoring program includes measuring performance against key performance indicators (KPIs) to give management insights into process effectiveness.

> # Deutsche Rentenversicherung Rheinland

Deutsche
Rentenversicherung
Nord Ost West
Informationstechnik

Deutsche Rentenversicherung Rheinland is a German regional insurance company that employs more than 4,000 people. Handling nearly seven million insurance policies, it is one of Germany's largest regional providers.

The company experienced a common problem, which was managing approximately 1.7 million paper-based business records with approximately 220 million documents in a central archive building. This presented problems every time an administrator requested a file, because the file had to be manually retrieved and this typically took five to seven days. Deutsche Rentenversicherung Rheinland made the decision to implement transactional process management because it provided the scalability and performance required to handle the large number of documents that the organization had.

One of the major benefits of the system is that locating documents now takes only a few seconds as opposed to days. This has enabled the company to optimize its customer service, offering clients much speedier responses. In addition, the electronic documents have been integrated into the Information Technology Working Group (AKIT) administration dialogue, which provides administrators with instant access to electronic files for insurance transactions. With an interface tailored to meet user requirements, the new system is much simpler to work with and documents are easier to find. That, in combination, results in providing much better customer service, a reduction in cost, and also a significant reduction in the staff required to deal with the huge amount of documents.

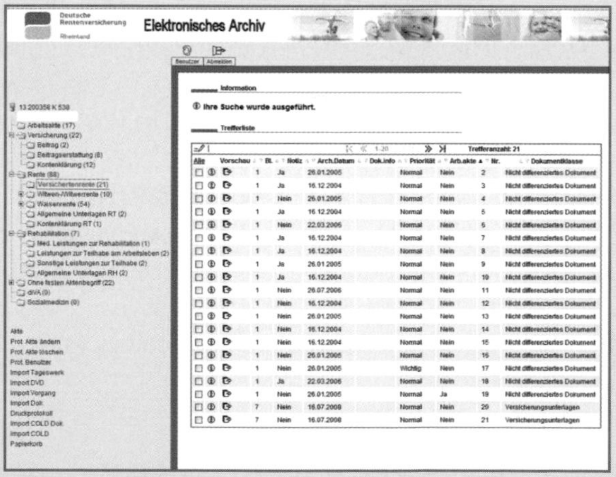

Figure 11.10: Process Management at Deutsche Rentenversicherung Rheinland

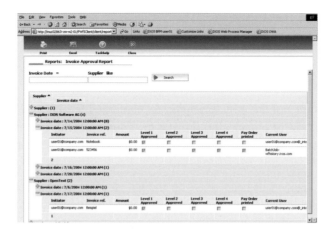

Figure 11.11: Online Reporting Based on Process Data

Web Services and SOA

With the introduction and succession of Web-based services and SOA-related standards, organizations can achieve a new standard of application integration. SOA architecture and Web-based services allow for the fast integration of widely disparate systems. Instead of reconfiguring ERP as their commercial environment evolves, organizations can use BPM to build processes that adapt to new market conditions. SOA helps to create an organization that can rapidly respond to new challenges by creating new processes.

Most automated business processes are too inflexible to keep pace with quickly changing markets, models and practices. Processes should be able to evolve as business requirements change. Emerging technologies such as BPM mashups are delivering solutions for quickly building and deploying structured and unstructured business processes. These lightweight applications deliver basic BPM functionality without the high end monitoring, simulation and integration usually found in BPM suites. By deploying process automation solutions in weeks as opposed to months, BPM mashups can be used to manage small departmental custom processes that connect with legacy ERP applications.

A cost-effective and timely solution, process mashups also provide relief for a resource-constrained IT department because they can be developed by management or process analysts with minimal IT skills.

By separating the management of processes from the underlying infrastructure, BPM endorses a process-driven view of IT. This distinction gives organizations the ability to find the gaps between systems and identify which gaps are caused by human interaction with these systems. As a result, processes can be more clearly defined, controlled and monitored. In addition, best practices can be identified, modeled and distributed across the organization in the form of BPM centers of excellence.

Web 2.0 and Social BPM

Process mashups are not the only emerging technologies to affect BPM. Web 2.0 technologies have lured BPM outside the firewall for developments that include the use of cloud computing, or BPM-as-a-Service, and social software functionality to support business processes.

BPM-as-a-service allows business users to model, develop and execute process management in the cloud. Accessing BPM as a service gives organizations the opportunity to control processes that extend across on-premise solutions, legacy applications and cloud services, considerably reducing IT requirements, cost and barriers to adoption. Different cloud service offerings that have recently surfaced run the gamut from hosting modeling processes in the cloud to vertical or horizontal workflow solutions available on a pay-per-use basis. For more information on cloud computing, please refer to Chapter 13.

As BPM embraces the cloud, social networking capabilities are finding their way into a number of BPM offerings. This is because participation in complex business processes usually involves multiple interactions between people, making BPM a social as well as a highly structured application. Completing a process involves numerous communications via email, instant messenger and voicemail. The synergies between structured processes such as workflow and BPM and unstructured processes like social networking are quickly emerging, producing the integration of instant messaging, wikis, discussion forums, and collaboration with BPM. These ad hoc collaborative capabilities function on top of structured solutions to provide a rich and collaborative context for process management.

This holistic marriage of structured and ad hoc collaboration gives workers a highly contextual workplace powered by BPM. Social collaboration provides BPM with the tremendous ability to provide real-time feedback to refine processes by giving people access to the context of conversations that occur in a process instance.

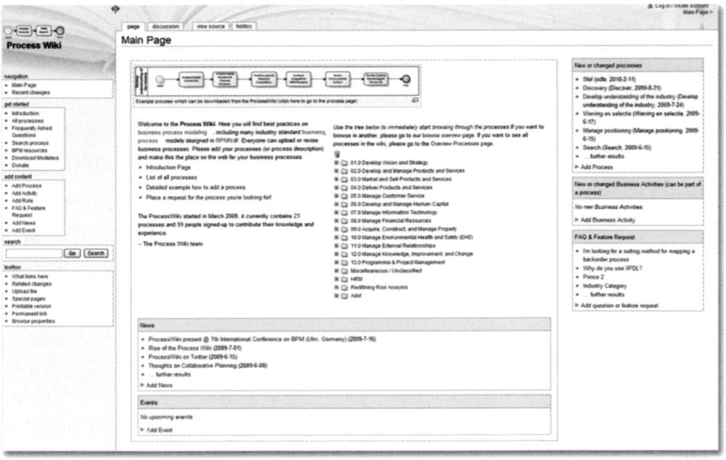

Figure 11.12: An Example of a Process Wiki

Technologies such as process wikis allow users to update and refine process information as conditions change. Effective for connecting geographically dispersed teams, process wikis can document the procedural flow of compliance, for example, to establish best practices, build online centers of excellence and optimize processes for compliance.

As Web-based applications become increasingly prominent, BPM will move to the cloud. Solutions will be flexible enough to adapt to change in real time as processes are being executed – giving BPM the ability to re-define itself in process. Modeling tools will evolve into semantically rich multi-dimensional models to communicate complex processes and relationships between people, information and processes. Business intelligence capabilities will increasingly map the process and extract KPIs, which in turn will be leveraged to optimize processes. Lightweight APIs and mashups will power process discovery and integrated social software technologies will capture tacit interactions between participants within the BPM environment. Functionality will extend to integrate collaboration using RSS and IM and mobile access will make BPM seamless and ubiquitous.

Mobile BPM

Integrating BPM with rich content gives employees access to a highly contextual business environment. Mobility plays a role in creating this rich environment by making BPM portable.

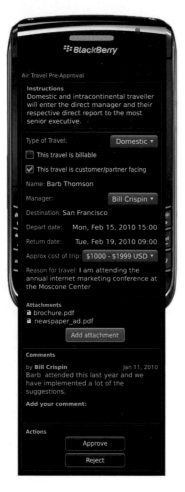

In today's fast-paced business environment, mobile professionals need to make informed decisions to keep processes and productivity on track. The ability to interact with business processes in real time has been a challenge for enterprise executives who travel or are out of the office frequently. Decision-makers can use mobile BPM to access, review, digitally sign and approve steps in business processes in a secure and compliant manner from any location. With Mobile BPM, management can access, engage with and act on the critical information and processes that drive their business, bringing the mobile workforce a step closer to seamless access to BPM.

BPM and ECM

Successful organizations need to be knowledgeable enterprises. They need to track processes and measure their effectiveness. Senior management needs to know when deadlines are missed, why there are delays and the status of approvals and outstanding issues. Only with this timely information can management can make informed decisions. And making fast, accurate decisions gives organizations a definite advantage. The ability to do this is directly related to optimizing operations by improving business processes.

Figure 11.13: Mobile BPM

BPM delivers support for cross-functional business processes. It is built on a platform for collaboration and content management to support interactions between people, processes and information. Using BPM, organizations can map their business processes to their business objectives to control the flow of content throughout an organization. Part of this process involves looking at how well an organization's underlying content supports these business activities. ECM solutions that provide document and records management, and contextual awareness and search capabilities, integrate well with BPM systems to optimize business processes and improve operational performance. By linking processes with people and content, ECM organizations can exchange transactional information and respond more quickly to new or changing business requirements.

Figure 12.1: Enterprise Content Management and Enterprise Applications

The enterprise ecosystem combines business content (for example, documents) with business context (transactional data in ERP and CRM systems), enabling organizations to extract the maximum value from content stored in Enterprise Applications. This chapter explains the business benefits experienced when an organization integrates ERP-based numerical information with a comprehensive ECM system. Sample applications and innovator stories are used to illustrate these benefits.

ECM ECOSYSTEM: ENTERPRISE APPLICATIONS

As Web technologies have inundated the consumer market, enterprise applications have undergone their own kind of evolution. They have matured from traditionally isolated, point solutions supporting a single enterprise resource or business function into comprehensive solution suites, serving the entire enterprise and its business operations.

Today's enterprise applications are complex, scalable, component- or service-based, distributed and mission-critical. They may be deployed on a variety of platforms across corporate networks, intranets, or the Internet. Enterprise applications are transactional, structured and data-centric, and must meet stringent requirements for security, administration and maintenance.

Pervasive Enterprise Content and Business Processes

Businesses, organizations and government agencies run their operations on enterprise applications. These foundational enterprise applications include enterprise resource planning (ERP), customer relationship management (CRM), supplier relationship management (SRM), supply chain management (SCM), and product lifecycle management (PLM). These enterprise applications focus on optimizing business processes, often in a transactional environment, where significant investment has been made.

Structured Data	Application Area	Unstructured Data ECM Solution
ERP	HR	DM – Policies and Procedures
ERP	Legal	DM – Contracts Management
ERP	Accounting	Image Management – Invoice Tracking
CRM	Customer Support	Collaboration – Call Center Tech Manuals
SCM	Component Tracking	DM – Contracts Management

Systems like business intelligence, analytical applications, and business activity monitoring complement enterprise applications by providing visibility into operations and business processes in a timely fashion. This type of transparency is crucial to streamlining business performance, improving agility and capturing new opportunities.

Despite these requirements, the growing volume of information which constitutes the lion's share of enterprise information often remains unmanaged. Along with its unstructured content, an organization is required to manage the structured data generated from its enterprise applications. In order to streamline the flow of information across an organization, and make it more accessible, transparent and compliant, the content from both enterprise applications and content management systems should be integrated. This enables the enterprise to effectively control the unstructured information in the context of their enterprise business processes – and this is what this chapter will focus on.

The Evolution to Business Process-Centric ECM

To carry forward the fundamentals of ECM technologies introduced in the previous chapters, it serves to place them in context of the enterprise ecosystem, which is made up of enterprise applications and end-to-end business processes.

Linking documents to transactions to provide a business process with context adds tremendous value. However, as far as complexity and scale of systems are concerned, only an integrated ECM solution extends this value by enabling the enterprise to fully leverage all of its content.

Integrating enterprise content and business processes at their very core offers the most effective approach and is delivered by leading ERP application suites today.

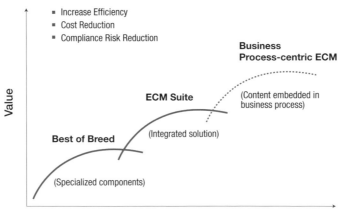

Figure 12.2: Evolution to Business Process-Centric ECM

An extended ECM solution enriches business processes by integrating unstructured business content. This approach enables the management and control of unstructured enterprise content in its business context, throughout the complete lifecycle of content – from creation to publication to archival and eventual disposition. It also promotes adoption and improves access to content by providing a unified view into business information. Key functionality includes document management, records management, archiving and collaboration.

Figure 12.3: Integrating Enterprise Content with Business Processes

Document management is discussed in Chapter 5. It serves the enterprise application ecosystem by enabling electronic documents and/or images of paper documents to be accessed within relevant business context.

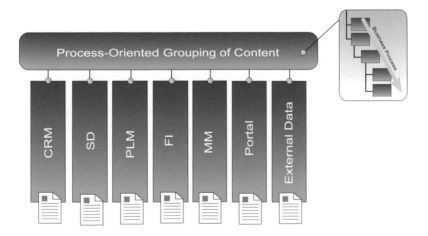

Figure 12.4: The Process-Centric Organization of Enterprise Content

In a larger business context, business documents are shared assets of interest to many stakeholders in an organization. From a technical standpoint, document integration into enterprise applications delivers the ability to share business content across applications without extensive application development or customization. An underlying ECM system provides a central storage facility for all business content and grants access to various enterprise applications.

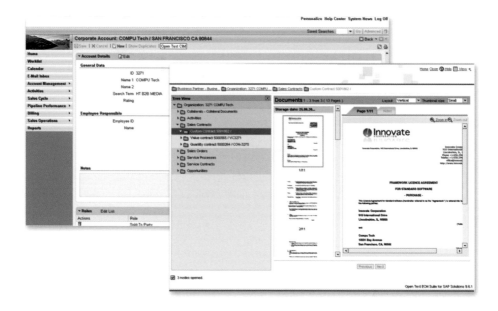

Figure 12.5: A CRM System Provides a Unified View to Customer Information

Obviously, content should be instantly accessible to some but not to everyone. Employee-related content, including resumes and salary histories, for example, is saved to a core Human Resource (HR) Management System as unstructured information. In this form, unauthorized access must be prevented to protect employees, support company policies and fulfill legal requirements. For this reason, an enterprise application should be configured to deliver the appropriate security provisions for content. This is heightened by the shift in enterprise security from a role-based to a rules-based approach.

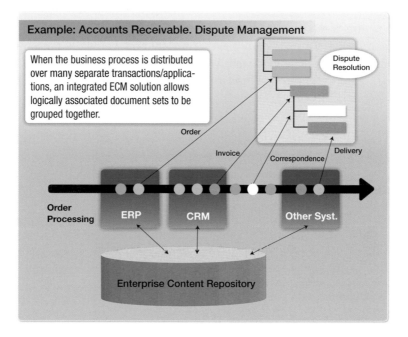

*Figure 12.6: A Process-Centric Organization of Related Documents
Across Enterprise Applications*

Chapter 5 is dedicated to the lifecycle management of business content. Content Life-cycle Management (CLM) builds on core DM functionality, adding capabilities that recognize that information exists in context that imparts different meaning to content as it changes over time. Technologies such as archiving and records management are enablers for gaining control over enterprise content and assets, along with traceability and readiness for compliance. Auditable content control and retention are necessary to comply with various regulations. Extended ECM mitigates these risks.

As explained in Chapter 8, advanced collaboration functionality delivers support for the management and optimization of unstructured business processes. This includes project team workspaces, discussion forums, workflows, tasks, blogs, and wikis, which are extended by secure extranet environments, workspaces and online communities – all of which enable knowledge exchange in various formats.

INVISTA is one of the world's largest integrated fibers and polymers businesses with a global presence. The company delivers exceptional value for customers through market insight, technology innovations, and a powerful portfolio of some of the most recognized global brands and trademarks in their respective industries. INVISTA needed a solution to streamline their accounts payable operations and simplify and automate their invoice processing.

INVISTA faced a number of business challenges including inadequate accounts payable process control, excessive cost-per-invoice and difficulty in preparing accruals. Additionally, they were looking to improve vendor discount opportunities and vendor relations.

According to the project lead, the "Vendor Invoice Management (VIM) has allowed INVISTA to streamline and improve our process of managing vendor invoices. We have seen a reduction in our cost-per-invoice and our percentage of overdue invoices has dropped each month since VIM went live. Our accruals are more accurate and less labor intensive and we've seen an overall improvement in our vendor relations."

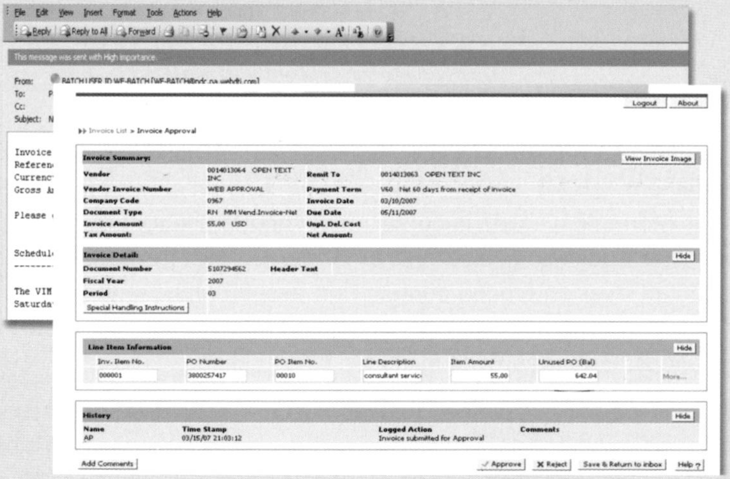

Figure 12.7: INVISTA's Web-based Invoice Approval

Example Scenario: Enterprise Asset Management

In highly regulated sectors like utilities and energy, organizations are required to have all documentation in place before technicians visit a plant, an oil rig, or a refinery to perform maintenance. These organizations need to manage their facilities and equipment across diverse locations – often on a global level. To do so, they need to be able to manage large volumes of information covering these assets, including engineering drawings, manuals and operating instructions for maintenance reports. Although there are plant maintenance (PM) applications, the authors who write operating manuals more than likely are not aware of all the processes related to managing the lifecycle of all these assets. An extended enterprise application ecosystem allows the technicians who consume this information to access It more readily, along with the authors who are required to share this information and work in other (PM) applications.

ECM streamlines plant maintenance (PM) processes and enables business process transformation. For capital-intensive industries, this contributes to improved productivity, reliability, compliance, and reduced cost and environmental impact.

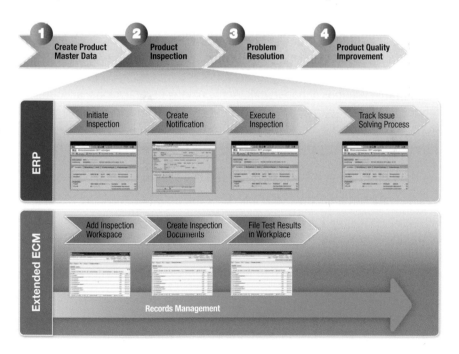

Figure 12.8: Optimizing Plant Maintenance Activities

Realizing the Business Value

Now that we have explored key capabilities of business process-centric ECM, we can examine the business value of enterprise content integration. When content is integrated across the enterprise ecosystem, it delivers improved business operations and competitive advantage. Organizations are able to improve efficiency in key processes, manage compliance, consolidate IT systems and reduce their total cost of ownership (TCO).

A holistic, value-based and integrated approach to managing enterprise content in the context of business processes yields benefits by reducing risk and achieving compliance and governance with internal, industry and legal regulations and standards.

In volatile economic times, the mandate to add value to business performance governs all enterprise resource management units, including financial departments, corporate services, operations and human resources. The following integrated applications demonstrate the resulting top line growth and bottom line profitability realized from improved efficiencies across an integrated enterprise ecosystem.

Improved Operational Efficiencies and Productivity

In most accounting departments, core business operations revolve around optimizing working capital by efficiently handling receivables and managing payables, which encompasses dealing with volumes of paperwork. Across many organizations, accounting departments rely on counterproductive, resource-intensive and error-prone manual processes that increase costs, facilitate employee mistakes and decrease overall efficiency.

Accounts Payable: Taking Advantage of Cash Discounts

Most organizations find it increasingly difficult to manage the accounts payable process, since it involves numerous transactions and associated paper documents. Every invoice passes through several people for review, content edits and final sign-off before payment is made. Initially designed to ensure accurate appropriation and accounting, this process can cause missed due dates, incur late fees and missed eligibility for cash discounts on invoices.

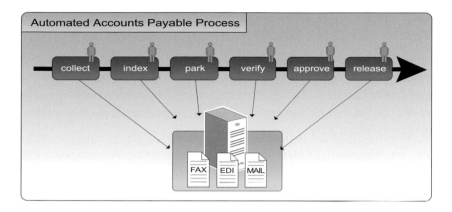

Figure 12.9: Central Electronic Document Storage Eliminates Manual Paper Handling

An integrated ECM solution streamlines standard invoice verification, enabling paper documents to be scanned into the system in original format upon receipt, linking invoices to related documents in an ERP system and triggering the initiation of a workflow.

This workflow informs each appropriate agent of the invoice status, tracks the agent's activity and, when resolved, automatically sends it to the next agent until the process is complete and the final agent sends out payment. In minutes, an agent can validate the invoice electronically against order documents, since all relevant documents are scanned into the ECM repository. Robust document and records management capabilities enable the ECM system to maintain an audit trail of related activity for each invoice, so that agents can immediately review their status and perform invoice verification on an exceptional basis.

Accounts Receivable: Increasing Profitability by Reducing DSOs

The accounts receivable world revolves around collecting payment. The longer a payment remains outstanding (known as Daily Sales Outstanding or DSO), the less likely it will paid in full. An inefficient collection process prolongs collection time, increases bad debt and erodes bottom line revenue.

Employees in accounts receivable departments need supporting information from multiple sources to reconcile differences between customers and invoices. They must review account information generated throughout the organization before they can effectively field customer questions, troubleshoot problems and facilitate timely collection. Traditional processes have forced accounts receivable agents to manually pull relevant documents from multiple departments and filing systems, query colleagues and wait for information to be faxed or sent to them.

An integrated ECM solution streamlines the accounts receivable process by integrating disparate accounting, sales and support information into a central repository and providing a single point of access to it. The ECM solution captures order information as soon as it is entered or scanned into the system, links it to corresponding customer information and then archives this information.

In addition, an integrated ECM solution across the enterprise ecosystem can deploy monitoring and measurement tools to track user activity and deliver an overview of the status of each process. This audit history helps accounts receivable agents understand and monitor the progress of each step in the collection process to identify where or why issues arise.

Reducing Operational Costs in Human Resource Departments

Many organizations have already transformed their human resources (HR) department to a more modern structure to lower TCO and align with an evolving business strategy. In HR, this is especially true with regard to the day-to-day business transactions and administrative work that can be standardized, automated or even outsourced.

HR professionals devote about 70 percent of their time performing routine administrative tasks such as changing address information, obtaining approval for travel or vacation, and fielding employee questions regarding payment statements. These tasks require searching through stacks of paperwork, matching each document with the appropriate employee or candidate, populating forms and re-entering data into an HR system.

Integrating ECM with HR applications improves the overall performance of standard HR operations, while alleviating the demand these daily tasks place on HR staff. Integrated solutions also increase HR employee productivity and reduce costs by streamlining employee administration, automating key business processes and offering self-service tools. The HR department is relieved from manually processing standard requests, enabling it to reassign staff to focus on more strategic tasks. Tight security controls enable organizations to comply with privacy regulations. All relevant information about an individual, whether applicant, employee or former employee, can be stored and maintained in a protected environment, reducing the risk of losing or misplacing confidential documents. ECM integrates this information with key business process applications to expedite the recruiting process, for example, and reduce the risk of losing good candidates due to a lengthy and complex hiring process.

> Barclays Bank

Since its establishment over 300 years ago, Barclays Bank has earned a reputation as a leader in technological innovation. So, when mounds of accumulated HR paper documents started to threaten efficiency and the quality of service the organization offered to employees, Barclays Bank turned to technology for help.

Barclays implemented an ECM solution as their information hub that scans, stores, and links email and employee-related information and then, using a workflow, forwards it to the appropriate agent as an activity request. All 75,000 employee-related HR records are captured in a centralized repository and secure electronic access is provided to authorized users.

Records are now quickly retrieved and the need for many paper-based processes has been eliminated. As a result, response times to employee requests have significantly improved. In general, operational costs and resources have considerably decreased, while efficiency and productivity have increased.

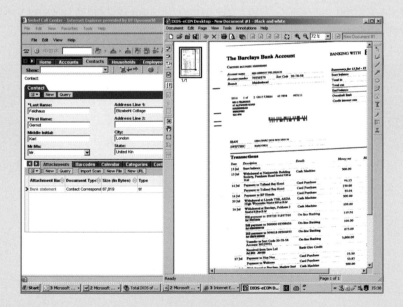

Figure 12.10: Example of Employee Information Access within an ERP System

Reduced IT Consolidation and Maintenance Costs

Managing Transactional Data

Every business process generates data and typically increases the volume of an enterprise application's database. The growing volume of data hampers system performance and slows down access to information. The prolonged backup and restoration of information adds to an administrator's workload and increases costs.

An integrated ECM solution offloads old data from an enterprise application, providing long-term access to archived information that is stored in a durable, tamper-proof format. This helps companies lower both the costs and risk associated with meeting data retention and disposal requirements. In addition, offloading data facilitates fast backup and recovery times, reduces administrative and hardware costs and decreases the time it takes to implement enterprise application upgrades.

When an ECM solution offloads application data, it deletes it from a database, freeing up resources and space while allowing this information to be easily accessed. Users working within a transaction can access both online and offline data within seconds. Administrators can archive data when necessary and even schedule data archiving to enhance the application's performance.

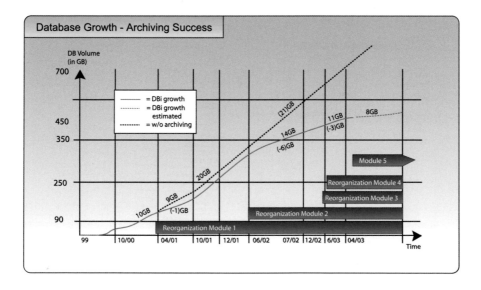

Figure 12.11: An Example of Data Archiving for Enterprise Applications

> Multiquip

Multiquip is one of the largest and most diversified suppliers to the construction, entertainment and equipment rental industries. Multiquip and its divisions sell products in more than 70 countries, with company offices located throughout the United States, Canada, Mexico, England, Brazil and China.

Customer-centric Multiquip realized that staying competitive meant delivering real-time services and information to both customers and employees. Using ECM, Multiquip developed a sales portal to help improve the sales process and reduce time-to-market for new products. The sales portal puts real time interactive reports from internal ERP and CRM systems directly into the hands of the sales team no matter where they are located. Employees can access and manage content generated from various systems with a single sign-on, benefiting salespeople and their customers with real-time information related to product deliveries, specifications and pricing.

Today at Multiquip, new products get to the market much faster than before and call center activity has been reduced. Operational efficiencies have improved significantly with a move towards customer self-service and collaboration. With the availability of real-time tracking of information, customer and employee satisfaction is strong. Multiquip now has the platform and flexibility to grow and launch MQ Web 2.0 which will entail a mobile portal, and customer and supplier-facing portals.

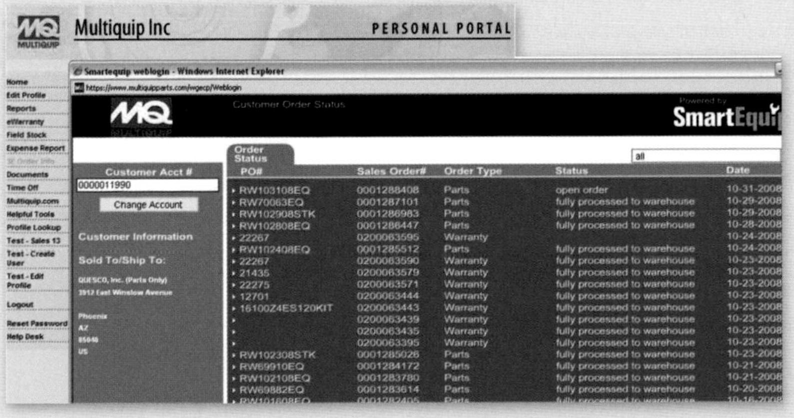

Figure 12.12: Real Time Access to ERP Order Information

Ensuring Compliance and Reducing Risk

Although regulations vary from country to country, they consistently require that organizations track, manage and retain critical business information and present it upon request. Developing and implementing best practices for compliance requirements not only protects organizations from risk but helps to streamline operations, reduce administrative costs and proactively prepare to comply with emerging regulations. An integrated ECM solution plays an integral role in fulfilling evolving legal requirements by securely storing content for designated periods, linking related information, providing an audit history for each document and enabling organizations to access any document on demand.

Securely Retains Documents, Books and Booking Records/Vouchers

Financial records in accounting practices exemplify a core compliance requirement. Even though organizations generally store financial documents for extended periods, they fail to fulfill many current regulations with long-term storage alone. Organizations must also be able to present requested financial records on demand, demonstrate how each record was used and which other records contributed to the designated process.

An integrated ECM solution addresses these transaction-related requirements and satisfies fundamental storage requirements by archiving all documents in a central repository. The solution enables organizations to prove that financial records are accurate by linking these scanned records to related financial records. Employees can instantly retrieve purchase orders, customer requests, correspondence, supplier orders and amounts and distribution information to verify the accuracy of the amounts on the requested document.

An ECM solution also enables companies to link documents like invoices or lists to respective sections in an enterprise application. If an auditor requests a specific invoice, employees can quickly pull up all supporting documents to confirm the invoice's accuracy and justify its use. An audit trail will trace the activity path for each requested document. An ECM system ensures secure, unalterable retention of documents in their original form, enabling organizations to benefit from aged ERP data that is maintained separately from the production environment and available on demand.

The Ecosystem and Enterprise 2.0

Market dynamics, business landscapes and emerging technologies dictate how an enterprise designs its business and information architectures. Successful enterprises must be ready to manage change to transform business operations into new opportunities.

Current innovations in technology are impacting the way the enterprise does business. Enterprise 2.0 is demonstrating value by driving the convergence of business content and processes, along with their underlying infrastructure.

> Delhaize Group S.A.

Delhaize Group S.A. is a Belgian international food retailer with locations in seven countries on three continents and 138,000 employees. Delhaize had a vision for its European financial operations, located in Belgium, Greece, Romania, and Luxembourg. The company wanted to simplify, optimize, and integrate its complex, non-integrated finance and IT landscape, which included more than ten accounting applications. So Delhaize Group embarked on a multiyear, multiphase transformation.

As part of its transformation, Delhaize wanted to reengineer invoice management to optimize its accounts payable (A/P) processes, increase invoice status visibility, and automate data entry. Each member of Delhaize's accounting staff, comprising 100 people, processed nearly 10,000 invoices each per year for a total of 1 million invoices per year. Delhaize wanted to improve this performance and reduce cost.

With the improved functionality of its new integrated software, Delhaize is experiencing significant benefits from its greatly improved A/P processes. "We've minimized manual data-entry errors and reduced selling, general, and administrative expenses," Jean Luc Vandebroek, the VP of accounting, financial systems, and change management for Delhaize Group explains. "We've also shortened financial closing time and lowered IT costs by retiring legacy software." Perhaps the most dramatic improvement has been to process cycle times. Staff members process nearly 30,000 invoices each per year. And thanks to an integrated ECM and ERP solution, Delhaize is much more compliant with Sarbanes–Oxley (SOX).

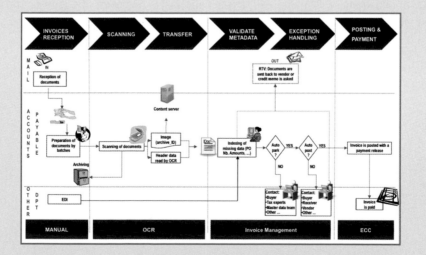

Figure 12.13: Reengineering Invoice Management at Delhaize

Mashups, for example, deliver a lean approach to extending the value of existing enterprise applications by designing applications to extend existing business processes to new channels to extend market reach. Mashups are, in a sense, a form of application syndication. A defining characteristic of mashups that sets them apart from other forms of application integration is that they source content or functionality from established systems without supporting their own native data store or content repository.

Cloud computing represents another emerging technology service that presents a compelling business model for IT, especially with regards to economies of scale. The concept of outsourcing IT services is appealing for the promise of improved accessibility, decreased investments in technology infrastructure and ease of deployment, however the model is fraught with concerns around security, privacy and performance when applied to the enterprise ecosystem. The Cloud is examined in greater detail in Chapter 13.

The Ecosystem and ECM

As part of an integrated platform, ECM promises to manage all business content – from paper documents, such as incoming vendor invoices and electronic records processed using an ERP system, to online documents, records, Web content and more. Enterprise application extensions enable employees to perform invoice verification and other routine procedures more effectively, using ECM to instantly access unstructured or structured content within enterprise applications. ECM gives organizations tight control over information in order to optimize business operations. By building a bridge to extend enterprise applications, ECM enables organizations to minimize the costs, risks and resources inherent in deploying disparate technologies and enterprise applications.

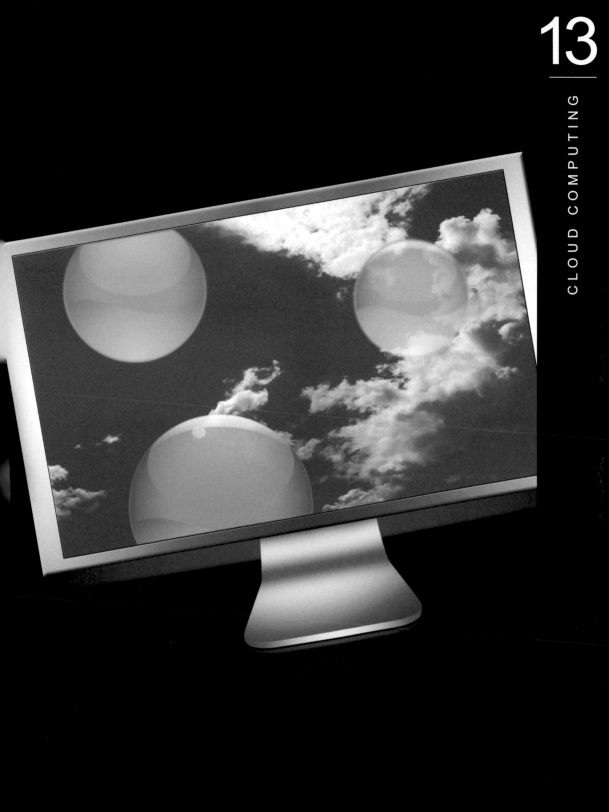

Figure 13.1: ECM and Cloud Computing

Cloud computing has been championed as the next revolutionary stage in information technology. In the near future, the majority of computing activities will not take place on PCs at home or in the office, but instead they will occur in the "cloud". Many of us spend time in the cloud on a daily basis without even realizing it. Web-based e-mail services, social networking sites, photo and video services and online applications are all services that run on a cloud computing component, and can be accessed through browsers, smart-phones or other client devices.

But what exactly is the cloud? And what are the implications of managing content in the cloud? This chapter offers a broad definition of the term and examines both opportunities presented and barriers to adoption for the enterprise as it embraces the cloud to manage content, collaborate and drive processes.

CLOUD COMPUTING

The term "cloud computing" is a metaphor that was inspired by the cloud symbol used to represent the Internet in flow charts and diagrams. The cloud represents an abstraction of the underlying structure of the Internet, as shown in the illustration below.

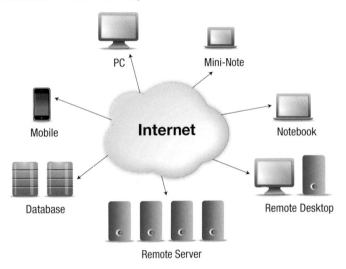

Figure 13.2: The Cloud

Basically, cloud computing is a term used to describe the disruptive transformation of IT toward a service-based economy, driven by economic, technological and cultural conditions[1].

Cloud computing offers a variety of services, with people using cloud computing for storing and sharing information, managing databases and deploying Web services. While their services may differ, all cloud computing services are delivered on demand over the Internet from data centers.

---

[1] Wardley, Simon. *Cloud Computing - Why IT Matters*, YouTube, 2009

A key benefit – and what is the premise for how cloud computing will revolutionize IT – is the ability to "rent" computing services from a third-party provider, rather than owning and maintaining the physical infrastructure. Hardware or software resources are consumed as a service and unless the service is free, consumers pay only for the resources they use or are billed on a subscription basis. For this reason, cloud computing is analogous to how traditional utility services like electricity or hydro are consumed as a metered, pay-as-you-go service.

Figure 13.3: Cloud Computing Resources

Cloud computing is the commercial version of utility computing, delivering highly scalable and accessible computing resources while reducing any user interaction with underlying technologies. In concept, cloud computing represents a shift in consumption, where users – including global corporations – are not required to have knowledge of, expertise in, or management of the technology infrastructure. And while the concept of utility computing appeals to the enterprise, especially with respect to reducing over-head and labor costs, organizations still want to maintain a high level of control over their content and applications.

Where is the Cloud?

The origin of computing is based on mainframes with so-called "dumb terminals." In the seventies, the early computers that housed central processing units and memory were called mainframes. In the eighties, when hardware became affordable, technology shifted to client-server operated PCs. Today, with more affordable and powerful processes and ubiquitous connectivity, technology is moving again toward the mainframes of the seventies. This infrastructure is what makes the cloud so notable. Cloud services combine thousands of computers and storage networks, or public mainframes, into "server farms".

The power of the cloud lies in its immense server infrastructure. Facebook, the second most-trafficked Web site, runs thousands of databases in one of the largest server installations in the world. Google owns over one million servers spread across the globe to support its services. All major software vendors run server farms. These data centers represent the largest collection of information and computer resources in the world. In the US alone, there are close to 7,000 data centers. Some of these data centers are so large they require their own power generators.

To manage growing amounts of data and transactions, organizations have built data centers which consist of thousands of servers with infrastructure required for storage, networking, and cooling. Over the years, these companies have gained expertise in large scale data management and the technical development, infrastructure, and processes required to operate these large data centers. Cloud computing represents the commercialization of these data center developments.

Over the last decade, the tremendous growth and popularity of the Internet has resulted in new and technology-driven challenges for organizations. While these include the need to support millions of simultaneous e-commerce transactions and millions of concurrent search queries, there has been tremendous rise in traffic due to large files being shared. The whole configuration of the Internet has changed to meet people's needs to access complex content files such as video and music files. What has driven this change is the need to distribute traffic around the world.

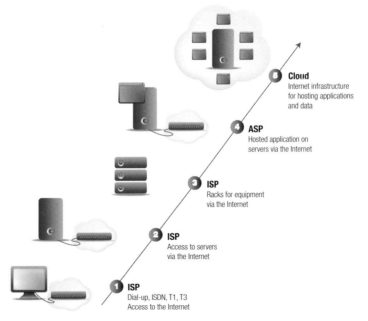

Figure 13.4: The Evolution of the Cloud

As traffic increases and files get larger, organizations will leverage cloud services to enable the global distribution of content. The enterprise's content distribution strategy will involve Content Delivery Networks or CDNs. A content delivery network is a system of computers containing copies of content, placed at various points in a network to maximize bandwidth for access to content from clients throughout the network. A client accesses a copy of the data near to the client (proximity is key), as opposed to all clients accessing the same central server. CDNs differ from server farms because they are much more distributed; they are in essence sophisticated versions of multiple caches throughout the world.

As an increasing number of organizations tap into the cloud, the challenge will be to distribute content quickly and effectively enough to deliver a positive end user experience. Consumers now expect to download content in 2 seconds, down from a previous 4 second threshold. When we take into account that mobile access speeds are only 20% of computer speeds, a positive mobile experience will also drive organizations to adopt cloud computing for content distribution.

The Delivery of Cloud Computing

A clear definition of the cloud is obscured by its many components, including infrastructure, platform and application. What follows are cloud services divided into broad categories.

Cloud Infrastructure

Cloud infrastructure, or infrastructure as a service (IaaS), refers to providing a computer infrastructure as a service. Vendors offer storage and virtual servers that IT can access on demand. Because customers can pay for exactly the amount of service they use, IaaS is also referred to as utility computing.

Cloud Platform

Cloud platform, or platform as a service (PaaS), describes delivering a computer platform or software stack as a service. Developers can then create applications using the provider's Application Programming Interfaces (APIs).

Cloud Application

In this instance, the cloud provider gives its customer access to its applications. This is also commonly referred to as Software-as-a-Service (SaaS). This type of cloud computing delivers a single application to a large number of customers using a multi-tenant architecture. Multi-tenancy allows for the sharing of resources across multiple redundant sites to improve reliability. As cloud solutions develop, fail-over and data recovery options will need to be guaranteed by service level agreements (SLAs) to protect critical business content against loss or destruction.

Hardware as a service (HaaS) enables individuals and organizations to purchase space for applications, games and other types of software to run in the cloud rather than taking up space on a computer. Managed service providers (MSPs) deliver another form of cloud computing, offering IT departments access to applications, rather than end users.

Finally, service commerce platforms deliver a service hub that allows users to order services from a platform, and coordinates service delivery and pricing to deliver a complete solution.

Types of Cloud Computing

There are three types of clouds: marketplace, workplace and hybrid.

The public (marketplace) cloud delivers computer resources on demand over the Internet using Web services or applications from a third-party provider who bills on a utility computing basis. A private (workplace) cloud emulates cloud computing services on private networks. While security, compliance, governance and reliability issues can be more closely managed in the private cloud, users do not benefit from minimal investments in technology because they are required to purchase and manage the technology infrastructure. A hybrid cloud is made up of internal and external cloud providers. With investments in legacy and existing technology infrastructure, the enterprise will most comfortably adopt a hybrid approach to cloud computing, completing some computing tasks internally, possibly in a private cloud, while other tasks will be offloaded to the public cloud.

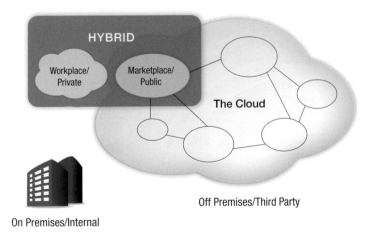

Figure 13.5: Types of Cloud Computing

Servicing more than one million residents in the area, the City of Edmonton needed a Web site that reflected the vibrancy of the city while providing user-driven architecture, easy-to-find content, rich media and Web 2.0 compatibility.

The City of Edmonton decided on a different approach to implement the technology, opting to outsource its Web operations – partnering with Software as a Service (SaaS) provider, Yellow Pencil. Yellow Pencil manages hosted environments, providing comprehensive consulting and development services.

"In our IT department, we had a fundamental shift in thinking. About 75 percent of our IT time was spent babysitting servers with just 25 percent on customer solutions' work. So the decision was made to completely outsource our Web site. It was probably the best decision we've ever made," explains Paul Strandlund, Web Operations Manager, City of Edmonton. Using Web content management and working with partner Yellow Pencil, the City of Edmonton upgraded the look and feel of its Web site and the technologies behind it, making it Web 2.0 compatible and easy for content authors to contribute to.

Figure 13.6: City of Edmonton's Hosted Web site

The Cloud and Open Source Software

While integration technology is in its infancy in the cloud, there are organizations working to connect cloud providers to deliver integrated solutions to organizations. In reality, the cloud consists of isolated services that consumers, organizations and IT departments connect to individually. Despite this fact, cloud computing integrators are already moving the concept of loosely connected services running on scalable and accessible infrastructure closer to reality. One example of this is open source integration with cloud computing services, based on a SaaS model of delivery.

Open source software (OSS) is computer software for which the source code and certain other rights normally reserved for copyright holders are in the public domain. Open source is not the same as "open standards"; open source is open code whereas open standards are open protocols or standards for development. While the waters between the two are often muddied, to simplify: open standards include HTML, CSS, XML and JavaScript; Mozilla Firefox is an open source Web browser.

Open source software has provided the foundation for cloud computing implementations. By offering processing, storage and other services on demand over the Internet, cloud computing providers are making it easier and more affordable for open source suppliers to develop solutions at lower costs. The cloud and open source complement one another, and in the future, this symbiotic relationship will bring enterprise infrastructure and business software solutions together. Before this happens, issues of security will have to be addressed. While open source software components should adhere to licenses like the General Public License (GPL), they are often developed without following best practices. Often, cloud providers are unable to detect the components that make up open source software solutions and cannot ensure that the software meets full requirements for licensing.

As far as ECM is concerned, many organizations in the market for a comprehensive and standards-based solution do not have the time to invest in an open source solution. It would require too much IT investment to be cost effective and often the risks outweigh the benefits. As far as open source and open standards are concerned, ECM systems should support the standards that are available, tested and widely accepted.

ECM and the Cloud

Cloud computing demonstrates a profound shift in the way organizations acquire and use technology. Seeing the benefits of "renting" over the capital expenditures required to purchase and run software, corporations are increasingly using content management and collaboration services in the cloud. Assigning computing tasks such as document management, archiving and workflow to a remote location allows organizations to focus their time and resources on activities that drive significant business value.

> # Bundesrechenzentrum (BRZ)

The Bundesrechenzentrum (Federal Computing Centre of Austria, BRZ) plans, implements and runs a broad range of eGovernment services for federal ministries, universities, social security providers and other public organizations. With 1,200 employees and a total annual turnover of 226 million Euros, the BRZ is the leading IT service provider for the public sector in Austria.

In most administrative processes, documents submitted to the public sector play an important role. As they were often transmitted on paper or by email, the management of unstructured data became more important for both individual applications that cover the specific government processes and for standard applications. To optimize the administrative processes, it became necessary to provide the means to handle all the relevant data in the business processes electronically.

Typical examples for this were the land and commercial registers of the Austrian Ministry of Justice, which was managed digitally and could be viewed on the Internet after payment, but paper documents were stored at each court house. Besides huge costs for archive maintenance, there was also a risk of losing the original documents. Along with the need for document archiving from the ERP applications for the Austrian Government, this provided for the initial business case for setting up a common ECM infrastructure.

As a service provider to the Austrian federal administration, the main objective of the BRZ is to provide a flexible, reliable and scalable ECM infrastructure for the various needs. To ensure that their platform is widely adopted, the archive and document management service was actively promoted at several eGovernment events and the BRZ made individual presentations to their main customers. A transparent ASP pricing model allows them to make attractive offers for all kind of customers.

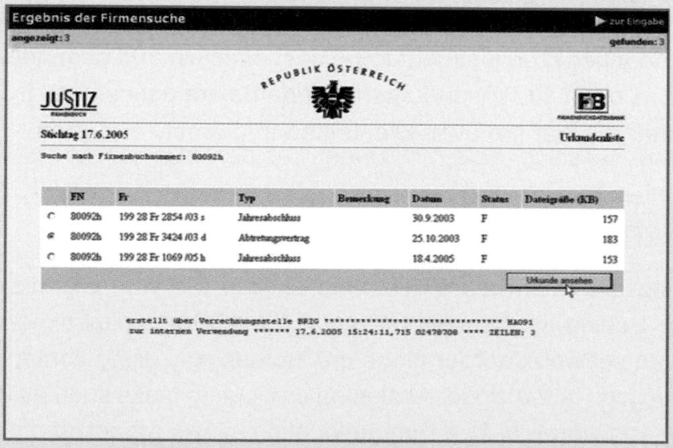

Figure 13.7: ECM as a Service at BRZ

ECM in the cloud helps organizations bypass the investment required in infra-structure and ongoing administration and frees them up to respond strategically to customer needs and changes in the market. As more organizations seek out packaged ECM solutions, the ability to add Web services or build custom applications that augment existing legacy systems becomes a clear business advantage. There are, however, significant issues with cloud computing in a business context. Concerns such as data pro-tection, operational integrity, business continuity and disaster recovery present a strong barrier to entry for many enterprises.

Content in the Cloud

The advent of cloud computing aligns directly with the expansion of ECM and the economies of scale required to manage the tremendous volume of information available in digital format today. Many of the early adopters of cloud computing – genomics researchers with huge amounts of sequence data for example – require inexpensive and accessible ways to share information. By separating enterprises from their computers and offering universal access to servers, cloud providers can bundle computing with value-add services that run the gamut from point solutions to fully outsourced IT solutions.

Cloud platforms give IT departments the ability to remove hardware implementation from the overall ECM equation. As a result, organizations can deliver new applications without having to purchase the hardware, software and consultants required to set up and run corporate systems. In-house solutions can take months to acquire, install, configure and deploy. Being able to instantly deploy solutions gives businesses the agility to have ECM applications up and running in less time than it takes to develop solutions in-house. By outsourcing IT tasks such as managing email or Web content, organizations can focus on core competencies. While business agility is a definite advantage, it can be contrasted to the slow connection times that can result from accessing data hosted in the cloud and transmitted from remote locations around the world.

While the economies of scale are compelling enough for enterprises to embrace ECM in the cloud, larger organizations will be slow to adopt cloud-based solutions because data integrity is not guaranteed. The concept of cloud computing creates new challenges for security because sensitive data no longer resides behind the firewall on dedicated hardware. Whether for software services or storage capacity, security and reliability must improve before organizations accept large scale cloud computing services.

Collaboration in the Cloud

As discussed in Chapter 9, social computing applications, including wikis, blogs, RSS feeds and social networking are being increasingly adopted as productivity tools for the enterprise. This is because they are creating flexible and exciting new ways for people to connect, interact and collaborate. The pervasiveness of the Internet and innovations in software architecture has made it possible to procure collaborative functionality from the cloud.

Collaboration in the cloud promises fast, reliable and easy access to a global network from a desktop PC, laptop or mobile device. What is so revolutionary about collaborating in the cloud is that it crosses geographical, cultural and organizational boundaries, offering a solution that puts the user in control. This is what has made Web 2.0 technologies so popular.

Ironically, it is exactly this control that organizations do not want to compromise. The enterprise is not willing to entrust the management, performance and recovery of applications or data to external organizations. User generated content, the byproduct of collaborating in the cloud, gives organizations good cause for concern around data security, transparency and regulatory compliance. As users bypass IT departments for solutions outside the firewall, organizations run the risk of exposing confidential or sensitive information. While opportunities to collaborate in the cloud will only increase, organizations should outline expectations around usage into their information governance and compliance strategies.

Process in the Cloud

Large software vendors are offering cloud platforms that enable organizations to create mashups. Mashups combine content or functionality from external sources to create a new service that addresses a specific business problem. Organizations are using these services to operate in the cloud and are connecting with the operations of other companies also using the cloud. This is creating the potential for organizations to develop business processes as they expand collaboration to include other businesses in the cloud in their own processes. As companies seek ECM solutions, the ability to build custom applications and add Web services which integrate with legacy applications and existing infrastructure becomes a business advantage.

While opportunities to develop solutions exist, cloud-based applications may not offer the depth of solution required by organizations, especially when it comes to work flow. While setting up project teams on the fly and collaborating are a good fit with the cloud, many complicated processes necessitate the tight management of content. In some cases relying on documents created in the cloud is just not viable.

Who Owns the Data?

In the cloud, an organization's data and applications reside on the "cloud cluster," a centralized network of computers and services owned by the cloud provider. But who "owns" the data?

Organizations in certain industries must maintain strict control over their data to protect against liability and comply with regulations to ensure business continuity. The Health Insurance Portability & Accountability Act (HIPAA) sets regulations for the security and privacy of health records. Sarbanes-Oxley is another regulation that governs corporate financial reporting.

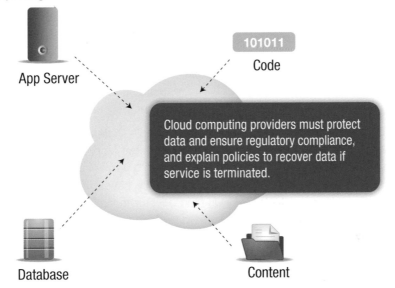

App Server

101011
Code

Cloud computing providers must protect data and ensure regulatory compliance, and explain policies to recover data if service is terminated.

Database

Content

Figure 13.8: Cloud Computing and Security

Privacy is another key concern. Policy issues in the US are focused around national security and privacy, requiring adherence to the USA PATRIOT Act and the Homeland Security Act. While data that a cloud computing provider collects about its users can provide marketing intelligence, consumers today are concerned about the abuse and violation of privacy. As a result, organizations will need to be able to access and log their data wherever it resides for protection and compliance purposes.

Along with privacy and compliance, intellectual property is another key concern when it comes to cloud services. In some cases, the cloud provider owns the infrastructure or the applications, while the user owns the data. But this delineation is not always clear. Open source software and mashups often combine data and code and it is not always clear who owns rights to what.

> Davis + Henderson

Davis + Henderson

Founded in 1875, Davis + Henderson provides innovative programs, products and technology-based business services to customers in the financial services industry. The company's technology focuses on Credit Lifecycle Management for the retail lending, small business lending, commercial lending and equipment finance industries, and within this space, Davis + Henderson is an industry leader in solutions to the mortgage industry. During 2009, Davis + Henderson launched its next generation collaborative document management solution – Exchange 2.0 – to respond to the Canadian mortgage industry's growing requirements for automation, data security and performance.

Exchange 2.0 is a Web-based application built on top of ECM, a powerful, fully integrated document management system that delivers the essential capabilities for managing business-critical documents. Hosted on Davis + Henderson servers, Exchange allows mortgage brokers and lenders to share and collaborate with everyone touching a deal in a highly secure environment. Based on a Software as a Service (SaaS) delivery model, they are able to provide a solution that allows clients to complete a mortgage transaction electronically, securely and very quickly.

Immediate benefits for Davis + Henderson clients include increased productivity, decreased administrative effort, and reduced paper and storage costs – within a secure environment. Organizations can realize a 70 percent cost savings in document handling processes and going paperless not only saves clients time and money, it also enables the convenience of real-time access to deal with documents anytime, anywhere.

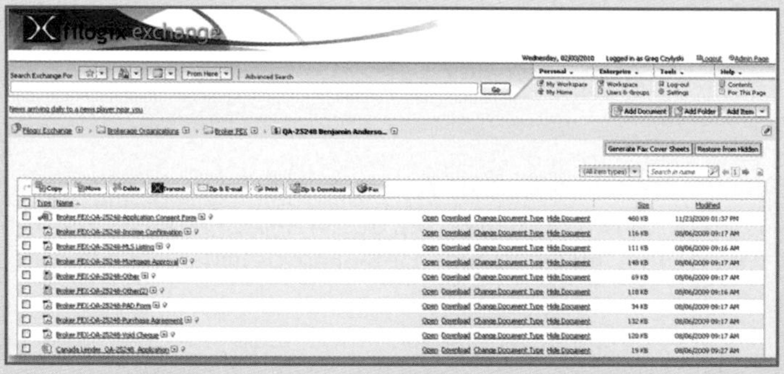

Figure 13.9: A Service (SaaS) Delivery Model Cuts Costs by 70%

Finally, the environmental impact of cloud computing should also be examined. Data Centers require massive amounts of energy to operate. In the 90's, data centers consumed one to two megawatts of power. Today, data centers can consume as much as 200 megawatts. Access to electricity and cost will dictate where data centers are located, and carbon emissions from data centers are set to quadruple in the next decade. Use of content systems will reduce this negative impact as improvements in bandwidth can reduce an organization's carbon footprint.

ECM as a Service

People are already using cloud based services to store huge amounts of pictures, videos and corporate data. As the cloud business model expands to the enterprise, the ECM landscape will experience a dramatic shift.

Utility computing will be the future as infrastructures are outsourced due to economies of scale. The consolidation of data centers and the virtualization of servers will give organizations the opportunity to concentrate their efforts on building secure and protected solutions. Security will focus on content and how this content is accessed, stored and shared. Access to information will be facilitated by cheaper and more powerful processors, and faster networks.

ECM 2.0 in the cloud empowers organizations to collect, correlate and analyze data in previously incomparable ways. This difference in computing capacity is clear when we compare the tens of trillions of computations per second of a popular Internet search site to the PC's 3 billion computations per second. Cloud computing offers tremendous capacity in using technology to connect people across dispersed locations to store and share information.

Until security, privacy and reliability are guaranteed, however, the enterprise adoption rate of cloud computing services will be slow. Software as a service is still evolving, and the IT department is not quite ready to make the move to provisioning in the cloud; there lies great disparity at the operational level between outsourcing via cloud computing and the processes involved in procuring on-premise solutions. Despite this fact, over the coming years, organizations will develop their own cloud capacity, or opt for hybrid cloud solutions. In the meantime, the enterprise will use cloud services for the rapid deployment of prototype sites for collaboration and bring these sites in-house for full production and use.

Figure 14.1: Mobility

This chapter provides an overview of mobile content. It traces the transformation of knowledge workers into the mobile workforce – and the implications this presents for the secure access, management and exchange of enterprise content. The innovator stories included in this chapter illustrate how mobile access combines with ECM to deliver relevant content to users whenever they need it, improving productivity, operational efficiency and organizational agility.

MOBILITY

The use of mobile content has gained momentum with the surge of high-speed 2.5G, 3G and wifi network support, and the wide-scale deployment of smart mobile devices. With improved connectivity, higher bandwidth, unrestricted accessibility and powerful devices, the enterprise is going mobile. As the world boasts close to 5 billion mobile subscribers, organizations are increasingly using mobile devices and applications to enhance productivity. The knowledge worker has evolved into the mobile professional and connecting across geographic, cultural and organizational distinctions has become the standard for work. To facilitate this, global organizations will be required to deliver high value ECM 2.0 solutions directly to mobile devices and users.

The Mobile Workforce

The enterprise is witnessing a wide adoption of smartphone devices and, along with it, the mobilization of both remote and traditional office workers. As more advanced devices are produced, such as the BlackBerry® and iPhone® and mobile platforms like Google's Android™, Symbian OS and Windows® Mobile, there is an increased capability to support content management, processes and social applications using mobile devices. By extending the reach of corporate content to mobile users, functionality moves beyond the simple exchange of emails and text messages to the secure delivery of critical information to mobile professionals in context.

The escalating use of smartphones means that more and more enterprise applications are being accessed by handheld devices. The smartphone is a mobile phone that offers advanced, PC-like capabilities. RIM's BlackBerry is an example of a smartphone and has become the enterprise standard for most North American organizations. Along with smartphones, Apple's iPhone is used throughout the world, with millions of users and billions of downloadable applications. Despite these usage numbers, the mobile application market is fairly new and rapidly evolving.

All trademarks found above are owned by the respective trademark owners and the authors of this book do not intend to imply that any such trademark owners are endorsing any specific ECM software product.

Figure 14.2: Mobile and Secure Social Networking

Mobile applications are discreet programs created to solve a specific purpose with little or no back-office type server or content integration. They are designed to solve problems in a moment of need, and allow users to save time and effort by enabling tasks that might normally require access to a PC with an Internet connection. As the volume of digital content increases, consumers expect unlimited and immediate access to it – whether on their PC, TV or mobile device. What is available on the desktop should be available on a mobile device. Mobile workers require powerful mobile applications that deliver functionality and access to vital enterprise content, expertise and resources.

By leveraging the best capabilities of devices available today and anticipating shifting trends in the mobile platform market, ECM is evolving to drive end user adoption and organizational efficiency through better access to information in a secure, managed and easy to use way.

A Pervasive Interface

To fully understand the potential and benefits of mobile content, it is important to consider the mobile device as a "pervasive" interface to content.

Professionals interact with many different application user interfaces (UIs) to complete their daily tasks. To decrease the amount of time it takes to complete a task and increase productivity, organizations are always seeking to optimize UIs for specified tasks. Traditional applications have used a single UI for access. Technology developments that include the Web and mobile devices have caused vendors to provide additional interfaces based on different interaction models. While mobile applications in the future will be built to support multiple user interfaces, they will share a common interaction model. This will provide end users with a seamless experience, regardless of context, location or device.

On the UI development continuum – from PCs to cell phones and eventually television – mobile devices present the next step in the evolution of content access, whether it is accessed using a rich client, Web interface, or other mechanism. As the demand for mobile applications grows, organizations will need to support a variety of mobile devices and platforms.

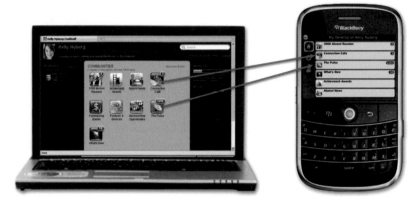

Figure 14.3: Mobile Devices Emulate the Way People Work Online

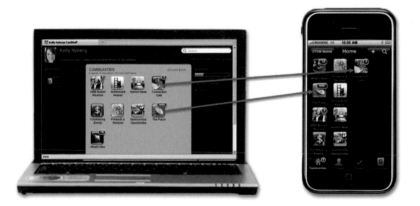

With the limited screen size of mobile devices, an appealing UI that displays information is critical to creating a positive user experience and driving adoption. Being able to view, filter and sort information easily and intelligently on a mobile device is a key requirement. When accessing a content repository, for example, mobile professionals will not be able to easily consume a terabyte of information on a single screen. The amount of real estate on a mobile device is often limited, offering the end user the option to expand views of information displayed. Innovative interface design, the QWERTY keyboard, email access, and calendar capabilities are some features that have made the mobile device popular in consumer sectors. As consumer and enterprise usage converge, mobile devices will be much more varied. To support this, organizations will need to deliver a matrix of applications across multiple platforms and devices.

User behavior drives UI development and mobile users are embracing touch screens as technology moves away from the mouse and keyboard paradigm to provide a richer and more intuitive experience. The iPhone, for example, is a gesture-based device that offers a touch screen for users to execute commands. Touch screen devices are becoming increasingly popular for delivering a very compelling, immersive end user experience with the ability to interact with a device and its applications at a touch. As touch screens becomes more prevalent, UI development will evolve to support immersive three dimensional interfaces. Users will navigate through these screens in a very intuitive way to view and manipulate – at a touch – objects, media assets, videos, Web content, processes and more.

Mobile ECM – A New Business Model

Organizations are increasing the efficacy of their workforces by providing secure, managed mobile access to enterprise systems. Extending ECM to mobile users enables a workforce to consistently engage with the resources they need to do their jobs effectively. With a secure content infrastructure in place, mobile professionals can create, manage, find and publish content in a compliant and secure fashion. Organizations can accelerate the velocity of business by mobilizing processes and extending application data out to field professionals at any location.

Having critical information immediately available will revolutionize content management and mobile computing. By combining traditional content management functionality with compliance, records management, social media, process management and other applications, organizations are able to deliver critical information in context. Mobile ECM gives mobile users the ability to immediately tap into the content and enterprise resources they need when they require them.

Established in 1992, Emergency Medicine Physicians (EMP) is one of the leading providers of emergency medical services in the United States. EMP is a physician staffing company focusing on emergency rooms. EMP began with one hospital partner in 1992; currently they staff 31 locations in eight states.

EMP sought to redesign their intranet in order to provide physicians with improved access to applications, an effective navigational structure and a more personalized end user experience. Emulating the iPhone interface, the "mypulse" intranet experience would provide on one-click access to information and applications, with a focus on optimizing the interface for mobile devices to provide access via a BlackBerry smartphone, for example.

The new site design delivers a unique interface which allows for a fully customizable experience, enabling users to drag and drop portlets to build their own personalized home page. Additional features include integration with social software and applications such as wikis, a notification system which allows messages to be sent to the intranet or a user's phone, and an RSS feed reader from which administrators and users can select feeds for display.

Figure 14.4: EMP's Intranet, Optimized for the Mobile Experience

Figure 14.5: Mobile ECM Extends the Enterprise

Extending ECM to mobile involves more than merely mobilizing existing applications. A number of important factors should be considered when moving powerful enterprise systems outside of office and IT environments. These issues include offline storage and access to content, the use of mobile capabilities, performance and security of content.

Storage and Access to Content

From an enterprise perspective, organizations will need to provide persistent device storage and secure mobile access to existing enterprise infrastructure via a virtual private network (VPN). A VPN enables mobile devices to access network resources and software applications on home networks when they connect via other wireless networks. Mobile VPNs are used when workers need to keep application sessions continuously open, as they suspend and resume work or connect using a number of networks, carrier-based or wifi.

Leveraging the Capabilities of Mobile Devices

Mobility goes beyond delivering improved access to information. It extends the reach of ECM by providing opportunities to leverage intelligent devices to manage information. For example, location-based systems (GPS), ring tones and alerts can be used to support improved responsiveness and efficiency. A sales representative located at a hotel several kilometers from a customer site, for example, stands to benefit greatly from a combination of mobile features, applications and enterprise content. Using a smartphone's GPS system, the device can complete a semantic analysis to determine the location of the customer site and identify a meeting scheduled with this customer in the calendar. A customer folder on the mobile device can then be pre-populated with all of the documents the sales rep needs to prepare for the meeting: user documents, transactions conducted with this customer, any outstanding contracts and any other relevant information. In an intelligent way, mobile access anticipates what the salesperson may need and provides content within context to ensure a successful meeting.

Performance

Performance on a mobile device depends upon connections, from wifi to 3G or even 4G connections. Enterprise content is manipulated on the server side, leveraging an organization's IT infrastructure or data storage in the cloud, and rendered for delivery on a mobile device. Documents, for example, are translated into a format that is appropriate for mobile access, transmitting only fragments of a document as they are requested in real time. Transmitting content this way allows the system to be responsive and the user to be productive by viewing content as it is transmitted in real time. Differences in performance depend upon the device being used, the network being accessed and how much bandwidth is available.

Figure 14.6: Mobile ECM Leverages Enterprise Security

Security

Security on a mobile device is a combination of security over-the-air, over-the-wire and permission-based access to the ECM system. When information is transmitted to a mobile device, it follows an extremely secure and proprietary protocol used by telephone and wireless vendors. If this information is from an enterprise content repository, security depends upon a user being identified by the system (via directory services, Active Directory Services, LDAP or NTLM) as a trusted member who is permitted access based on permissions assigned by system administrators. Mobile platforms will verify permissions much in the same way a Web browser checks access permissions to an ECM system. As data is transmitted or collaborative spaces accessed, the platform ensures that version history, audit capabilities, reports, security and permissions contained with the system translates directly to the mobile device.

Mobile ECM Applications

As mobile technology improves to support enhanced capabilities, organizations will be able to extend ECM applications to mobile professionals and improve collaboration and productivity by making people, processes and content more accessible. The mobile use case scenarios for ECM are rich, unlimited and compelling. To illustrate mobile ECM in action, let's examine some mobile ECM applications:

Mobile Compliance and Governance

Mobile records management empowers organizations to comply with regulatory standards and corporate governance policies and procedures. Records management and compliance policies can be applied to content from a mobile device for dispositions, legal document holds and location-based physical records management. The application is fully integrated with enterprise records management, so that when a retention period ends, for example, users are able to access a disposition approval workflow and take the appropriate required action.

Mobile professionals can search, store and retrieve email messages and attachments directly from the enterprise archive to the mobile device to ensure that email is effectively managed and archived.

Mobile Media Management

With mobile media management, professionals can search, retrieve and view digital assets, including high-resolution marketing assets, full motion video and complex engineering file formats. Processes are fully integrated, as marketing professionals, for example, can initiate, review and submit a production workflow directly from their mobile device. A smartphone's video and still camera capabilities can also be leveraged. Documents, objects and content can be stored in the device's local memory, allowing for access and reuse.

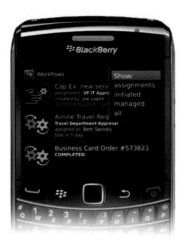

Figure 14.7: View, Sort and Manage Workflows from a Mobile Device

Mobile Process Management

Mobile professionals can view workflow assignments and update critical processes in real time. Workflows can be initiated, reviewed and executed using mobile devices from any place at any time to improve efficiencies across the enterprise. To illustrate this, consider an executive who spends a tremendous amount of time traveling and typically receives numerous workflows or processes in a week. If this person is able to receive content and make sound business decisions based on this information, regardless of location, the organization realizes significant benefits of streamlined efficiencies, improved agility and increased competiveness.

Mobile Web Content Management

Mobile applications for WCM deliver frameworks for the quick and easy development of custom applications, along with public Web site content review, modification and approval, and integration with enterprise process management systems.

ERP System Integration

Being able to access and view files from a trusted enterprise repository using a mobile device in real time is a fundamental benefit of mobile content. A mobile ERP system integration application gives mobile professionals access to vital corporate content from multiple systems, allowing them to manage travel expenses, vendor invoices, human resources management and customer information from a mobile device.

> Open Text

OPEN TEXT

Open Text Corporation is a leading provider of enterprise content management software (ECM 2.0) solutions, helping organizations manage and gain the true value of their business content.

Mobile ECM gives Open Text the ability to extend content into business processes, social networks and more – connecting its mobile workforce across organizational and geographical boundaries. Social media features such as blogs, wikis and profiles are combined with mobile capabilities such as GPS systems, calendars and notifications to keep the sales force connected to dynamic information 24/7. Field sales is able to stay on top of customer account information and can connect on a daily basis with product managers and developers to keep pace of product innovations and properly prepare for customer meetings and product demonstrations. What's more, because the company is leveraging a secure ECM infrastructure, all information is guaranteed to be secure and compliant.

Mobile ECM enables Open Text professionals to improve their productivity by as much as 15 hours in one week. Significant productivity benefits have also been experienced by field services and executive management. By delivering mobile access to content management, and combining this with social media tools, Open Text is able improve its overall responsiveness to new opportunities, lower the costs of inefficient communications and collaboration, all while ensuring that critical content is secure.

Figure 14.8: Open Text Improves Productivity with Mobile ECM

Figure 14.9: Mobile Access to Enterprise Content from Multiple Systems

Mobile Collaboration and Social Media

As mobility extends the reach of enterprise content, it also promises to extend the functionality of social software to mobile professionals. In every organization, the ability to share information with the right individuals at the right time is paramount for success. Mobile social media exposes the knowledge and expertise of an organization to the entire workforce. Mobile professionals can be as effective and information aware as they are in the office, while bringing immediate benefits from connecting in context – on location at a job site, for example, or with a customer. Mobile social media helps organizations to drive bottom-line revenue by making their employees more productive, efficient and knowledgeable.

Mobile access to online communities and social media functionality helps mobile professionals make connections, collaborate with colleagues, and view people's profiles to understand their interests, skills and expertise. Once expertise is located, critical information can be shared to solve pressing issues, stimulate innovation, drive awareness and foster a sense of community within an organization. As an enterprise identifies these self-formulating networks that bind its workforce, the organization gains insight into the connections that drive how people share information, make decisions, collaborate and innovate.

Figure 14.10: Mobile Profiles

Mobile social media delivers productivity gains for the enterprise. In some situations, social media tools are replacing emails as people are having conversations and sharing information using comments, rating, polling, sharing, via blog comments, and more. Accessing a persistent online community using a mobile device can reduce the number of emails people generate in an organization. As a result, time can be better spent on more pressing tasks rather than managing email inboxes.

Figure 14.11: Mobile Blogging

Along with traditional collaborative or shared project workspaces, wikis, blogs, discussion forums, alerts and notifications can all be mobilized as part of a fully integrated ECM solution. By leveraging enterprise infrastructure, social media content becomes auditable to guarantee compliance with regulations and corporate governance. Being part of an ECM solution ensures enterprise-class management of social content for future review and litigation risk management.

In addition to mobilizing the baseline functionality of social media, mobile devices allow users to exchange and formulate ideas, discuss and solve problems and leverage the cumulative social experience, knowledge and capabilities of every employee in the organization in real time. This reduces costs, mitigates risks and imbues the knowledge, power and capability of the entire organization in an individual, regardless of physical location.

As the Millennials enter the workforce, they will expect to use the same tools in the office as they do at home. Global organizations will need to support mobile access to social media applications. Traditional social networks and online communities will give rise to new, mobile communities based on a shared proximity, location and behavior. We are already seeing this as marketers are using proximity-based programs to advertise goods and offer promotions to mobile users based on location, or being in the right place at the right time, with mobile access to timely information.

Figure 14.12: Mobile Wikis

Mobility and the Cloud

Mobility as an interface to the cloud gives users any place, any time access to applications, media and content while the cloud vendors are responsible for deploying, managing, connecting and supporting mobile workers with built-in security and compliance features for transparency and accountability. As the market develops, vendors will be required to deliver fast, perpetual connectivity to users to satisfy critical use within the enterprise. Mobility and the cloud are a good fit because applications in the cloud gain persistency, enabling services to be delivered across a wide range of environments and runtime scenarios. What does this mean for ECM? As the mobile workforce grows, organizations will benefit from implementing a mix of cloud-based services and on-premise solutions to satisfy diverse content access and management requirements for professionals across the enterprise.

The demand for higher speed connectivity and cross-platform services will continue to expand. Cloud-based mobile services stand to deliver both strategic and tactical benefits for the enterprise, including immediate access to applications, scalability, improved productivity and business agility and increased cost savings. With guaranteed "always-on" data mobility, organizations can achieve a whole new level of productivity as users are no longer limited by time or location to do their jobs. Outsourcing IT or having the cloud manage the "heavy lifting" – data storage and infrastructure – saves organizations substantially on deploying, managing and supporting on-premise solutions. Organizations may also be able to eliminate current in-house networks and systems and the cost of supplying remote office infrastructure.

As with other platforms and infrastructures delivered in the cloud, security is a key concern. Real-time policy enforcement, remediation, and compliance reporting can eliminate security and operational gaps and improve efficiency and scalability of mobile deployments. Connectivity, management and security will be given equal play by cloud vendors, and as different levels of security are required, organizations may opt for public, hybrid and private cloud services – or a combination of all three. For more information on cloud services, please see Chapter 13.

Extending the Reach of ECM 2.0

By integrating mobile applications with the rich and powerful capabilities of ECM systems, organizations can extend mission critical aspects of their records management, compliance and legal solutions directly to the hands of every employee. This means that sensitive, controlled enterprise information can be stored, retrieved and managed immediately regardless of the mobile user's activity or location.

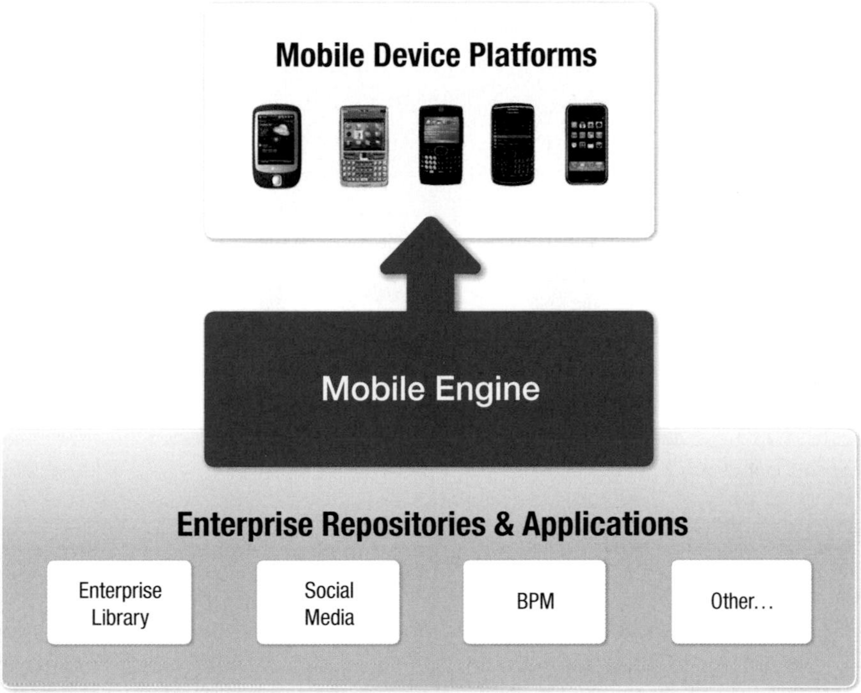

Figure 14.13: The Mobile Enterprise Framework

ECM provides an extensible content infrastructure, giving mobile users access to applications which leverage the entire enterprise ecosystem – from ERP systems to the enterprise library to process and content management solutions. With a connection to these back end repositories, mobile ECM gives users fast, easy and seamless access to an organization's IT environment, trusted corporate repository and enterprise processes directly on a mobile device. A mobile platform integrates with secure services like directory services to authenticate users and deliver all of the capabilities of an organization's back-end infrastructure directly to users on their mobile device. This model ensures that the content that is most important to an organization is managed securely and delivered expediently. This ability is not limited to documents, text and traditional content types; it also includes the ability to sort, manage and classify non-traditional content types such as social media and other rich media experiences, including high definition video.

Figure 14.14: Mobile Access to Digital Media

Mobile ECM delivers flexible solutions and applications for today's mobile workers who require constant up to date information from their enterprise. Users can quickly and easily communicate and collaborate with team members. Increased access to resources significantly improves productivity, as organizations can seize new opportunities, improve customer services and retention, and mobilize the applications its users depend on to keep business agile, responsive and moving forward.

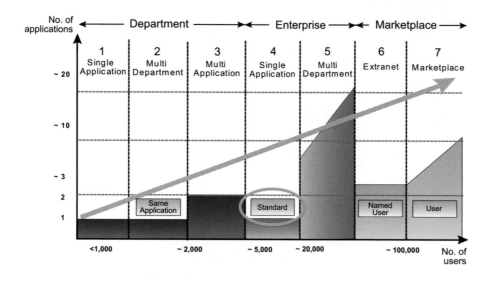

Figure 15.1: The Stages of ECM Adoption

The diagram above illustrates the stages of ECM adoption within an enterprise. It is organized along two dimensions: users and application deployed. This graph reveals the gradual adoption path of ECM, starting from a simple department application and ending with an online marketplace.

At the enterprise level, it is important to understand the process by which the organization adopts ECM solutions. As with other forms of learning and technology adoption, ECM is typically adopted within organizations in a very distinctive, staged manner.

In this chapter, we explore the complexity of enterprise deployments and outline an architectural approach that enables organizations to scale ECM to support the enterprise. To illustrate the issues encountered when installing ECM at the enterprise level, we trace the global adoption of ECM across all stages at Siemens.

CHAPTER 15

ENTERPRISE ADOPTION

With the maturation of the ECM market, it is possible to identify trends in how large Global 2000 organizations implement ECM. As more business applications are delivered using the same underlying technology, organizations will adopt enterprise-wide strategies for ECM to reduce the total cost of ownership and increase the effectiveness of existing deployments.

ECM Adoption Stages

ECM adoption can be defined in seven stages that range from the simple adoption of a departmental solution to the most complex adoption involving an entire marketplace. There are very distinct phases that an organization must go through to evolve from a single departmental deployment to a marketplace deployment.

The table below lists the basic attributes of each stage:

Stage	Description	Organization Level	Users	Applications
1	Application	Department	<1,000	Single solution
2	Multi-Department	Division	2,000+	Single to many departments
3	Multi-Application	Department/Division	2,000+	Multiple applications to one department
4	Application Standard	Enterprise	5,000+	Single application for company
5	Multi-Application	Enterprise	10,000+	Multiple applications for company
6	Extended Applications	Extranet to named users inside the firewall	20,000+	Single external application for a department
7	Multiple Extended Applications	Online Marketplace	100,000+	Multiple applications with guest access in a non-secure market

Figure 15.2: An Overview of ECM Adoption Stages

From Stage 1 to Stage 7 at Siemens

In the mid 1990s, Siemens began experimenting with ECM technologies. Initial deployments managed growing amounts of content in Web-based repositories. At the time, Siemens was adopting Web-based search technology well before these tools were on the market. With this base of experience, Siemens' IT Department introduced ECM technologies to various departments throughout the corporation. The following excerpts illustrate the evolution of departmental installs into the enterprise-wide deployment of ECM that occurred at Siemens.

Stage 1: Sales and Marketing

Most organizations adopt ECM initially to solve a departmental problem, such as accounts payable processing or customer support. At Siemens, one of the most important early applications of ECM took place in departments related to customers in sales and marketing.

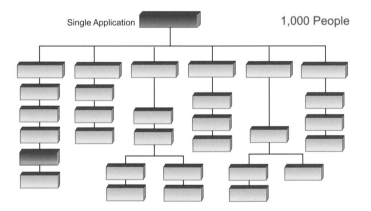

Figure 15.3: Stage 1 – Department Application

Siemens Industrial Solutions & Services (I&S) is a global supplier of electrotechnical equipment, drive systems, automation and IT solutions. To support the lifecycle of offer preparation and tendering, Siemens I&S created a customized workflow and project template. When users initiate a new offer tendering process, the system automatically creates a project and populates it with the framework for an offer in the form of a compound document. The workflow uses process steps and a dynamically generated address to send email notification to key people throughout the process.

Siemens is a global powerhouse in electrical engineering and electronics. The company has 434,000 employees working to develop and manufacture products, design and install complex systems and projects, and tailor a wide range of services for individual requirements. With a presence in 190 countries, Siemens has one of the most geographically complex and comprehensive ECM deployments in the world. The organization's global solution will provide the backdrop for effective methodology throughout this book.

"As a global company with employees all over the world, it is critical to provide our teams with tools for virtual collaboration and knowledge sharing across geographical and organizational boundaries. The ECM system serves as the backbone of the company-wide Siemens ShareNet and complementary divisional solutions, delivering capabilities that support our ability to work faster, smarter and more efficiently," says Siemens' Corporate Knowledge Officer.

Siemens' IT department introduced various ECM technologies to different business areas within the organization in a step-wise fashion. As the departments began realizing significant benefits including time and resource savings as well as improved efficiency and productivity, the final step in the ECM implementation was the creation of a corporate-wide knowledge strategy led by C-level management.

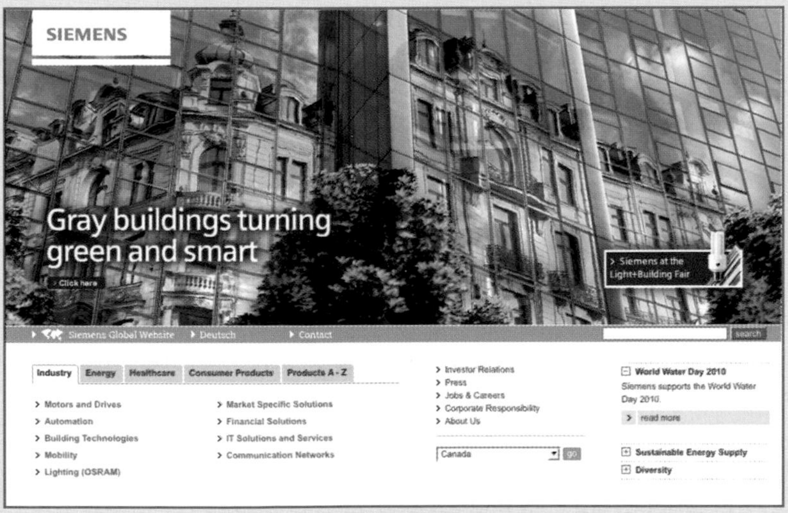

Figure 15.4: Siemens' Web Site

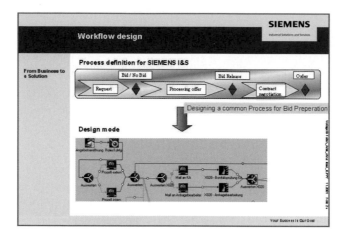

Figure 15.5: Workflow Design Drives the Bid Process at Siemens

Stage 2: Additional Departmental Applications

Stage 2 involves the adoption of the same ECM solution across departments.

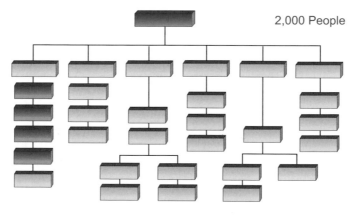

Figure 15.6: Stage 2 – Multiple Departments Deploying the Same Application

Working on cross-divisional projects, Siemens Netherlands sells, manages and executes building projects, offering professional services and consulting. To reduce the amount of time spent setting up new projects and ensure that consultants and engineers were all working from the most current version of a document, Siemens Netherlands implemented technology to facilitate collaboration within user communities and cross-divisional project teams. Capturing knowledge from collaboration means that customers benefit from best practices, project time savings and improved productivity.

At this stage, Siemens Enterprise Networks was able to develop an application called EZA. EZA pulls together all Siemens activities for a single engagement with a customer, from the time a prospect becomes a lead, through installation and final confirmation of the arrangement. As a unique approach to sales and customer engagements, the solution aids the sales force in their ability to interact with customers, business partners and internal employees.

Stage 3: Multiple Applications in Different Departments

Stage 3 is the adoption of additional solutions within the same department, as shown in Figure 15.7.

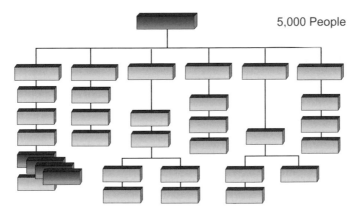

5,000 People

Figure 15.7: Stage 3 – Multiple Applications

After sales and marketing, Siemens adopted ECM at the production level in areas where employees required quick and easy access to technical information, within and outside of the organization. By this time, the sophistication of ECM deployments increased and applications included workflow and BPM elements closely integrated with content management. Collaboration began to take on a more important role in the early versions of content repositories when advanced search techniques were implemented.

OSRAM, a subsidiary of Siemens AG, is one of the leading lamp manufacturers in the world. As customers grew highly knowledgeable about the sophisticated materials and technology used to develop lighting solutions, access to technical information became increasingly important. Using content management, OSRAM's marketing department developed a solution to support its sales force with detailed technical information on thousands of lighting products. Today, when a customer asks a technical question, the sales representative has immediate access to product-related documentation that provides the answer.

Research and Development

As the need to produce technical information in electronic format increased within Siemens, the next logical step was the deployment of ECM to research and development departments. As this happened, the use of more creative forms of collaboration became widespread to increase the effectiveness of teams as they worked in shared content repositories.

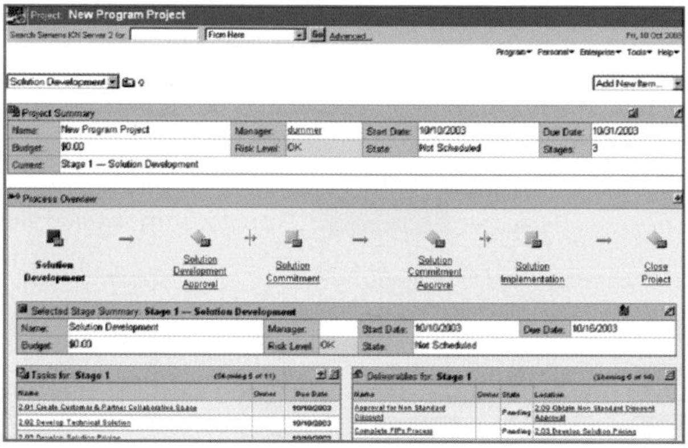

Figure 15.8: Program Management in Research and Development

Stage 4: Enterprise Standards Begin at Administration

Stage 4 represents the first time that an organization decides on an ECM solution as an enterprise standard. This stage involves the IT Department and the senior-level management team, since the implementation occurs across all departments.

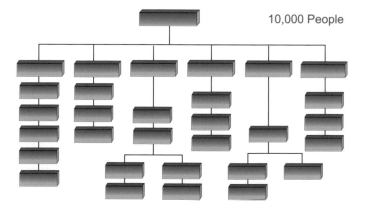

Figure 15.9: Stage 4 – Adoption at the Enterprise Level

As more divisions and departments came to rely on the Internet for communications, the administration department at Siemens followed suit and deployed an ECM solution. Company-wide, the need for compliance-driven documentation extended ECM applications to include records management and content lifecycle management technologies.

Stage 5: Enterprise Collaboration across Departments and Business Units

Stage 5 in the ECM deployment cycle at Siemens began with a corporate-wide inventory and evaluation of ECM technologies, as well as other applications that could be made more efficient. This evaluation led to the creation of a corporate-wide knowledge strategy which was led by C-Level Management. By this time, virtually all elements of an ECM system were in use at Siemens at various department and division levels. Cost reductions could be achieved by organizing these technologies into common standards across the enterprise.

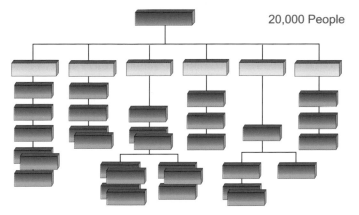

20,000 People

Figure 15.10: Stage 5 – Multi-Application Enterprise

ShareNet is the global intranet solution for Siemens Financial Services (SFS). Based on ECM technology, ShareNet provides extensive business process support, from selling products and solutions to quickly responding to customer requests and finding experts across the organization. Building efficient processes across business units and regions based on best practices, SFS can set up new projects using predefined templates in minutes.

Replacing 26 document management systems, **Siemens Enterprise Networks** developed a single, integrated knowledge management and Web publishing application for all of its product documentation, process, and procedure materials. Keeping its internal people knowledgeable about products and changes in processes, this solution for finding and disseminating key documentation is a critical part of Siemens' solution for collaborative communication with partners and customers.

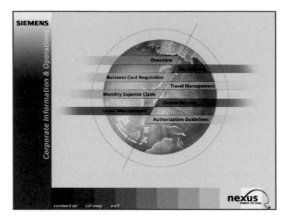

Figure 15.11: Siemens' Nexus Project

Using ECM technology, Siemens Singapore hosts a centralized standard solution called Nexus for the entire Siemens Asia and Australia region. Nexus is a Web-based, employee self-service solution that automates administrative approval processes, such as travel booking, expense claims, leave management, asset management, recruitment, purchase requisition, timesheets, and more. Tightly integrated with its ERP system, Nexus helps ensure adherence to business rules and policies.

Stage 6: Extranet Solutions by Division Application

Stage 6 extends enterprise collaboration, content and processes to include external parties, outside of the organization, in an extranet or online marketplace.

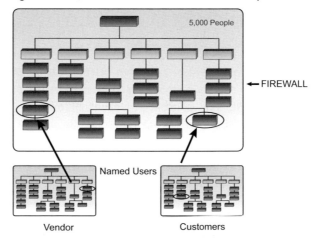

Figure 15.12: Stage 6 – Extranet

As the Systems Engineer for total solutions, **Siemens Building Technologies (SBT)** needed to collaborate and share information with seven locations and six divisions. Using an extranet solution, the organization manages all information related to building and construction projects online. ECM technology has enabled SBT to address productivity and customer satisfaction challenges caused by time consuming searches for documentation, data and images during building projects.

Stage 7: Online Marketplaces

The seventh and final stage is the Online Marketplace Stage, in which a series of extranets are extended to include a broad range of market participants, including partners, suppliers, customers and even competitors. An online marketplace functions as the main clearing house for all of the issues of a particular industry.

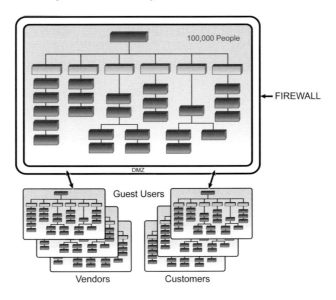

Figure 15.13: Stage 7 – Online Marketplace

Siemens Automation and Drives knows that world-class customer care is a critical part of the sales process – customer acquisition and retention. To that end, the division built a knowledge management system that relieved its Customer Support Hotline staff of supplying daily routine answers to Frequently Asked Questions (FAQs), leaving them free to aid customers with critical issues. The extranet was designed to host answers in five languages for problem-solving, downloadable software updates, and technical documentation such as end-user or service manuals.

Using the 10 years of online experience at Siemens with ECM, we have illustrated how an initial ECM deployment occurs at the department level and expands to other departments and divisions. After consolidating several applications on a common infrastructure, organizations begin to consider a full enterprise-wide implementation of an ECM solution.

ECM Solutions Framework

The diagram below shows how different ECM solutions can be built on an ECM Solutions Framework. This Framework provides a layer of software services that link corporate applications to repositories of information, no matter where they reside. The three key services are engagement, lifecycle and transaction.

Figure 15.14: ECM Solutions Framework

The ECM Solutions Framework is completed by integrating these user interfaces and foundational services with business services such as content management, records management and Web content management. Competitive advantage is created because the framework simplifies the deployment of ECM solutions that span the enterprise and extend into the supply chain. Solutions built on the ECM Solutions Framework provide a consistent view of content to the user regardless of what device they are using to access applications – in the office on a PC or on the road using a smartphone – with access controlled by their role as defined for each process.

> Motorola

Motorola is a global leader in integrated communications solutions and embedded electronic solutions. A consolidated ECM system serves as the foundation for Motorola's COMPASS system, a global intranet that acts as a central repository for information and a place for collaboration and enterprise-level communication. "COMPASS gives us a way to bring people and information together under one system. It's the primary location where people share information and collaborate. Improved communication and access to information are helping project teams work together more effectively and that, ultimately, has a positive effect on the way we serve our customers," says the Manager of Content Management and Collaboration Systems, Motorola.

With databases dispersed throughout the company, it was important for Motorola to centralize its information repository and make it accessible from anywhere throughout the organization. When Motorola implemented ECM, their system had to support 55,000 plus users and logins for guests and 35.5 million documents at 86.6 terabytes. Motorola's deployment of COMPASS may well be one of the largest in the world.

Motorola's ECM system has allowed them to build project areas that could be extended to include their customers, suppliers and business partners in a secure extranet. In just the first month of implementation, 308 project areas and 833 external users were added to the system.

Figure 15.15: Centralized Access to Global Content, Resources and Expertise

Scaling to the Enterprise

The evolution toward connecting more people with more computers places new demands on ECM technology; not the least of which is the burden placed on a system to accommodate an increasing number of users. Functionality within a system has to scale to accommodate each new user, their associated files and memory requirements.

For example, a search technology that can handle 1,000 people and their documents may not scale to handle 100,000 people and their documents. This is a key issue when considering the eventual usage profile and patterns of single departmental ECM deployment and how this will evolve over time within the enterprise. All of the component technologies for ECM must scale. If one component technology fails to scale, the entire ECM implementation will fail. The chain is only as strong as its weakest link. The technologies required to scale ECM deployments include the cost of network connections, bandwidth, memory and CPU. Innovations in ECM have been driven by the enabling technologies of bandwidth and server performance. Today, deployments supporting 100,000 people or more and terabytes of data are possible.

A large part of Motorola's success is due to their continuous monitoring of system availability and response time, as illustrated in the chart below.

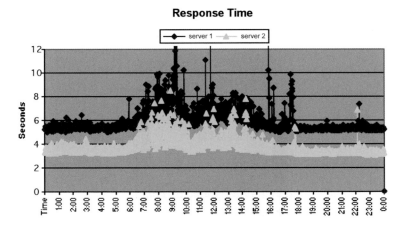

Figure 15.16: Server Response Times

Today, Motorola's system configuration includes a central cluster consisting of multiple tiers and a global network that also performs routing and caching functions for optimal access regardless of office location. The cluster architecture includes a grid of load balancers, Web servers, front-end application servers, background process servers, database servers and storage servers that has expanded over time to meet growing usage requirements.

Planning Enterprise Deployment

How can you ensure success when deploying ECM technology throughout a large, multinational corporation and across its supply chain? It is obvious that such an endeavor requires careful planning and ongoing change management. Best practices, along with user training and tying ECM to business processes are critical success factors. An examination of large-scale ECM deployments reveals the best practices that can help to organizations gain user acceptance of ECM systems in a properly structured enablement program.

Organizations seeking to deploy an ECM solution across the enterprise should understand and communicate the business needs that will be addressed by the ECM system and understand and address barriers that may affect adoption by new users, such as usability issues or required integration with other systems. In order to track the success of rollout, an organization should establish quantitative indicators and measures throughout the system's lifecycle.

Training is essential in helping the enterprise roll out an effective ECM system. A training requirements assessment can help organizations to:

- Improve user adoption by providing executive sponsors, managers, users and administrators with the business context and strategic benefits of the application and clear learning paths beyond the initial setup and deployment to business units.

- Reduce time to train and to prepare training. Acquiring specific and detailed learning objectives for each learning group reduces the time it takes to develop and deliver training.

- Ensure the sustainability of training through tools that enable the organization to continue to support users, for example quick reference guides, videos and e-learning, with each reflecting the business context and processes of the organization.

- Reduce reliance on help desk support staff. With an improved level of knowledge in the day-to-day use of the tools, a reduction in technical support can be anticipated.

- Ensure a healthy, secure ECM environment by providing knowledge managers, trainers and system administrators with the right training to use new tools effectively.

- Improved quality and value of information. Users that understand the value of the system will store and extend information that is valuable.

The following user story featuring the European Investment Bank illustrates the effective employment of these best practices.

> European Investment Bank

European Investment Bank

The European Investment Bank (EIB) finances capital investment in European Union policy objectives – the bricks and mortar that are constructing an integrated Europe. The bank also partially funds operations in approximately 150 countries outside Europe. This means that remote access to documents is operationally important, especially for countries with relatively weak telecom networks.

To improve access to content, EIB has implemented an ECM solution called GED as part of a broader IT reengineering program affecting all of the major processes in the bank: borrowing, lending and administration. The integration of GED with the other systems and with the user's work environment is critical to its success. For that reason, GED is fully integrated with other IT systems.

To ensure that users would adopt the ECM system, the project team planned how to market the system, developing an "elevator speech" to ensure that everyone understood that "all vital documents in the bank must be created, modified, signed, stored, indexed and available in structured folders" within the system. However, they soon realized that it was not practical for people to use the GED system for vital documents only. The system is in fact destined to receive all electronic documents in the bank, regardless of their importance.

Very early on in the GED project, the implementation team realized that a design is never finished and that the iterative process is unavoidable. They adopted a system approach that relies heavily on process analysis and the interpretation of more than 550 varieties of documents produced by the organization.

"I call this practice corporate hermeneutics," says GED's Project Manager. "In the spirit of Gadamer, hermeneutics means looking at an answer to find the question that it responds to. This is a very interesting activity to carry out on corporate documents and one which has not been formalized anywhere yet."

In planning for the GED system, the EIB developed a bank-wide taxonomy, the most visible element of which is the file plan. The EIB taxonomy follows international best practice and more specifically the DIRKS methodology and is consistent with ISO 15489. An access control model was developed for the higher levels of the taxonomy. The taxonomy model has become the basis for content management. The taxonomy fully describes the bank processes. In parallel, the permission model indicates who needs to have access to what to be able to work most efficiently. The combination of the two models and the mapping of the roles onto the file plan produces the knowledge map of the organization.

The GED project adopted a gradual approach over an eight-month period. In particular, training was carried out by two certified, in-house trainers over a six-month period.

There is also a plan to give an internal official recognition to users who have reached a particular proficiency with the system.

Virtually everyone in the bank was trained, including senior management. There was a conscious decision to cater simultaneously, but sometimes with different means to all levels of the organization. It was essential not only to convince top-level executives, but also to ensure that secretaries willingly adopt the new tool. Therefore, the project team included users from the start. In addition to the traditional steering committee, a high-level working group contributed directly to the design. This group, made up of mostly secretaries, met every two weeks and was instrumental in keeping people at all levels informed on the status of the project. They contributed very significantly to the development of the taxonomy and continue to constitute a network of proficient users who help the system develop.

At the outset of the project, the team set quantitative indicators of the project's success. Two months into the launch of the GED system they were able to measure that their user adoption was 20 percent higher than expected. 100 percent of vital documents and new lending and borrowing operations were being supported and there were already 600,000 documents in the system – increasing at a rate of 100,000 documents per week.

Globalization

Enterprise deployments also present another challenge when managing content: language. Unlike databases where one plus one equals two in any language, the subtleties of human language and culture play a role in the effectiveness in global deployments of content management systems. Every technology covered in this book is affected by language, whether it is searching for words in another language, or holding an online meeting over the Internet in multiple time zones with multiple languages. This is particularly true for symbolic languages which are generally found in Asia. Japanese and Chinese are examples of languages with symbolic character sets. This presents unique challenges in how an entire enterprise can make use of all information within it, regardless of source language.

ワークフローマップ: ワークフローマップ
移動 ...
マップエディタ
ワークフローマップ
スタート
開始者
評価
開発グループ
マイルストーン
グループ2
プロパティ
保存
名前を付けて保存 ...
開始
開発第一課
開発第2課
サブワークフロー

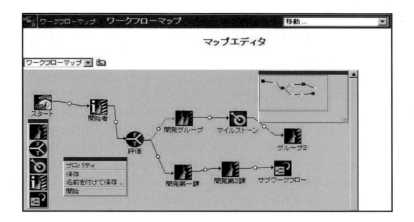

Figure 15.17: A Workflow Written in Japanese

Each ECM application may need to provide multiple user interfaces in the various languages of the individuals who participate in a global process. Content must be stored, searched and displayed regardless of the language in which it was originally written. If necessary, ECM applications can be designed to store content that is translated into multiple languages so that anyone can perform their tasks in their own language. Other globalization challenges that must be considered when designing ECM applications include: date formats, time formats, time zones, currency and advanced language-specific search features (for example, natural language query parsing, stemming and thesaurus).

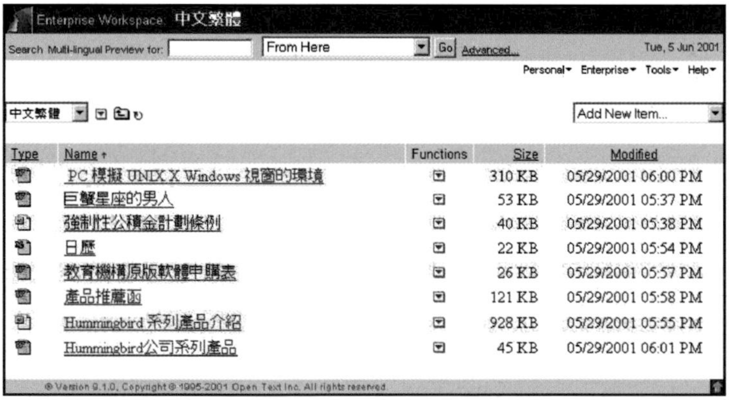

Enterprise Workspace: 中文繁體
Search Multi-lingual Preview for:
From Here
Go
Advanced...
Tue, 5 Jun 2001
Personal Enterprise Tools Help
中文繁體
Add New Item...
Type Name Functions Size Modified
PC 模擬 UNIX X Windows 視窗的環境 310 KB 05/29/2001 06:00 PM
巨蟹星座的男人 53 KB 05/29/2001 05:37 PM
強制性公積金計劃條例 40 KB 05/29/2001 05:38 PM
日曆 22 KB 05/29/2001 05:54 PM
教育機構原版軟體申購表 26 KB 05/29/2001 05:57 PM
產品推薦函 121 KB 05/29/2001 05:58 PM
Hummingbird 系列產品介紹 928 KB 05/29/2001 05:55 PM
Hummingbird公司系列產品 45 KB 05/29/2001 06:01 PM
® Version 9.1.0, Copyright © 1995-2001 Open Text Inc. All rights reserved.

Figure 15.18: A Collection of Documents Written in Traditional Chinese

Sprint, a global communications company, required an infrastructure to consolidate the use of servers and centralize the storage of electronic documents – essentially, the telecommunications giant wanted to create a common path for "knowledge discovery" within Sprint.

Sprint deployed ECM to create a Web-based knowledge repository to store customer circuit data in its Network Operating Center (NOC), allowing the company to move from a paper-based system to an electronic document management solution. ECM provides a Web-based repository for storing accounts payable invoices and managing Sprint employee expense report receipts linked to an intranet-based reimbursement system.

Today, Sprint has developed an ECM solution that is based upon an enterprise scalable platform for document management, project coordination and process improvement. The ability to search and retrieve information online empowers Sprint employees to leverage the company's core competencies to efficiently solve business problems.

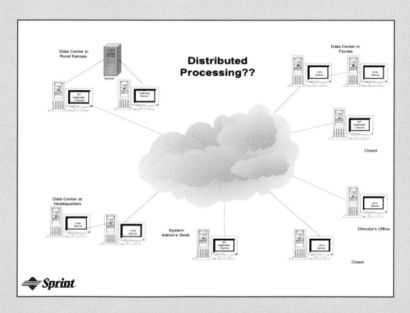

Figure 15.19: Distributed Processing at Sprint

A global consortium of interested parties has developed a universal character set, called unicode that supports every written language used on earth (and even some that are not). The broad adoption of unicode across the various ECM technologies will make it easier to support global applications.

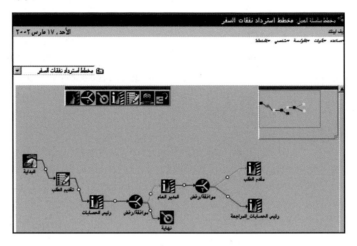

Figure 15.20: A Workflow Written in Arabic

ECM at the Enterprise Level

In this chapter we reviewed how some of the largest organizations in the world are adopting ECM to increase productivity. Previous chapters have demonstrated how ECM improves business operations by enabling organization to achieve compliance with various government regulations and standards. As ECM is adopted on a wider scale, the total cost of ownership (TCO) is reduced and further deployments gain increasing economic leverage to deliver applications. As witnessed with other technology adoptions – from email to Web sites and digital media – organizations throughout the world are adopting ECM at the enterprise level to maintain competitiveness in the face of compliance and productivity pressures.

Figure 16.1: The Future of ECM

As illustrated throughout this book, organizations are rethinking their content strategies based on growing volumes of content, networks being formed inside and outside the firewall, technology developments and the storage systems required to house enterprise content. ECM 2.0 is already being transformed by advances in Web-based, search and mobile technologies. ECM 3.0 will be based on applications of Web 3.0 technology; it will be personal, portable and immersive.

So now that you know something about ECM, what will tomorrow look like? Read on to discover how our future will be revolutionized by ECM, social media in the cloud, and wireless technologies.

CHAPTER 16

ECM AND THE FUTURE

ECM 3.0 will be driven by applications that exploit the growth and sophistication of Web 3.0 technologies like social networking, cloud-based services and mobility. Web 3.0 is the Semantic Web, which delivers an intelligent online environment that understands the meaning and context of content as it is being consumed. This last dimension delivers a new freedom for computing, and the implications will be substantial.

Search engines are the hub of the Semantic Web. Semantically-based search engines will understand queries by filtering out ambiguous terms from a searcher's true intent, as well as the structure, entities, concepts and relationships between all content in a document or on a page. Text mining functionality, including entity extraction, sentiment analysis and ontology, promise to transform search on the Semantic Web by adding a layer of analytics to deepen the understanding of content and meaning.

Content is instilled with value when the human element is introduced to search technologies, as social networks, immersive reality and mobile access are combined with text mining and concept-based search. Social media will be increasingly applied for its ability to improve how organizations discover and organize knowledge; Facebook is already outpacing Google in total site "hits" and may overtake search sites on the Internet for human-intervened search.

Web 3.0 application design will focus on cloud computing and Web-scale programming as enablers for innovation. Organizations will quickly and easily prototype and test lightweight applications. Service-oriented access will allow these applications to scale and be customized. User generated content is already being replaced by user generated applications, or the ability to create Web-based applications like mashups.

Within the enterprise, Web 3.0 applications will be required to address specific business needs to be widely adopted. A Web that understands meaning and context benefits users, systems and organizations. When we consider the network effect of tagging and linking content across the organization, Web 3.0 technologies hold great potential to enrich content by providing referential value.

> ## Compassion International

Compassion International is a child advocacy ministry that works to help more than one million children in 26 countries by partnering with churches, parents, and communities to teach, train and mentor children in third-world and developing countries.

Compassion's globally dispersed partner offices help to produce a mixture of marketing collateral, including newsletters, flyers, brochures, mailers, and a magazine a couple of times a year, so an integrated, globally sharable solution is essential to managing these and other marketing assets. Although the organization already had a digital asset management solution, it was unable to continue meeting the organization's needs as it grew; search, control, and usability requirements were not being met, and Compassion knew it was time for change. Out of frustration, people started coming up with their own workarounds: an FTP site, emails, network drives, disks, and so on. All of the organization's material was widely dispersed, loosely controlled and no one had any idea what media and marketing materials Compassion really had.

To manage their marketing assets, Compassion implemented a Media Management solution. By centralizing their content, Compassion partners and employees can efficiently repurpose photos, articles, Web site content, and digital audio and video media to reduce research time and increase productivity. Users can easily find, access, edit, share, reuse, distribute, and archive their digital assets, all within unique workflows and using the desktop applications of their choice.

Figure 16.2: Compassion's Media Management System, "MAX"

Future Trends

In the future, ECM 3.0 will deliver relevant, social, multi-channel, immersive and secure content experiences. This vision will be based on the following aspects:

Relevance

Search engine sites are now capturing more than one trillion Web pages. Many organizations make hundreds of thousands of content items available on their Web sites. Large commerce sites handle several thousand products. Intranets store incredible amounts of unstructured data. The challenge is helping users find the exact information they are looking for. People expect a Web experience that gives them the content they desire, based on their needs, their persona and their intent. If this happens at home; it should happen in the office as well. Millennials as "digital natives" will exert tremendous influence on ECM 3.0 technologies; as they enter the workforce, they will expect to connect with their network on topics that are relevant to them. Accordingly, the online experience will become much a more tailored and personalized experience.

Multi-Channel

Every year a growing percentage of mobile customers are using smartphones with large screens, high speed Internet access and powerful browsers to access Web content. Beyond phones, Web content is being published to car navigation systems, intelligent devices, widgets, RSS feeds and other channels. As the devices used every day get smarter and more connected, consumers have almost unlimited access to information in more places and in more convenient ways.

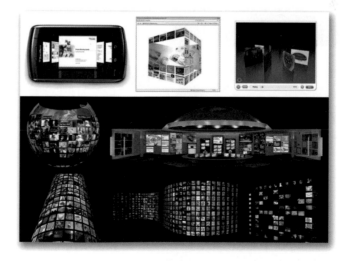

Figure 16.3: Access to Content Crosses Applications, Devices and Platforms

Mobile smartphones, social networks, blogs, and wikis are just some of the capabilities that require organizations to support the distribution of and access to content across applications, devices and platforms. One can envision more than a trillion devices being Internet-protocol ready for content.

Based on Web 3.0 applications, digital experience management (DEM) will support cross-platform distribution, facilitating next-generation immersive collaboration, viral distribution and document syndication. The combination of Web syndication with content management and the enterprise repository will transform media management into the mainstream enterprise enabler for all types of rich media-oriented use cases – from creation through to consumption. Web content management, as another distribution channel, has great potential to embrace Web 3.0 capabilities and deliver immersive digital experiences to help organizations attract customers. Social media will continue to be used for viral distribution and mashups of video content will enable the reproduction and redistribution of content.

Figure 16.4: Immersive Digital Media

In the future, organizations will be required to develop business models that support the widespread sharing of content and simultaneously, ensure that this content can be managed and tracked as assets across repositories, social networks, Web sites and more.

Accessible

Instead of sending emails in the future, people will be sharing ideas in face-to-face conversations hosted by rich media technology. This evolution will improve productivity as the technology becomes more intuitive and easier to use. As a result, ECM 3.0 will be available on a mass level, heralding the final stage of ECM adoption throughout the computing world. Because rich media places greater demands on bandwidth, storage and processing power than other forms of media, it will become an increasing challenge for organizations to manage. As digital media develops, ECM architecture will integrate "slow zone" collaboration with "fast zone" bandwidths until the transition is complete. The ability to search on these objects will require further advances to be made in retrieval algorithms. While this is achievable, it remains a growing challenge in the implementation of ECM solutions.

Social

The original Web was about companies publishing information and marketing materials online. In the e-commerce days, the Web supported transactions between one user and one company. Web 2.0 made the Web a place where people connect to each other, where users are empowered to create and share content and where customers expect to find content created by companies and other consumers, like themselves.

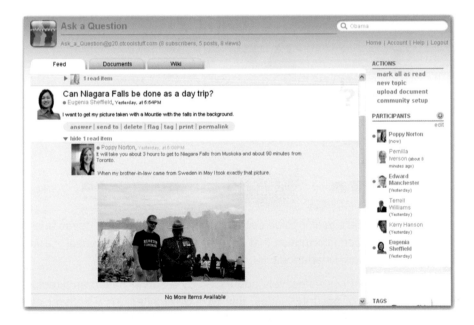

Figure 16.5: Influential Content is Valuable Enterprise Content

As social media is increasingly accepted inside the firewall, security is another factor that will impact ECM 3.0 and the rest of the computer industry. Peer-to-peer or influential content will be regarded as valuable enterprise content, and organizations will need to deliver an interface that allows people to move easily and securely between workplace and marketplace content, resources and expertise.

Secure

As applications move from the consumer sphere into the world of business, issues around security will need to be addressed to enable adoption and integration of Web-based applications and services. As content is distributed, across a variety of mediums, applications and repositories, organizations will need to guarantee that content is secure and protected. Permissioned access to information, based on roles and profiles within an organization will have to be guaranteed at the granular level, across workplace and marketplace networks.

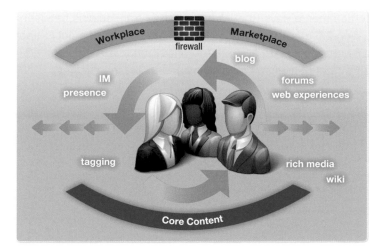

Figure 16.6: Seamless and Secure Access to Workplace and Marketplace Content

Privacy is a key issue that sits alongside security when we consider the devastating effects of lost, stolen or misplaced information that is either personal or confidential – from both a personal and organizational standpoint.

Security issues are most cost-effectively addressed by a server-based architecture. With heightened awareness of security issues, this type of architecture – content stored on central servers with user access via desktop GUIs – is becoming the standard. A server-based architecture also makes it easier to control the information needed for regulatory

> Royal Shakespeare Company

The Royal Shakespeare Company (RSC) is one of the world's best-known theatre companies, performing every year to a million theater goers across the world. The RSC's ultimate mission is to bring the works of Shakespeare to life for audiences in the 21st Century. In the last ten years, the Company has mounted 171 new productions, given 19,000 performances, sold 11 million tickets, and played in 150 towns and cities in the UK and around the globe.

The Company was quick to recognize that an engaging, dynamic Web site would be the most effective way to communicate and interact with its growing worldwide audience. The site was already considered to be at the heart of the Company, however keeping it up to date with the latest information was proving to be an arduous and time-intensive project. Traditionally, the RSC's eight-strong technical team, together with the RSC Web Editor, was responsible for handling everything from advance bookings and online gift shopping to managing the 500-plus pages of content on the site, which include 3,500 images.

To improve the Web site's usability, functionality, and overall user experience, RSC managers implemented a Web content management solution. The intuitive technology enables content management to be placed firmly in the hands of the experts, writers, and editors who are now in charge of developing new material for the site – with minimal training. The robustness of the solution was demonstrated when the RSC exported its intuitive navigation tools to link seamlessly with the Company's Box Office, improving the online shopping functionality on the site. Following the rapid implementation of the WCM solution, the technical team has dramatically reduced its support to the Web site and content can be uploaded to the site in a fraction of the time.

Figure 16.7: Royal Shakespeare Company's Web Site

compliance. Many regulations require an audit trail of information and actions. This involves enforcing higher levels of security for content storage and access.

Legislated

A significant trend affecting ECM is the global increase in legislation. Regulators are seeking good governance and accountability through transparency. Transparency is achieved by the diligent recording of all decisions made, including the collaborative pro-cesses and documents involved. This will extend across every form of corporate commu-nication – from email to instant messaging (IM) to social computing. If it is digital, it will be discovered; virtually all content will be recorded with a proper audit trail. This will continue to be a challenge for ECM in the future.

Organizations in key industries need to demonstrate that they are compliant with all regulations, both old and new. The amount of work required to comply is enormous. Amendments made to the FRCP legislation, for example, have created an immense change in the way public corporations monitor and record decision making and reporting. Increased regulation means that organizations will receive more inquiries in the form of discovery orders, audits and so on. The information required often spans multiple applications and storage devices. ECM 2.0 delivers a consolidated window into all enterprise content, enabling a timely and cost-effective solution for information governance and regulatory requirements.

Immersive

Simulation and gaming environments present complex, multi-component systems, enabling users to create new identities and immerse themselves in new realities. Computer simulations have been used in engineering, as well as for training in the military and aviation industries for decades. In an enterprise environment, this kind of simulation can accelerate learning, facilitate knowledge transfer and allow users to extract meaning from complex systems.

Figure 16.8: Immersive Access to Content

> California Public Utilities Commission

The California Public Utilities Commission (CPUC) regulates privately owned electric, natural gas, telecommunications, water, railroad, rail transit, and passenger transportation companies in addition to authorizing video franchises. This involves filing and managing thousands of documents for new applications, complaints, investigations, and policy rulemakings. Filers range from law firms and utilities to small businesses and individuals. The paper files involved in these processes was very intensive, and the CPUC needed a system that enabled quick and easy filing, more efficient management of the documents, and better access for the general public.

In terms of compliance, the CPUC knew they needed to do something to keep their files in order. Because they are required by law to retain and archive the files, they needed to make sure that files, which are official records of the CPUC, are intact and easy to find. Electronic filing with document management provides the CPUC with not only better access to public information, more efficient management of documents, and a major savings in paper, it also has had the added benefits of reduced processing time, greater opportunities for staff and very satisfied clients.

The CPUC has an impressive 92 percent e-filing rate. They have somewhere around 6,000 or 7,000 electronically filed documents per year, representing around 1,000 unique filer names. It took CPUC staff approximately two days to process a paper document as opposed to only a third of a day to process an e-filed document. With an ROI like that, the CPUC is pleased with their results.

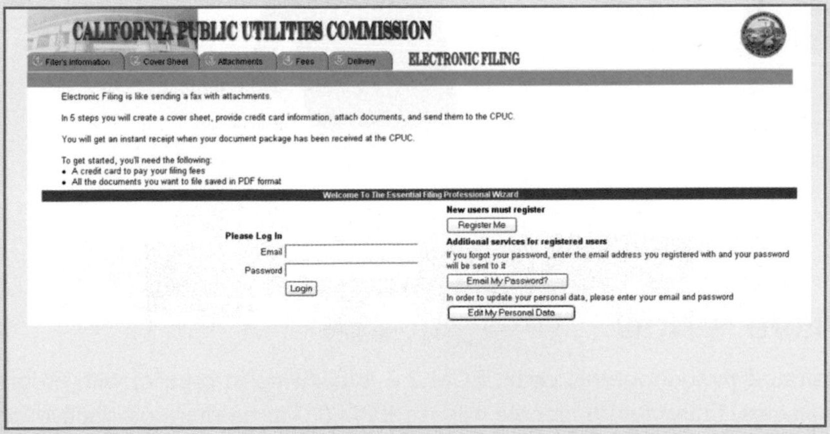

Figure 16.9: California Public Utilities Commission's E-File Web Site

As we have seen with gaming environments, 3-dimensional renderings are replacing 2-dimensional virtual experiences. Internet users are already able to adopt a virtual identity or avatar and create, modify, share and customize every aspect of their virtual world, as in Second Life (www.secondlife.com), a 3-dimensional dedicated social network. In the future, these virtual scenes will interoperate with an office environment, integrate with social networks and permit mobile access to rich and integrated digital media. Users will be able to interact virtually to combine online and offline experiences.

Virtual reality does more than create presence-awareness between users online. Within a business context, virtual reality gives users the ability to find things using a location metaphor. This becomes very powerful as users will be able to intervene on a search and "lead" searchers to information. Virtual reality leads to enhanced information discovery, and people will be able to find things faster and more easily.

Figure 16.10: People Assume Virtual Reality Identities Using Avatars

The Future is Now

As demonstrated throughout this book, ECM 2.0 is evolving in parallel with progressive Web technologies. In the future, people will use ECM 3.0 to be more productive; companies will deploy ECM to become more efficient and agile. Because it defines a better way to work, ECM 2.0 will continue to expand in scope and scale. In the future, millions of ECM users will become billions of users as ECM becomes commonplace.

Organizations will build trust by bringing together employees, customers, partners,

Open Text Corporation is a leading provider of enterprise content management software (ECM 2.0) solutions, helping organizations manage and gain the true value of their business content. Following its customer-centric approach, Open Text has been offering customers access to their own "brand network", called the Knowledge Center, run on Open Text's ECM 2.0 platform.

Delivering mission-critical services to Open Text customers and partners, the site supports over half a million documents and 52,000 users from all over the globe – Asia/Pacific, Europe, Middle East, North and South America, everywhere – making it one of the top 20 systems in the world. Customers use the site for support; it facilitates logging, updating, and reporting on all issue tickets; downloads for all core product upgrades; patches and fixes; and it offers completely secure social collaboration for customer projects – with social media tools like wikis, communities and an online forum called the Discussion Zone. Using these tools, customers can interact with one another and the brand, providing feedback and making feature requests directly to developers, trainers and consultants within the company. The Knowledge Center as a brand network enables customers to collaborate and innovate with one another to deepen relationships and build trust with the organization.

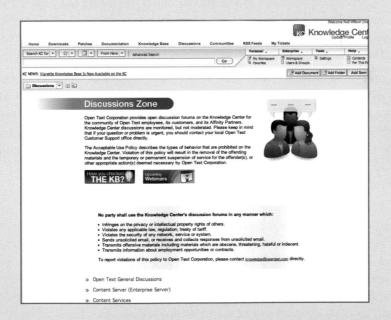

Figure 16.11: Using Social Media to Facilitate Customer Conversations

suppliers and other stakeholders using the Web as a platform for improved collaboration and communications.

Proximity marketing and complex analytics will drive customer engagement. Marketing organizations will track, monitor and measure consumer behavior and sentiment to deliver tailored and targeted experiences based on role, industry or personal preference. Peer influence will continue to grow in importance. Tools such as blogging and online forums are already enabling direct participation with customers at a very personal and trusted level.

Brand experience is being taken to a whole new level as organizations give up control over content and empower their customers to interact directly with one another. Organizations are already using social media to create trust and build "brand networks" around consumers and brands. While marketing leads the way, customer support and research and development departments will follow suit to interact more directly with customers to collect feedback and ignite collaborative conversations. These conversations will form the basis of innovative products and services, and sustain competitive advantage. Videos will replace traditional paper-based manuals. Simulation and advanced gaming environments, along with digital media, will dramatically impact the common understanding of cognition and learning processes.

The social marketplace will extend to include partners and suppliers – building loyalty between all organizations involved in the supply chain. Involving external stakeholders in an online community will streamline production, development and efficiencies. Critical information will be transparent, secure and easy to access. Improvements will take place globally as organizations are seamlessly incorporated into an organization's processes.

Inside the social workplace, retention rates, employee satisfaction and overall productivity will improve as networks form organically around areas of expertise, topics of interest and projects. If social collaboration is not available inside the enterprise, digital natives will bring these technologies to the enterprise. This has already happened with mashups and the development of composite applications. As content becomes more dimensional, digital and portable, ECM 3.0 will follow suit – becoming more flexible, multi-platform and secure.

So now you know that the next great idea, the next breakthrough, the next innovation, resides within the collective knowledge of connected people. This is the motivation that has driven ECM innovations from the start. By enabling great minds to work together across organizational and geographical boundaries, ECM 2.0 unleashes potential and gives businesses room to grow. It ensures that companies evolve according to defined procedures and in accordance with standards and regulations. For this reason, ECM is currently being used by every sector of the economy, by all industries and by firms of all sizes. It makes global companies as nimble as start-ups and gives small firms the global reach to deliver sophisticated, professional products and services using immersive, social networks.

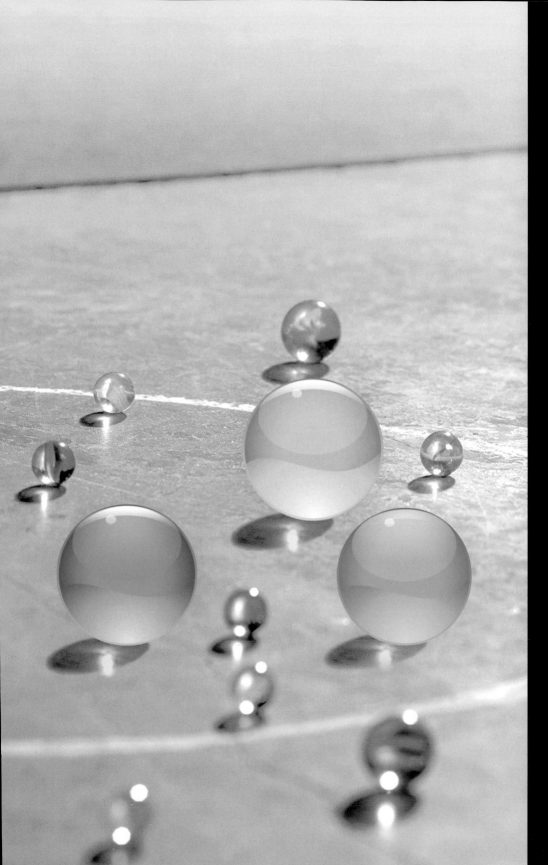

GLOSSARY

3D Virtual Environments – See Virtual Reality.

3G (also 3rd Generation or International Mobile Telecommunications-2000 (IMT-2000) - A family of standards for mobile telecommunications defined by the International Telecommunication Union. Services include wide-area wireless voice telephone, video calls, and wireless data, all in a mobile environment. Compared to 2G and 2.5G services, 3G networks deliver simultaneous use of speech and data services and higher data rates, allowing network operators to offer users a wider range of more advanced services while achieving greater network capacity.

Adobe Acrobat - A program that converts electronic files to Portable Document Format (PDF). PDF files can be viewed and printed via Adobe Reader on a variety of platforms.

Advanced Search - A variety of software tools that allow users to get more relevant search results. These tools include Boolean Operators, Stemming, Adjacency and Proximity Searches, Thesauri and Synonyms.

AJAX – See Asynchronous JavaScript and XML

API – See Application Programming Interface.

Application - Software or programs used to execute tasks on computers.

Application Programming Interface (API) - An interface implemented by a software program to enable interaction with other software, much in the same way that a user interface facilitates interaction between humans and computers.

Application Service Provider (ASP) - A company that offers Internet access to applications and related services that otherwise would have to be present on users' personal or enterprise computers.

Archive (verb) - Systematic transfer to alternate storage media of digital data of continuing value that is no longer required to be immediately accessible. Often stored on Computer Output to Laser Disk (COLD) systems.

Archives (noun) - Records and digital assets systematically identified as having enduring legal, evidentiary or historical value and permanently preserved in the context of their creation as evidence of action, decision and transaction. 'Archives' also refers to the department or institution entrusted with this task.

Asynchronous JavaScript and XML (AJAX) - The development of dynamic, interactive Web sites through communication between browsers and Web servers via XML.

Automatic Categorization - Classification of information based on pre-defined or user-created taxonomies.

Avatars –With the increased personalization and the abstraction of different roles within different contexts, Web 2.0 permits an advanced form of identification of similar roles or functions. The use of avatars permits the assumption of changing role identities where appropriate, such as assuming a role in a call center or an attendee at a virtual conference.

Bandwidth - The volume of information per unit time that a computer, person or transmission medium can handle.

Blog (also Web Log) - A chronological and topic-oriented collection of entries posted on a Web page. Typically, blogs communicate an author's point of view and solicit feedback in the form of comments which can be posted with the blog.

Blogosphere - All blogs as a connected community on the Internet.

Boolean Operators - Logical connectors used within advanced search software to obtain more relevant results.

Broadband - Relating to or being a communications network in which the bandwidth can be divided and shared by multiple simultaneous signals (as for voice or data or video).

Browser - See Internet browser.

Business Activity Monitoring (BAM) - Configurable dashboards that aggregate and present real-time information about process execution, such as throughput, service-level agreements, and backlog. Business activity monitoring (BAM) dashboards typically present gauges, charts, and graphs that combine process data with business data.

Business Applications - Software programs used to solve business needs such as word processing, accounting or customer relationship management.

Business Intelligence (BI) - A technology for analysis of information contained in structured data. It is the structured counter-part to content analytics.

Business Process Management (BPM) - Refers to aligning processes with an organization's strategic objectives, designing and implementing process-centric tools or architectures and determining measurement systems for effective process management.

Calendaring - Collaboration software used to schedule time on an individual, team or enterprise basis.

Cascading Style Sheets (CSS) - A style sheet language used to describe the look and formatting of a document written in a markup language. It is most common application is to style Web pages written in HTML and XHTML.

Categorization - Technology that maps content assets into categories of a taxonomy. For records management, 'classification' does mapping of a record (content asset) against a category in a file plan (taxonomy).

Central Processing Unit (CPU) - The part of a computer that does most of the data processing. The CPU and the memory form the central part of a computer to which peripherals are attached.

Chat (also Instant Messaging or IM) - Real-time instant messaging and other forms of chat within the context of an overall topic, Web site or meeting space.

Classification - A technology that groups content into classes, usually based on dynamic clusters resulting from the patterns in the content sample.

Client Server - A system of sharing files and executing applications within a local or wide-area network.

Cloud Computing ("The Cloud") – A metaphor inspired by the cloud symbol used to represent the Internet in flow charts and diagrams, Cloud computing describes the disruptive transformation of IT toward a service-based economy, driven by economic, technological and cultural conditions.

Cluster Computing - A group of linked computers, working together closely so that in many respects they form a single computer. The components of a cluster are commonly connected to each other over fast local area networks. Clusters are deployed to improve performance and/or availability over that of a single computer, and are more cost-effective than single computers of comparable speed or availability.

Collaboration Software - Programs that link processes and individuals across different locations and time zones to create an environment where team members work together to share ideas, experiences and knowledge.

Commenting - Adding online comments to social media to add value, including commenting on online documents, blogs, wikis and more.

Community of Practice (CoP) - A self-organizing collection of people who collaborate and share resources to support work in a specific field. Organizations develop communities of practice to facilitate knowledge transfer and collaboration between employees, promoting productivity and fostering innovation through the act of sharing, refining and distributing best practices.

Compliance - Adherence to a body of regulations, government legislation or standards (for example, ISO 9000).

Composite Applications - Model-driven development environments that rely on graphical process modeling tools to support direct interpretation of the models into executable code. The technical concept can be compared to mashups, however, composite applications use business sources of information, while mashups typically rely on Web-based sources.

Compound Documents - Large, complex documents that are authored in chapters or sections, with different organizations, departments or individuals responsible for each component.

Compound Objects - Documents and images converted to a Web-viewable format and treated as a single object.

Concept Extraction - The capability of content analytics to identify phrases, keywords, nouns, etc. Also known as speech tagging.

Conferencing - Real-time meetings between groups over the Web. In organizations, these meetings facilitate the exchange of synchronous information, such as collaboration around presentations or spreadsheets, on white boards and shared screens.

Connectors - In database management, a link or pointer between two data structures.

Content Analytics - A technology for analysis of information contained in content. It allows customers to optimize user experience by dynamically serving up content based on automatically created content relevance.

Content Lifecycle Management (CLM) - The combination of document management, records management, workflow, archiving, and imaging into a fully integrated solution to effectively manage the lifecycle of content, from creation through to archiving and eventual deletion.

Content Management - Storage, maintenance and retrieval of HTML and XML documents and all related elements. Content management systems may be built on top of a native XML database and typically provide publishing capabilities to export content not only to the Web site but to CD-ROM and print.

Content Syndication (also Web Syndication) – A form of syndication which makes Web site content available to multiple sites, often in the form of Web feeds delivering summaries of recently added or updated content.

Contextual Information (Collaboration) - Smaller services/objects that can be embedded in business applications.

Control - A program module or routine that enhances program functionality. A control can be as small as a button on a user interface or as large as a complicated forecasting algorithm. The term is often used with regard to user interface functions such as buttons, menus and dialog boxes.

Controlled Vocabularies - Provide a way to organize knowledge for information retrieval. They are used in subject indexing schemes, subject headings, thesauri and taxonomies.

Converters - An application that converts data from one code to another.

Cross-Platform - Refers to developing for and/or running on more than one type of hardware platform. It implies two different processes. The first is programming source code that is compiled into different machine environments, each of which has to be supported separately. The second method is with the use of an interpreter such as the Java Virtual Machine.

CSS – See Cascading Style Sheets

Customer Relationship Management (CRM) - Enterprise-wide software applications that allow companies to manage every aspect of their relationship with customers. The goal of these systems is to assist in building lasting customer relationships and to turn customer satisfaction into customer loyalty.

Cyber Attack - Cyber attacks target vulnerable computers to make them inoperable by disrupting data flows across the Internet and involved organizations, institutions or government agencies.

DAM - See Media Management.

Data Archiving - Data archiving offloads historic data from the online database and archives it for future access on a secure media.

Data Center (also called Server Farm) - A collection of computer servers usually maintained by an enterprise to accomplish server needs far beyond the capability of one machine. Server farms often have backup servers, which can take over the function of primary servers in the event of a primary server failure.

Data Integrity - A term that can mean ensuring data is "whole" or complete. Put simply, data integrity is the assurance that data is consistent, correct and accessible.

Data Loss Prevention (DLP) - Systems that identify, monitor and protect data in use by preventing the unauthorized use or transmission of confidential information.

Data Mart - A subset of a data warehouse often created for just one department or product line.

Data Warehouse - A database designed to support decision making in an organization. Data from the production databases are copied to the data warehouse so that queries and analysis can be performed without disturbing the performance or the stability of the production systems.

Database - A collection of data arranged for ease and speed of search and retrieval.

Deep Web (also called Deepnet, the invisible Web, or the hidden Web) - Refers to World Wide Web content that is not part of the surface Web, which is indexed by standard search engines.

Desktop - The area of the monitor screen in a graphical user interface (GUI) against which icons and windows used to run applications appear.

Digital Asset - Describes any subdivision or collection of content and meta-data that holds value to the owner. Digital assets may include photos, video, audio, Web pages, text documents, Microsoft® PowerPoints or graphics.

Digital Asset Management (DAM) - See Media Management.

Digital Experience Management (DEM) - Using tools such as widgets to embed digital media, DEM presents significant content distribution opportunities for organizations outside the enterprise as well as enabling emerging social collaboration tools within the enterprise.

Digital Media - The term encompasses a wide variety of content types – photos, graphics, audio files, video clips, Flash animations, PDFs, PowerPoint files and design layouts.

Digital Native – Describes people who grew up accustomed to using digital technologies.

Disposition - Final deletion of content when it reaches the end of its lifecycle.

Document - A piece of work created with an application, such as by word processor. A computer file that is not an executable file and contains data for use by applications.

Document Management (DM) - Involves the capture and management of documents within an organization. The term traditionally implied the management of documents after they were scanned into the computer. Today, the term has become an umbrella under which document imaging, workflow and information retrieval fall.

Document Repository - A database that includes author, data elements, inputs, processes, outputs and interrelationships.

Document Summarization - A statistical summary of the document is automatically generated.

Dynamic Clustering - Similar results are automatically placed into groups.

Early Payment Discounts - Commonly, vendors give customers an optional early payment discount. If vendor invoices are being paid within a certain time frame, customers can reduce the payment by a certain predefined percentage.

ECM - See Enterprise Content Management.

ECM 2.0 - Managing content that is from Web 2.0 social networks.

ECM Applications - Applications that are usually tailored to address line-of-business problems or customized for specific vertical markets.

eDiscovery or Electronic discovery - Refers to discovery in civil litigation which deals with information in electronic format also referred to as Electronically Stored Information (ESI).

Electronic Reports Management (ERM) - Accounting software that helps manage tax estimation/preparation, balance sheets, and profit and loss statements.

Email - One of the first and most popular uses for the Internet, email (electronic mail) is the exchange of computer-stored messages by telecommunication.

Email Management - The application of content lifecycle management to emails to manage the creation, archiving, storage and disposition of email messages.

Encapsulated PostScript (EPS) - A graphics file format typically used in print layout and design.

Enterprise 2.0 (E2.0) - The use of emergent social software platforms, such as social networking, blogs and wikis, and other Web 2.0 technologies within companies, or between companies and their partners or customers. Also called enterprise social software.

Enterprise Application - A computer program designed to perform specific functions, such as inventory control, accounting, payroll, material management, etc.

Enterprise Content Management (ECM) - Systems that capture, store, retrieve, print and disseminate digital content for use by the enterprise. Digital content includes pictures/images, text, reports, video, audio, transactional data, catalog and code.

Enterprise Resource Planning (ERP) - Any software system designed to support and automate the business processes of medium and large businesses. This may include manufacturing, distribution, personnel, project management, payroll and financials. ERP systems are accounting-oriented information systems for identifying and planning the enterprise-wide resources needed to take, make, distribute and account for customer orders.

Entity Extraction - An entity extractor locates and extracts places, people, organizations, and more. Controlled vocabularies and linguistic rules are used to identify and extract all occurrences of an entity type. Entity types can include product names, company names, proper names, geographic locations, dates, times and more.

Extensible Markup Language (XML) - An initiative from the World Wide Web Consortium defining an "extremely simple" dialect of SGML suitable for use on the World Wide Web. See also HTML and SGML.

Extranet - An IP network that provides secure connections between remote users and a main site, or among multiple sites within the same company, including connectivity to business partners, customers and suppliers.

FDA - Food and Drug Administration (FDA) (United States). FDA's mission is to promote and protect the public health by helping safe and effective products reach the market in a timely way while monitoring products for continued safety after they are in use.

Firewall - A firewall is a part of a computer system or network that is designed to block unauthorized access while permitting authorized communications.

FOIA (Freedom of Information Act)(USA) - The implementation of freedom of information legislation in the United States which allows for the full or partial disclosure of previously unreleased information and documents controlled by the US Government.

Federated Search - The simultaneous search of multiple online databases or Web resources, federated search is an emerging feature of Web-based library and information retrieval systems.

File Plan - A classification scheme for the physical arrangement, storage, and retrieval of files.

Folksonomy - A system of classification based on collaboratively creating and managing tags to annotate content. Also referred to as social tagging.

Forums – Online discussion forums in which users post "articles" to forums organized around a topic, typically in question and answer format resembling an offline discussion.

Full-Text Retrieval - Software that allows users to search the entire text portion of digital information and retrieves files that match the user's search criteria. Document-retrieval systems store entire documents, which are usually retrieved by title or by keywords associated with the document. In some systems, the text of documents is stored as data. This permits full text searching, enabling retrieval on the basis of any words in the document.

Gen-Xers - Generation X, commonly abbreviated to Gen X, is the generation born after the baby boom ended, with birth dates ranging from 1961 to 1981.

Gigabyte (GB) - The gigabyte is a multiple of the unit byte for digital information storage. One gigabyte is 1000MB or one thousand million bytes. The unit symbol for the gigabyte is GB or Gbyte.

Global Positioning System (GPS) – A U.S. global navigation satellite system. It provides reliable positioning services to worldwide users on a continuous basis anywhere on or near the Earth which has an unobstructed view of four or more GPS satellites.

Graphics Interchange Format (GIF) - A filename extension used to describe digitized images.

Graphical User Interface (GUI) - A type of user interface that allows people to interact with programs in more ways than typing such as computers; hand-held devices such as MP3 Players, Portable Media Players or Gaming devices; household appliances and office equipment with images rather than text commands.

Hardware as a Service (HaaS) - HaaS enables individuals and organizations to purchase space for applications, games and other types of software to run in the cloud rather than taking up space on a computer.

Hosting - Maintaining a computer system and its applications at a third-party site.

Hypertext Markup Language (HTML) - A structured document format in which elements (commonly referred to as "tags") are embedded in the text. Tags are used for presentation formatting to delimit text which is to appear in a special place or style. HTML is an extension of SGML.

Index - In data management, the most common method for keeping track of data on a disk. Indexes are directory listings maintained by the operating system, RDBMS or the application. An index of files contains an entry for each file name and the location of the file. An index of records has an entry for each key field (for example, account number or name) and the location of the record.

Information Governance - The set of multi-disciplinary structures, policies, procedures, processes and controls implemented to manage information on all media in such a way that it supports the enterprise's immediate and long term regulatory, legal, risk, environmental and operational requirements.

Infrastructure as a Service (IaaS) - IaaS refers to providing a computer infrastructure as a service. Cloud infrastructure delivers virtual servers with unique IP addresses and blocks of storage on demand

Instant Messaging (IM) – See chat.

Internet - An interconnected system of networks that connects computers around the world via the TCP/IP protocol.

Internet Browser - The program that serves as the client front end to the World Wide Web.

Interoperability - Refers to diverse systems and organizations working together (inter-operating).

Intranet - An "internal Internet" configured behind a firewall to connect individuals and departments. A privately maintained computer network that can be accessed only by authorized persons, especially members or employees of the organization that owns it.

IP address - An Internet Protocol (IP) address is a numerical label that is assigned to devices participating in a computer network utilizing the Internet Protocol for communication between its nodes.

JPEG, JPG - A file extension typically used for an image that appears within the body of a Web page. Most graphical Web browsers can display both GIF and JPG images online.

Keyword - A term used as a keyword to retrieve documents in an information system such as a catalog or a search engine.

Knowledge Management (KM) - An umbrella term for making more efficient use of the human knowledge that exists within an organization. The major focus is to identify and gather content from documents, reports and other sources and to be able to search that content for meaningful relationships. Knowledge Management also concerns the ability to identify high-value individuals within an organization.

Knowledge Repository - A database of information about applications software that includes author, data elements, inputs, processes, outputs and interrelationships.

Knowledge Worker - One who works primarily with information or one who develops and uses knowledge in the workplace.

LAN - Local Area Network.

The Long Tail – A consumer demographic in business, the Long Tail is a concept used by Chris Anderson in an October 2004 Wired magazine and later in his book *The Long Tail: Why the Future of Business Is Selling Less of More*. It is applied to retail in this book, as it involves the niche strategy of selling a large number of unique items in small quantities along with selling fewer popular items in large quantities.

Mainframes - Computers used mainly by large organizations for critical applications, typically bulk data processing such as census, industry and consumer statistics, enterprise resource planning (ERP), and financial transaction processing.

Mashups - A Web page or application that combines data or functionality from two or more external sources to create a new service.

Materials Management - A specific module within an ERP system used to process all material management related tasks.

Media Management (also known as Digital Asset Management, Brand Asset Management or Media Asset Management) - Media Management consists of the ingestion, storage, management, retrieval, production and distribution of digital assets.

Meta-data - Sometimes known as data about the data, meta-data describes and provides context for content.

Meta-data Extraction - Capability to generate meta-data from text-based content. This capability is delivered by combined content analytics and search.

Meta-data Tagging - Data that describes other data, including detailed compilations such as data dictionaries and repositories that provide information about each data element. May also refer to any descriptive item about data, such as the content of an HTML meta tag or a title field in a media file. Tags are a set of bits or characters that identify various conditions about data in a file. Tags are often found in the header records of such files.

Micro-blogging - Blog posts with a limited character set to keep messages short. Also called "tweets".

Millennials - Also called Echo Boomers, Millennials are the demographic group following Generation X with birth dates ranging from the mid 1970's to the early 2000's.

Mobile virtual private network (mobile VPN or mVPN) - Gives mobile devices access to network resources and software applications on their home network, when they connect via other wireless or wired networks.

Mobile ECM - Secure access to ECM technologies and functionality via a mobile device.

Multimedia - Integration of text, voice, video, images, or some combination of these types of information. Also called Rich Media.

Multi-tenancy - In a multi-tenancy environment, multiple customers share the same application, running on the same operating system, on the same hardware, with the same data storage mechanism. The distinction is achieved during application design, so that customers do not share or see each other's data. Contrast this with Virtualization where one or other of these components is abstracted so that each customer application appears to be running on a separate physical machine.

Natural Language Queries - Users type in a sentence or phrase or even cut and paste an entire paragraph into the query box.

Object tree - Objects within systems can be maintained in a hierarchal structure called an object tree which lists the parent-child relationships between objects.

Online - Connected to or accessible via a computer or computer network. Typically refers to being connected to the Internet or other remote service.

Online Community - A virtual community that exists online whose members form relationships, establish trust and exchange knowledge. Online communities combine social software functionality, including text-based chat rooms and forums that use voice, video text or avatars.

Online Discussion Forums – See forums.

Open Source Software (OSS) - Computer software for which the source code and certain other rights normally reserved for copyright holders are provided under a software license that meets the Open Source Definition or that is in the public domain.

Operating System - A computer's master control program that manages its internal functions controls its operation. An operating system provides commonly used functions and a uniform, consistent means for all software applications to access the computer's resources. Windows and Unix are operating systems.

Optical Character Recognition (OCR) - Recognition of printed or written characters by computer. Each page of text is converted to a digital image using a scanner and OCR is then applied to the image to produce a text file.

OSS - See Open Source Software.

OWL (Web Ontology Language) – A set of knowledge representation languages for authoring ontologies as endorsed by the World Wide Web Consortium .

PDA - See Personal Digital Assistant.

Permissions - Management of who can access a computer or network. The Access Control List (ACL) is the set of data associated with a file, directory or other resource that defines the permissions that users, groups, processes or devices have for accessing it.

Personal Computer (PC) - A computer built around a microprocessor for use by an individual, as in an office, home or school.

Personal Digital Assistant (PDA) - Also known as a palmtop computer, a PDA is a mobile device which functions as a personal information manager and connects to the Internet. The PDA has an electronic visual display enabling it to include a web browser, but some newer models also have audio capabilities, enabling them to be used as mobile phones or portable media players. Some PDAs employ touch screen technology.

Petabyte (PB) – A unit of information or computer storage that is equal to 1000 terabytes, or 1,000,000 gigabytes.

Phishing - In the field of computer security, phishing is the fraudulent process of attempting to obtain sensitive information like usernames, passwords and credit card information by masquerading as a trustworthy entity, typically professing to be from popular Web sites, such as social networking sites, auction sites, online payment processors or IT administrators.

Platform - The term originally concerned only CPU or computer hardware, but it also refers to software-only environments. A messaging or groupware platform implies one or more programming interfaces that email, calendaring and other client programs are written to in order to communicate with the services provided by the server.

Platform as a Service (PaaS) - PaaS refers to providing a computer platform or software stack as a service. Developers can then create applications using the provider's Application Programming Interfaces (APIs).

PLM - See Product Lifecycle Management.

Podcast - A series of digital media audio or video files that are released episodically and downloaded through Web syndication.

Polls - Refer to dynamic data collection and tabulation, including Web site user evaluations of topics, articles and other content.

Portable Document Format (PDF) - File format used by the Adobe Acrobat document exchange system.

Portable Network Graphics (PNG) - An extensible file format for the portable, well-compressed storage of raster images. PNG provides a patent-free replacement for GIF.

Portal - Within the enterprise, software that provides access via a Web browser into all of an organization's information assets and applications. Portals provide a variety of services including Web searching, news, white and yellow pages directories, free email, discussion groups, online shopping and links to other sites.

Portlets - Pluggable software components that are managed and displayed in a Web portal. Portlets produce fragments of markup code that are aggregated into a portal page.

Plug-in - A computer program that interfaces with a host application.

Process Management - The automation of business processes using a rule-based expert system that invokes the appropriate tools and supplies necessary information, checklists, examples and status reports to the user.

Process Modeling - A set of components and methodologies used to graphically depict and document business processes within a BPM environment. These components allow business and technical teams to collaborate on a shared model that describes how the business process will function.

Process Optimization - Set of components and methodologies that help organizations identify, evaluate, and implement improvements to key business processes. Process optimization and business activity monitoring (BAM) often go hand in hand.

Product Lifecycle Management (PLM) - An enterprise application for product lifecycle management.

QWERTY - The most used modern-day keyboard layout on English-language computer and typewriter keyboards.

Raster Image - A graphic consisting of sets of horizontal lines composed of pixels.

Rating - An online mechanism that allows customers, employees, and other visitors to provide direct feedback on the quality, relevance, or usefulness of content.

Real-Time Collaboration - Tools that let people to collaborate simultaneously. The primary data collaboration tools are electronic whiteboards, which are shared chalkboards and application sharing, which lets remote users work in the same application together. Some form of human communication is also necessary, so text chat, audio or videoconferencing is often part of the total system.

Really Simple Syndication (RSS) - RSS feeds deliver aggregated and syndicated Web content to Web-based or desktop clients called "readers." RSS readers inform users when Web sites, blogs, wikis, or news sources get updated.

Records Management (RM) - Refers to the creation, retention and scheduled destruction of an organization's paper and film documents. Email and computer-generated content also fall into the RM domain.

Redundancy - The duplication of critical components of a system with the intention of increasing reliability of the system, usually in the case of a backup or fail-safe.

Regulatory Requirements - Overseen by various governmental agencies to ensure compliance with laws, regulations and established rules. Examples relevant to content management applications include U.S. FDA 21 CFR Part 11, U.S. DoD 5015.2 Standard and HIPAA.

Relational Database - A database in which all the data and relations between them are organized in tables. A relational database allows the definition of data structures, storage and retrieval operations and integrity constraints.

Reporting - Metrics-focused analysis of user behavior (unlike Web analytics which is experience-driven).

Resource Description Framework (RDF) - A family of specifications designed as a metadata data model.

REST (Representational State Transfer) – A style of software architecture for distributed systems such as the World Wide Web.

Retention Schedule - Indicates how long corporate records should be kept, where the records are kept, who can access the records, who can file them, and who has the authority to dispose of them.

Return On Investment (ROI) - Traditional financial approach for examining overall investment returns over a given time frame (supports indexing and scoring).

Rich Content or Media - See Digital Media

Rights and Permissions - Identifies the circumstances under which a particular asset may be used. For instance, indicates who legally owns the asset, in what mediums it may be used (Web, print, TV) and the financial liabilities incurred to include the asset.

ROI - See Return on investment.

RSS Feeds: A format of XML that is intended to share information in a condensed format (such as a title, description and link to a new article). RSS feeds are good for syndication.

Scalability - Ability to reach high-performance levels.

SCM - See Supply Chain Management.

Search - A technology focused on user-driven information retrieval based on statistical occurrence of search keywords in text-based content.

Search Agents - Topics of interested are registered by users underlying technology sends alerts when topics of interest are found and results are aggregated.

Search Engine Marketing (SEM) - A form of Internet marketing which increases Web site visibility in search engine result pages through the use of paid advertising.

Search Engine Optimization (SEO) - Involves improving the volume and/or quality of traffic to a Web site from search engines organically or naturally by strategically placing keywords or phrases on Web pages across a site.

SEM - See Search engine marketing

Semantic Web – See Web 3.0.

Semantics – A term used often in the context of the Semantic Web which typically refers to RDF-based modeling of online user experience. In the context of content analytics, the term semantics is sometimes used to refer to the connotation of information contained in content or what is the information about.

Sentiment Analysis - Sentiment analysis detects the tones in content, identifying and displaying opinions that are expressed in clusters of sentences, phrases or entities.

SEO - See Search Engine Optimization.

Server - A server computer, sometimes called an enterprise server, is a computer system that provides essential services across a network, to private users inside a large organization or to public users in the Internet. Enterprise servers are known to be very fault tolerant, for even a short-term failure can cost more than purchasing and installing the system.

Service Oriented Architecture (SOA) - Describes applications which are based on code that is written according to "building block" SOA principles to permit easy re-purposing of code for other functions. A deployed SOA-based architecture will provide a loosely-integrated suite of services that can be used within multiple business domains.

SGML - See Standard Generalized Markup Language.

Shareware - Refers to proprietary software that can be downloaded from the Internet without payment on a trial basis.

Short Message Service (SMS) - Text messaging sent using this service, which allows a short alphanumeric message (160 alphanumeric characters) to be sent for display on a mobile or cell phone.

Similarity - Technology that relates similar particular content assets to other assets. This can be done in different way, e.g. based on keywords (in search), classification, content analytics, etc.

Simulation - The act of simulating something generally entails representing certain key characteristics or behaviors of a selected physical or abstract system. Simulation of technology is commonly used for performance optimization, safety engineering, testing, training and education.

Smartphone - A mobile phone that offers advanced, PC-like functionality such as email, Internet access, calendaring and viewing capabilities, along with a built-in full keyboard or external USB keyboard and VGA connector.

SOA - See Service Oriented Architecture.

SOAP - Simple Object Access Protocol, an XML protocol.

Social Bookmarking (also Social Tagging) - A way for Internet users to share, organize, search, and manage bookmarks of Web pages of interest. Tags and descriptions can be added to these pages to make them easier to find. Popular examples include Delicious. com and StumbleUpon.com.

Social Computing - Supports "computations" that are carried out by groups of people, an idea that has been popularized in James Surowiecki's book, *The Wisdom of Crowds*. More recently, it refers to the popularity of social software and Web 2.0 technologies.

Social Marketplace - Organizations use social computing to connect with customers, partners, and other stakeholders to enhance communications, provide improved quality of service and gain competitive advantage by directly interacting with customers and addressing their needs.

Social Media - Media designed to be disseminated through social interaction, created using highly accessible and scalable publishing techniques. Social media uses Internet and Web-based technologies to transform broadcast media monologues (one-to-many) into social media dialogues (many-to-many).

Social Networks - Web sites that facilitate connections of people based on self-generated user profiles. Facebook.com and LinkedIn.com are examples of social networking sites.

Social Network Aggregation - The process of aggregating content from multiple social network sites, such as MySpace or Facebook, into a single location.

Social Workplace - The social workplace uses Web 2.0 technologies to connect people with their peers and with critical content and information. Also referred to as Enterprise 2.0.

Social Software – Describes software programs that enable users to leverage the Internet to interact, collaborate and communicate. Examples include social sites like MySpace, Facebook, Flickr and YouTube, along with ecommerce sites Amazon.com and eBay. The terms Enterprise 2.0 (E2.0) and Web 2.0 are also used to describe this style of software inside the enterprise (for organizations) and outside of the enterprise (for individual consumers), respectively.

Social Tagging – See "Social Bookmarking".

Software - The programs, routines and symbolic languages that control the functioning of a computer and direct its operation.

Software as a Service (SaaS) - This type of computing delivers a single application through the browser to a large number of customers using a multitenant architecture.

Spam – Unsolicited email. See Spambot.

Spambot - Email spambots harvest email addresses from the Internet in order to build mailing lists for sending unsolicited email, also known as spam.

SPARQL - Stands for SPARQL Protocol and RDF Query Language and is considered a key Semantic Web technology.

Spoliation - Is the intentional or negligent withholding, hiding, alteration or destruction of evidence relevant to a legal proceeding, which is a criminal act in the U.S.

Standard Generalized Markup Language (SGML) - A language specification adopted by ISO (International Standards Organization) in 1986 as a means of defining and separating the structure, information content and presentation format of electronic documents. SGML is ISO standard no. 8879.

Structured Data - Data that resides in fixed fields within a record or file. Relational databases and spreadsheets are examples of structured data.

Summarization - Technology that automatically generates a summary of a content asset. This technology is used in search as well as in content classification.

Supply Chain Management (SCM) - An enterprise application for supply chain management.

Synchronous Collaboration - Relating to computer systems or applications that update information at the same rate as they receive data, enabling them to direct or control a collaborative process in real time.

Tag Clouds - A tag cloud is a visual depiction of user-generated tags.

Tagged Image File Format (abbreviated TIFF) - A file format for storing images, including photographs and line art.

Tagging - Enables users to assign keywords to content such as blogs, documents, forums and video files without following predefined terms.

Taxonomic Classifications - Laws or principles of classification; systematic division into ordered groups or categories.

Terabyte (TB) - A unit of computer memory or data storage capacity equal to one trillion bytes or 1,000 gigabytes (GB).

Text Analytics - Sometimes referred to as text data mining or text mining, text analytics as a subset of Content Analytics refers to a set of technologies for analysis of information contained in text-based content assets.

Text Extraction - The capability of a search engine to create an index which generates keywords from text using algorithms that analyze their statistical occurrence and weight.

Thumbnail - A low-resolution small size rendition of an image asset; or, small size textual rendition of a text asset.

Touch Screen - A visual display that can detect the presence and location of a touch within the display area.

Transaction - Synonymous with a specific business application, such as order entry, invoice information capture, etc. To create, change or display business information in an enterprise application, users have to call certain transactions in the system. See also - Transactional Data.

Transactional Data - Orders, purchases, changes, additions and deletions are typical business transactions stored in the computer. Transactions update one or more master files and serve as both an audit trail and history for future analyses. Ad hoc queries are also a type of transaction but are usually not saved.

Transformation - An operation applied to one or more assets that result in the construction of a new asset, called a Transformed Asset. The transformation embodies business rules that are applied during this construction.

Tweet – See Micro-blogging.

Unstructured Data - Data that does not reside in fixed locations. Free-form text in a word-processing document is a typical example.

User Generated Content (UGC) - Refers to various kinds of content or digital media produced by end-users and made publicly available. Also known as consumer generated media (CGM) or user created content (UCC).

User Interface (UI) - A user interface is the system people use to interact with a computer or other device. Typically, a system may expose several user interfaces to serve different kinds of users.

User Profiles - A collection of personal data associated to a specific user typically within an online community or corporate intranet. Profiles often contain a picture, relevant personal and professional information including knowledge, skills, abilities, department, projects, roles, other contacts and links.

Video - The technology of electronically capturing, recording, processing, storing, transmitting, and reconstructing a sequence of still images representing scenes in motion.

Virtualization - An umbrella term that describes software technologies that improve portability, manageability and compatibility of applications by encapsulating them from the underlying operating system on which they are executed.

Virtual Project (Workgroup) - A group of individuals who work on a common project via technologies such as email, shared databases, threaded discussions and calendaring. Virtual workgroups are mandated by company policy and employment requirements.

Virtual Reality or Virtual Worlds - Computer-based simulated environments or communities (such as Second Life), where users can interact with one another and objects in the environment. Also called "immersion" or interactive 3D virtual environments, where the users take the form of avatars for graphical display to others.

WAN - A wide area network (WAN) is a computer network that covers a broad area (i.e., any network whose communications links cross metropolitan, regional, or national boundaries.

Web - A shorthand way to refer to the World Wide Web and possibly its complementing technologies. For example, a Web authoring tool might be used to create documents that contain Hyper Text Markup Language (HTML).

Web 1.0 – Began with the release of the WWW to the public in 1991, and is the general term that has been created to describe the Web before the Web 2.0 phenomenon.

Web 2.0 – Refers to Web-based applications that enable new and emergent ways of searching, presenting and consuming information using the Internet. Web 2.0 is characterized by predominantly by technologies that use the Web as a platform for collaboration and communications. The term also covers applications that are participatory in nature, lightweight and easy to deploy (API's and mashups, for example) and are available online as a service.

Web 3.0 (also the Semantic Web) - The phase of Web application development directly following Web 2.0, which includes the ability for programs and systems to "understand" the meaning of content and services, to deliver highly personalized and relevant content and services to end users and computers. These highly personalized services will be accessible using ubiquitous connections and powerful mobile devices, including the Blackberry, iPhone, and Android.

Web Analytics - A technology for user behavior analysis (click-stream analysis). It allows customers to generate reports on user behavior on the site and to optimize user experience by dynamically serving up relevant content based on meta-data (= recommendations).

Web Browser - See Internet browser.

Weblog – See Blog.

Web Content – The content featured as part of the user experience on Web sites, including text, video, images, sounds and animations.

Web Content Management (WCM) - Systems designed to drive Web sites by separating content from presentation and providing the following capabilities - capacity planning, site design/layout, look/feel navigation, content development, production, delivery, session tracking and site evolution.

Web Editor - An HTML editor is a software application for creating Web pages. Although the HTML markup of a Web page can be written with any text editor, specialized HTML editors can offer convenience and added functionality.

Web Services - Web Services refer to the Web-based provision of services via open interfaces. This enables the integration of "third-party" applications with a Web site, giving rise to new sites or mashups.

Web Site - A collection of related Web pages with supporting images, videos or other digital assets that share a common domain name or IP address in an Internet Protocol-based network.

Widget - Highly portable Web applications which allow non-technical users to add dynamic content or functionality to Web pages. User-friendly Web sites are increasing their use of widgets to simplify and enhance the internet user's experience.

Wifi - A very high bandwidth connection. A Wifi-enabled device such as a personal computer, video game console, mobile phone, MP3 player or PDA can connect to the Internet within range of a wireless network connected to the Internet.

Wiki - A collection of articles that can be entered, edited, linked, and expanded by any authorized user. Wikis facilitate the open sharing of knowledge on a designated Web page.

Workflow - Using applications and technology to automate the execution of each phase in a business process.

World Wide Web (WWW) - An HTML-based Internet system developed at the European Center for Nuclear Research (CERN) in Geneva. Also relates to the complete set of documents residing on all Internet servers that use the HTTP protocol. The Web is accessible to users via a simple point-and-click system.

WSDL - Web Service Definition Language.

WYSIWYG (What You See Is What You Get) - Describes the presentation of content that appears very similar during edits and output.

XBRL - an open data standard for financial reporting. XBRL allows information modeling and the expression of semantic meaning commonly required in business reporting.

XML - see Extensible Markup Language.

BIBLIOGRAPHY

Anderson, Chris. *The Long Tail: Why the Future of Business is Selling Less of More*. New York: Hyperion, 2008

Bohn, Roger E. and James E. Short. *How Much Information? 2009 Report on American Consumers*. University of California: Global Information Industry Center, 2010

Carr, Nicholas. *The Big Switch*. New York: W. W. Norton & Company, 2008

Crump, James. *Passive vs. active compliance: active compliance mitigates cost, improves business and reduces risk. (Technology Strategies)*. Bank Accounting & Finance, 2007

Dunn, John E. *Internet now dominated by 'traffic superpowers'*: TechWorld, Oct 2009: http://www.itworldcanada.com/news/internet-now-dominated-by-traffic-superpowers/1390 70&sub=223407&utm_source=223407&utm_medium=top5&utm_campaign=TD

Email Statistics Report 2009-2013. The Radicati Group, Inc. Palo Alto, CA, 2009

Forrest, William, James M. Kaplan and Noah Kindler, *Data Centers: How to Cut Carbon Emissions and Cost*. McKinsey & Company, 2008: http://www.mckinsey.com/clientservice/ bto/pointofview/pdf/BT_Data_Center.pdf

Frank, Andrew and Mike McGuire. *Charting the Shift of DRM to Digital Experience Management*. Gartner Group, 2007

Gantz, John F., and others. *The Diverse and Exploding Digital Universe*. IDC Report, 2008.

Gartner Identifies Top Ten Disruptive Technologies for 2008 to 2012. Gartner Group, 2008: http://www.gartner.com/it/page.jsp?id=681107

Godin, Seth. *Tribes We Need You to Lead Us*. New York: Portfolio, 2008

Howe, Jeff. *Crowdsourcing: Why the Power of the Crowd Is Driving the Future of Business*. New York: Crown Business, 2008

Horrigan, John. *Use of Cloud Computing Applications and Services*. Pew Internet & American Life Project, 2008: http://www.pewinternet.org/pdfs/PIP_Cloud.Memo.pdf

Information Security Governance Guidance for Boards of Directors and Executive Management, 2nd Edition, IT Governance Institute, 2006

Jenkins, Tom. *Enterprise Content Management: Technology*. Open Text, 2008

Jenkins, Tom, Peter Jelinski and Bill Forquer. *Enterprise Content Management: Solutions*. Open Text, 2005

Jenkins, Tom, Walter Kohler and John Shackleton. *Enterprise Content Management: Methods*. Open Text, 2005

Library and Archives Canada (LAC). http://www.collectionscanada.gc.ca/index-e.html, June 2008

McAfee, Andrew. Blog: http://andrewmcafee.org/blog/

McAfee, Andrew. *Enterprise 2.0*. Boston, Massachusetts: Harvard Business School Press, 2009

McAfee, Andrew. *The Impact of Information Technology (IT) on Businesses and their Leaders*. May 26, 2006: http://blog.hbs.edu/faculty/amcafee/index.php/faculty_amcafee_v3/enterprise_20_version_20/

McAfee, Andrew. Enterprise 2.0: The Dawn of Emergent Collaboration. MIT Sloan Management Review, 2006: http://sloanreview.mit.edu/the-magazine/articles/2006/spring/47306/enterprise-the-dawn-of-emergent-collaboration/

McAfee, Andrew. *Enterprise 2.0 is vital for business*. FT.com, 2009

Mann, Jeffrey. *Maturity Model to Improve Enterprise Collaboration*. Gartner Group, 2007: http://www.gartner.com/DisplayDocument?doc_cd=153195&ref=g_rss

Phifer, Gene. *User Interaction – Spanning Portals, Ajax and Mobile Devices*. Gartner Portals, Content & Collaboration Summit, Gartner Group, 2007

O'Reilly, Tim. Blog: http://tim.oreilly.com/

O'Reilly, Tim. *What Is Web 2.0: Design Patterns and Business Models for the Next Generation of Software?*. September 30, 2005 http://www.oreillynet.com/pub/a/oreilly/tim/news/2005/09/30/what-is-web-20.html

Plummer, Daryl C., David W. Cearley and David Mitchell Smith. *Cloud Computing Confusion Leads to Opportunity*. Gartner, 2008: http://www.gartner.com/DisplayDocument?doc_cd=159034&ref=g_sitelink&ref=g_SiteLink

Porter, Michael. *Competitive Advantage*. New York: Free Press, 1985.

Scoble, Robert and Shel Israel, *Naked Conversations: How Blogs are Changing the Way Businesses Talk with Customers*. USA: John Wiley & Sons, 2006

Schooley, Claire. *The Millennials Are Here! Are You Prepared?* Forrester Group Report, 2009

Surowiecki, James. *The Wisdom of Crowds*. New York: Anchor, 2005

Shuen, Amy. *Web 2.0: A Strategy Guide*. O'Reilly Media, 2008

Siegel, David. *Pull, The Power of the Semantic Web to Transform Your Business*. New York: Portfolio, 2009

Tapscott, Don and Anthony D. Williams. *Wikinomics: How Mass Collaboration Changes Everything*, New York: Portfolio, 2007

Wagner, Stephen and Lee Dittmar, _The Unexpected Benefits of Sarbanes-Oxley_. Harvard Business Review. Boston, Massachusetts: Harvard Business School Press, 2006

Wardley, Simon. _Cloud Computing - Why IT Matters_. YouTube: http://www.youtube.com/watch?v=okqLxzWS5R4&feature=player_embedded

Weinberger, David. _Everything is Miscellaneous_, New York: Henry Holt and Company, 2007

Weinberger, David. _Small Pieces Loosely Joined: A Unified Theory of the Web_. Cambridge, Massachusetts: Perseus Publishing, 2002

Wikipedia: www.wikipedia.com

INNOVATOR STORY BIBLIOGRAPHY

Barclays. _Streamlining HR Processes_. Success Story. Open Text, 2004: www.opentext.com/ecmbook/innovator/barclays

BEHR. _BEHR Creates Ultimate Do-it-Yourself Web Experience with Open Text Solutions_. Press release. Open Text, 2009: www.opentext.com/ecmbook/innovator/behr

Buncombe County Government. _Implementing Electronic Document Management in Human Resources_. Content World Presentation. Open Text, 2008: www.opentext.com/ecmbook/innovator/buncombe

Bundesrechenzentrum (BRZ). _ECM as a Service: eGovernment Platform for the whole of Austria_. Success Story. Open Text, 2008: www.opentext.com/ecmbook/innovator/brz

California Public Utilities Commission. _The California Public Utilities Commission Improves Efficiencies With Electronic Filing_. Success Story. Open Text, 2009: www.opentext.com/ecmbook/innovator/cpuc

Canada 3.0. Presentation. Open Text: 2010: www.opentext.com/ecmbook/innovator/canada-3.0

Canadian Heritage. 2010 Winter Games (English and French Versions). _Canadian Heritage Goes for Gold with Open Text's Records, Document, and Information Management System (RDIMS)_. Success Story. Open Text, 2009: www.opentext.com/ecmbook/innovator/canheritage

Canopius. _Open Text Helps International Insurance Group Canopius Lead The Way In Electronic Trading_. Press Release. Open Text, 2009: www.opentext.com/ecmbook/innovator/canopius

CARE International. _ECM Strengthens CARE Canada's I Am Powerful Campaign_. Success Story. Open Text, 2008: www.opentext.com/ecmbook/innovator/care

Central Vermont Public Service (CVPS). *Central Vermont Public Service Manages Records and Meets eDiscovery Requirements*. Success Story. Open Text, 2008: www.opentext.com/ecmbook/innovator/cvps

City of Atlanta. *Atlanta Department of Watershed Management Uses Open Text for $4B Clean Water Atlanta Program*. Success Story. Open Text, 2009: www.opentext.com/ecmbook/innovator/city-of-atlanta

City of Edmonton. *A Site for All Citizens*. Success Story. Open Text, 2009: www.opentext.com/ecmbook/innovator/city-of-edmonton

Cohn & Wolfe. Success Story. Open Text, 2009: www.opentext.com/ecmbook/innovator/cohn-wolfe

Compassion International. *Compassion® International uses Open Text Digital Media Group to help break the cycle of poverty in developing countries*. Success Story. Open Text, 2009: www.opentext.com/ecmbook/innovator/compassion-intl

Cyberpresse. *Cyberpresse uses semantic navigation to offer an intuitive and relevant search experience that is enhanced by facets of semantic metadata*. Success Story. Open Text, 2010: www.opentext.com/ecmbook/innovator/cyberpresse

Davis + Henderson. *Open Text and Filogix Create Collaborative Document Management Solution*. Success Story. Open Text, 2009: www.opentext.com/ecmbook/innovator/davis-henderson

Deichmann Group. *From Archiving to Enterprise Content Management: Deichmann Supports International Expansion with Open Text*. Success Story. Open Text, 2010: www.opentext.com/ecmbook/innovator/deichmann

Delhaize. *Automating Invoice Management for Improved Efficiency*. Case Study. Open Text, 2009: www.opentext.com/ecmbook/innovator/delhaize

Deutsche Rentenversicherung Rheinland. *Open Text Transactional Content Processing*. Butler Group, 2009: www.opentext.com/ecmbook/innovator/deutsche-rentenversicherung

Electronic Arts. *Building the next generation gaming experience*. User Conference Presentation. Open Text, 2008: www.opentext.com/ecmbook/innovator/electronic-arts

Emergency Medicine Physicians (EMP). *Collaboration Product Overview*. Presentation. Open Text, 2009: www.opentext.com/ecmbook/innovator/emp

Energen. *Alabama Gas Streamlines Their Accounts Payable Processes in SAP*. Success Story. Open Text, 2007: www.opentext.com/ecmbook/innovator/energen

European Court of Human Rights (ECHR). *Open Text eDOCS Improves Access to Human Rights Knowledge Around the World*. Success Story. Open Text, 2008: www.opentext.com/ecmbook/innovator/echr

European Investment Bank. *Electronic Document, Records & Knowledge Management Solution for the European Investment Bank*. LinkUp Europe London 2004 Proceedings. Open Text, 2004: www.opentext.com/ecmbook/innovator/eib

Evolve24. *Evolve24 gauges public reactions and assesses risk to reputation using sentiment analysis*. Success Story. Open Text, 2010: www.opentext.com/ecmbook/innovator/e24

Genzyme. *Using ECM to Enhance Collaboration and Knowledge Management*. Success Story. Open Text, 2008: www.opentext.com/ecmbook/innovator/genzyme

Global Public Health Intelligence Network (GPHIN). *GPHIN uses text mining for its early warning system that detects human threats around the world*. Success Story. Open Text, 2010: www.opentext.com/ecmbook/innovator/gphin

Halliburton. *Halliburton Establishes an Email Management System to Meet Knowledge Management and Compliance Needs*. Success Story. Open Text, 2009: www.opentext.com/ecmbook/innovator/halliburton

Hatch. *Consultants at Hatch Connect with Livelink ECM™*. Success Story. Open Text, 2008: www.opentext.com/ecmbook/innovator/hatch

HBO. *Artesia Technologies Presents Digital Asset Management - Simplified at the AIIM EXPO 2004 SolutionCenter*. Press Release. Open Text, 2004: www.opentext.com/ecmbook/innovator/hbo

Hyatt. Success Story. Open Text, 2009: www.opentext.com/ecmbook/innovator/hyatt

INVISTA. *INVISTA Streamlines Accounts Payable Operations Using Open Text Vendor Invoice Management for SAP® Solutions*. Success Story. Open Text, 2008: www.opentext.com/ecmbook/innovator/invista

ISO Central Secretariat. *How ISO built one of the world's leading extranets*. Success Story. Open Text, 2006: www.opentext.com/ecmbook/innovator/iso

Junta de Andalucia. Success Story. Open Text, 2009: www.opentext.com/ecmbook/innovator/juntadeandalucia

Mercedes. Storyboard for Video. Open Text, 2009: www.opentext.com/ecmbook/innovator/mercedes

Motorola. *Consolidating Content and Collaboration Across the Enterprise. Motorola Compass: Availability, Scalability and Performance for the Enterprise and Beyond*. LiveLinkUp Orlando 2003 Proceedings CD-ROM. Open Text, 2003: www.opentext.com/ecmbook/innovator/motorola

Motorola. *Motorola Extends Use of Open Text's Livelink*. Press Release. Open Text, 2003: www.opentext.com/ecmbook/innovator/motorola

Mott MacDonald. *Open Text Constructs New Enterprise Content Management Solution for Mott MacDonald Group*. Success Story. Open Text, 2009: www.opentext.com/ecm-book/innovator/mott-macdonald

Multiquip. *Equipment Manufacturer Supports Large Field Workforce with Dynamic Intra-net*. Success Story. Open Text, 2008: www.opentext.com/ecmbook/innovator/multiquip

Mumbai International Airport. *Consortium Manages Modernization of India's Busiest Air-port with Open Text Fax Server, RightFax Edition*. Success Story. Open Text, 2009: www.opentext.com/ecmbook/innovator/mial

National Institute of Allergy and Infectious Diseases (NIAID). *The National Institute of Allergy and Infectious Diseases' (NIAID) integrated solution delivers functional, technical, compliance, and cost requirements*. Success Story. Open Text, 2009: www.opentext.com/ecmbook/innovator/niaid

Northrop Grumman. *Northrop Grumman Establishes Communities of Practice to Connect Knowledge and Expertise*. Success Story. Open Text, 2008: www.opentext.com/ecmbook/innovator/northrop-grumman

Ocean Conservancy. *Ocean Conservancy Cleans Up Digital Assets*. Success Story. Open Text, 2010: www.opentext.com/ecmbook/innovator/ocean-conservancy

Open Text. *Livelink ECM™ Provides Powerful Portal for Open Text's Own Customers and Partners. Success Story*. Open Text, 2008: www.opentext.com/ecmbook/innovator/opentext-extranet; www.opentext.com/ecmbook/innovator/opentext-mobility

OSFI. *Case Management at the Office of the Superintendent of Financial Institutions*. LiveLinkUp Orlando 2003 Proceedings CD-ROM. Open Text, 2003: www.opentext.com/ecmbook/innovator/osfi

RBS 6 Nations Rugby. *RBS 6 Nations Rugby Launch New Web Site Using Open Text*. Success Story. Open Text, 2009: www.opentext.com/ecmbook/innovator/rbs6nations

Roche. *Roche Streamlines Pharmaceutical Development with Livelink*. Press Release. Open Text, 2003: www.opentext.com/ecmbook/innovator/roche

Roche. *ShareWeb – Integrating Collaboration with Content Management*. LiveLinkUp Paris 2003 Proceedings. Open Text, 2003: www.opentext.com/ecmbook/innovator/roche

Royal Shakespeare Company (RSC). *Open Text Content Management System Performs for the Royal Shakespeare Company*. Success Story. Open Text, 2009: www.opentext.com/ecmbook/innovator/rsc

Siemens Automation & Drives. *ADEBAR Delivers Documents Immediately*. Success Story. Open Text, 2003: www.opentext.com/ecmbook/innovator/siemens

Siemens Enterprise Networks. *EZ-A: Easy Access to Customer Contracts, Engagement,*

Solutions, and Services. LinkUp Orlando 2003 Proceedings. Open Text, 2003: www.opentext.com/ecmbook/innovator/siemens

Siemens Financial Services (SFS). *Realizing a Paperless Office @ Siemens Financial Services*. LiveLinkUp Europe 2003 Proceedings. Open Text, 2003: www.opentext.com/ecmbook/innovator/siemens

Siemens Netherlands. *Enterprise Content Management at Siemens Netherlands*. LinkUp Europe London 2004 Proceedings. Open Text, 2004: www.opentext.com/ecmbook/innovator/siemens

Siemens. *Global network of knowledge*. LiveLinkUp Chicago 2002 Proceedings. Open Text, 2002: www.opentext.com/ecmbook/innovator/siemens

Siemens. *Integrating Livelink with SAP*. Live LinkUp Chicago 2002 Proceedings. Open Text, 2003: www.opentext.com/ecmbook/innovator/siemens

Siemens. *Supporting More than 80,000 Users*. LiveLinkUp Orlando Proceedings CD-ROM. Open Text, 2003: www.opentext.com/ecmbook/innovator/siemens

SNCF. *SNCF Infra Shares Best Practices Via a Single Portal*. Success Story. Open Text, 2006: www.opentext.com/ecmbook/innovator/sncf

Sprint. *Improving Business Efficiencies: Livelink as an Intranet Hosting Environment*. LiveLinkUp Las Vegas 2001 Proceedings. Open Text, 2002. www.opentext.com/ecmbook/innovator/sprint

STA Travel. *STA Travel Enriches Its Customer Offering With Help From IBM and Open Text*. Success Story. Open Text, 2009: www.opentext.com/ecmbook/innovator/sta-travel

Suffolk University. *Suffolk University Attains a Higher Degree of Web Content Management with Open Text*. Success Story. Open Text, 2009: www.opentext.com/ecmbook/innovator/suffolk

Timberland. *Open Text Optimizes Media Management at Timberland*. Success Story. Open Text, 2009: www.opentext.com/ecmbook/innovator/timberland

Time Warner Group. Open Text © 2004. http://www.opentext.com/ecmbook/innovator/time_warner

UBS AG. *An Interactive Information Platform*. Success Story. Open Text, 2006: www.opentext.com/ecmbook/innovator/ubs

INDEX

GPS, 167, 240, 244

Graphical User Interface (GUI), 41, 62, 83, 102, 122, 158, 175, 265, 278

H

Halliburton, 99

Hardware as a Service (HaaS), 223

Hatch, 155, 162

HBO, 177

Human Resources (HR), 8, 9, 11, 29, 132, 167, 208, 210, 243

Hyatt, 133

I

Image Management, 82, 83, 201

Immersive Collaboration, 72, 129, 134, 142, 176, 276

Information Governance, 36, 45, 48, 51, 53, 228, 280

Instant Messaging, 53, 129, 130, 134, 139, 196, 280

International Organization for Standardization Central Secretariat (ISO), 137

Intranet, 90, 129, 135, 140, 153, 201, 239, 259, 269, 275

INVISTA, 206

Invoice Management, 206, 215

J

Junta de Andalucia, 120

K

Knowledge Management, 15, 27, 50, 107, 259, 261

Knowledge Worker, 33, 76, 129, 141, 154, 176, 234, 235

L

Lifecycle Processes, 2, 20, 33, 48, 74, 90, 128, 200, 234, 272

Litigation, 47, 85, 93, 96, 99, 100, 136, 247

Long Tail, 159

M

Mainframes, 220

Manufacturing, 7, 14, 51, 136

Marketing, 6, 17, 132, 150, 162, 172, 177, 254, 284

Mashup, 68, 90, 129, 148, 176, 195, 228, 284

Media Management, 164, 168, 173

Mercedes-Benz USA, 117

Meta-data, 6, 10, 18, 62, 80, 91, 120, 170, 177

Michael Porter, 7

Micro-blogging, 151

Millennials, 148, 275

Mobile Device, 30, 52, 84, 114, 151, 235, 238, 242, 249,

Mobile ECM, 141, 238, 240, 241, 242, 244, 249, 250

Mobile Professionals, 141, 198, 238, 242, 245

Mobile VPN, 240

Motorola, 263, 264

Mott MacDonald Group, 12

Multi-tenancy, 222

Multiquip, 213

Mumbai International Airport, 84

N

National Institute of Allergy and Infectious Diseases (NIAID), 43

Nike, 157

Northrop Grumman, 161, 162

O

Ocean Conservancy, 181

Office of the Superintendent of Financial Institutions (OSFI), 49

Online Community, 23, 246, 284

Open Source Software (OSS), 18, 125, 225, 229

Open Text, 244, 283

P

Patrimoine Canadien: Jeux d'hiver de 2010, 88

Permissions, 57, 82, 120, 125, 132, 168, 241, 242

Personalization, 24, 68, 121, 122

Petabyte (PB), 4, 5

Pharmaceutical, 16, 17, 42, 50, 51, 190

Platform as a Service (PaaS), 222

Podcast, 116, 167

Portal, 120, 133, 140, 157, 172, 178, 213

Portlets, 68, 239

Process Management, 183, 194, 238, 243

Process Modeling, 189, 192

Product Development, 17, 136, 174, 186

Product Lifecycle Management (PLM), 7

Profile, 151, 184, 244, 264, 278

R

Rating, 148, 191, 203, 207, 227, 246, 262

RBS 6 Nations Rugby, 114

Really Simple Syndication (RSS), 122, 197, 227, 239, 275

Records Management (RM), 10, 25, 39, 53, 74, 90, 105, 198, 209, 242, 262

Regulatory Requirements, 18, 51, 139, 280

Retention, 75, 86, 99, 150, 160, 217, 242, 284

Retention Schedule, 33, 77, 86, 89, 99, 103

Rich Media, 4, 18, 97, 174, 224, 276, 277, 278

Risk Management, 12, 44, 49, 156, 159, 160, 247

Roche, 17

ROI, 188, 235, 281

Royal Shakespeare Company (RSC), 279

S

Sales, 6, 41, 104, 150, 177, 187, 200, 241, 254, 261

Sarbanes-Oxley (SOX), 37, 38, 46, 52, 192, 229

Scalability, 57, 194, 248

Search, 7, 15, 56, 78, 90, 116, 160, 210, 254, 267, 268, 282

Search Agents, 68

Security, 24, 44, 57, 84, 107, 146, 171, 210, 223

Semantic Web, 24, 68, 69, 70, 72, 273

Sentiment Analysis, 69, 70, 71, 273

Service Oriented Architecture (SOA), 149, 187, 195

Siemens, 252, 256, 259, 260, 262

Smartphone, 235, 240, 262, 275, 276

SNCF, 140

Social Collaboration, 16, 146, 148, 153, 176, 196, 283

Social Computing, 125, 141, 148, 153, 154, 155, 158, 160, 162, 227, 280

Social Marketplace, 146, 158, 159, 284

Social Media, 4, 18, 52, 80, 110, 145, 160, 238, 272, 283

Social Network, 52, 65, 147, 176, 218, 227, 247, 276, 284

Social Software, 52, 154, 196, 197, 239, 245

Social Tagging, 66, 123, 150

Social Workplace, 149, 151, 153, 154, 158, 284

Software as a Service (SaaS), 224, 230, 231

Sprint, 269

STA Travel, 150, 162

Storage, 38, 47, 78, 97, 160, 204, 220, 230, 248, 280

Structured Data, 76, 122, 168, 201, 202, 226, 275

Suffolk University, 124

Supply Chain Management (SCM), 41, 191, 201

Synchronous Collaboration, 26, 130, 131

Syndication, 116, 122, 175, 176, 178, 216, 276

T

T-Systems, 27

Tagging, 62, 123, 138, 150, 177, 273, 278

Taxonomy, 63, 64, 266, 267

Terabyte (TB), 4, 60, 76, 98, 166, 263

Tethered Content, 176, 178

Text Analytics, 64, 69

Text Mining, 56, 60, 70, 273

Tim Berners-Lee, 68

Tim O'Reilly, 148

Timberland, 174

Time Warner Book Group, 6

Training, 41, 132, 167, 265, 279, 280

Transaction, 30, 56, 126, 184, 202, 240, 262, 277

Transactional data, 191, 200, 212

Tweet, 151

Twitter, 4, 23

U

UBS, 46

User Experience, 20, 56, 96, 123, 128, 164, 184, 234, 272

User Generated Content (UGC), 4, 23, 65, 125, 147, 150, 159, 162, 228, 273

User Interface (UI), 24, 32, 115, 118, 152, 171, 236, 237, 262, 268

User Profile, 121, 152

Utility Computing, 220, 222, 223, 231

V

Value Chain, 7, 11

Video, 8, 12, 141, 148, 165, 174, 182, 218, 238, 265, 281, 284

Virtual Environments, 129, 142

Virtual Project, 130, 190

Virtual Reality, 56, 282

Virtualization, 91, 231

W

Web 1.0, 21, 22, 24, 159

Web 2.0, 18, 52, 66, 125, 138, 146, 161, 175, 196, 224, 277

Web 3.0, 21, 22, 24, 68, 70, 72, 167, 273, 276

Web Analytics, 123

Web Content Management (WCM), 22, 109, 121, 133, 224, 243, 262, 276, 279

Widget, 116, 120, 176, 182, 275

Wifi, 235

Wiki, 18, 148, 157, 196, 205, 227, 239, 247, 276, 283

Wikipedia, 148

Y

Yahoo, 57, 70

YouTube, 4, 148, 165, 166, 179, 180